Our Knowledge
of the
Historical Past

Our Knowledge of the Historical Past

Murray G. Murphey

The Bobbs-Merrill Company, Inc., Publishers

Indianapolis and New York

For

Allene

When you are old and grey and full of sleep,
And nodding by the fire, take down this book,
And slowly read, and dream of the soft look
Your eyes had once, and of their shadows deep;

How many loved your moments of glad grace,
And loved your beauty with love false or true,
But one man loved the pilgrim soul in you,
And loved the sorrows of your changing face;

And bending down beside the glowing bars,
Murmur, a little sadly, how Love fled
And paced upon the mountains overhead
And hid his face amid a crowd of stars.

—*Yeats*

Preface

This is a book about the nature of historical knowledge. The questions with which it is concerned are both philosophical and historiographical, and involve considerations as various as statistical hypothesis testing, componential analysis, and the problem of the synoptic gospels. Accordingly, some readers will find its range too broad while others will find it too narrow. But these considerations are all essential to an understanding of the kind of knowledge which we have respecting the historical past.

It may help the reader to have an outline of the contents of the book. Chapter I deals with four questions: the definition of history as a discipline, the reference of historical statements, the ontological status of the referents of historical statements, and the truth conditions of historical statements. Since the conclusions reached in Chapter I are at variance with traditional ideas about history, I have devoted Chapter II to a consideration of classical historiography. In Chapter III, three questions regarding historical explanation are discussed: the nature of the laws used in historical explanations, the logical structure of such explanations, and what such explanations explain. Chapter IV deals with the nature of historical interpretations. Chapter V deals with the general problem of confirming historical statements, and Chapter VI with the specific problem of confirming law-like statements about the historical past.

It is a pleasant duty to thank publicly those whose aid I have enjoyed in writing this book. Bruce Kuklick and Michael Zuckerman have read and criticized the entire manuscript and have given me invaluable suggestions on many points. Robert Zemsky made many helpful suggestions about the first four chapters. On particular topics, I have profited greatly from the aid and advice of K. S. Krishnan, Elizabeth Flower, Abraham Edel, and Michael Levine. And without the encouragement of my wife, this book would not have been written at all.

M.G.M.

Contents

I

The Truth and Reference of Historical Statements

Whatever their disagreements, historians as a group are agreed that history is a discipline which seeks to establish true statements about events which have occurred and objects which have existed in the past. Yet this claim, which seems so self-evident to historians, involves at least four major philosophical problems: (1) is history a discipline distinct from other disciplines?; (2) how can statements refer to objects and events which do not now exist?; (3) what is the ontological status of the referents of historical statements?; (4) how can a statement about past objects or events be said to be true or false? These questions are important for the understanding of the nature of historical knowledge, and so it is with these questions that our inquiry begins. In this chapter, we will deal with these four questions in order.

In 1943 Morton White published an article on historical explanation in which he dealt in an interesting way with the autonomy of history as a field of knowledge. White considered two ways of defining history as a field, and rejected them both on the ground that they did not succeed in distinguishing history from other disciplines. The first thesis which he analyzed was that "historical explanation explains facts prevailing at one time by reference to facts prevailing at an earlier time."[1] Against this thesis he urged the objection that "there are explanations which would be called physical, others which would be called chemical, and others which would be called biological, all of which must be called historical on this view."[2] That is, since there are explanations offered in many fields which explain an event by earlier events, history on this

1

definition would not be distinguishable from a large number of other disciplines. It should be noted that the thesis which White attacks is not identical with the historians' definition with which we began, for he speaks only of explanations, whereas our definition concerns statements; and he refers only to earlier events, not to events in the past. Nevertheless, the same objections which he raises against the thesis he attacks apply to the historians' definition, for there are statements in many fields of science which refer to events in the past.

The second position which White analyzes is more complex and rests upon a particular way of classifying theories. According to this method of classification, in order for a set of sentences S to constitute a theory belonging to a particular science T, there must be some sentences of S which contain terms in an essential way which are peculiar to T. By the phrase "in an essential way," White means that other terms cannot be substituted for the given term without changing the truth value of the sentence. Thus the term "cell" does not occur essentially in the sentence "whatever is a cell is a cell,"[3] since the truth value of this sentence is unchanged no matter what word is substituted for "cell"; on the other hand, the term "force" does occur essentially in the sentence "force equals mass times acceleration," since there are some other words the substitution of which for "force" would alter the truth value of the sentence. Now on White's view, the set S may contain many sentences which do not involve essential occurrences of terms unique to the science T. These sentences are regarded as borrowed from other sciences presupposed by T. Thus statements of logic and mathematics are presupposed by physics in the sense that they are employed in physics, even though they do not contain essential occurrences of purely physical terms. But if we are really doing physics and not mathematics, some statements must occur in our science which do involve purely physical terms in an essential way. Thus, for S to be classified as a theory of T, there must be sentences in S which contain essential occurrences of terms specific to T. But as White argues, it is impossible to find any peculiarly historical terms: "whatever the terms which are specific to history are, they are not any different from those of sociology, where the latter is construed as the science of society."[4] It follows, then, that history is not an autonomous field of study since there are no terms peculiar to history.

Several comments are in order with respect to White's argument.

With respect to the first thesis which he attacks, White takes it for granted that an explanation cannot belong to more than one discipline—hence to show that, if the thesis were granted, some explanations would belong both to history and to some other discipline is to refute the thesis. But why cannot a given explanation belong to more than one discipline? There are, I suppose, two arguments which might be advanced: it might be said that the names of disciplines are normally used in an exclusive fashion, so that it would be contrary to standard usage to hold this position, or it might be argued that unless there are explanations unique to a particular discipline, the use of a separate term to refer to that discipline is redundant and ought to be abolished. But the appeal to common usage is not compelling. We do commonly speak of "the history of the continent," "the history of the earth," "the history of the moon," "the history of the solar system," etc., where it is quite clear that whatever statements are to be offered in these "histories" must come from such sciences as geology, astronomy, and astrophysics, and where no one supposes that there are some special explanations involved which are not explanations of one of these sciences. The term "history" is thus used to refer to the past of a given entity, regardless of the specific discipline which provides the description or explanation of that entity. Hence the appeal to common usage is in favor of the thesis which White attacks rather than against it. Nor is the argument from redundancy any more compelling. It is easy to point out cases where an area of study is described as a distinct science even though every statement occurring in it also occurs in other sciences. This is certainly the case for astrophysics, biochemistry, geodesy, and many more well-recognized scientific fields. Redundancy is not, therefore, normally regarded as an adequate ground for refusing to regard sciences as distinct.

But these arguments do not meet White's attack on the second thesis, for that attack rests upon a special way of classifying theories. This way of classifying theories, however, is far from satisfactory. For to say that a theory is a biological theory just in case some of its statements contain in an essential way purely biological terms is to assert that we know what is and what is not a biological term antecedent to examining the theory. But how are we to establish what the terms of biology, physics, or any other science are? Suppose, for example, that I am confronted with a theory S* which contains in an essential way the term "cell." To what science, then, does S* belong? Unless I have some criterion for assigning "ell" to a science, the question cannot be answered. The only method which White suggests for determining what terms are peculiar to a science is enumeration. But what is to be enumerated? To say that we can enumerate the terms occurring essentially in theories belonging to that science assumes that theories can be classified as belonging to a given science by a criterion other than the terms which occur essentially in their sentences. But how else are we to determine what terms are specific to a given science? No other means are suggested.

These reflections cast doubt upon the method of classification used by White, and further reflection only suggests more doubts. His approach to classification is based upon the axiomatic formulation of theories. A theory is said to be axiomatized when its sentences are divided into two sets—a set of sentences called axioms which are logically independent of each other, and a set of sentences called theorems which are logically derivable from the axioms. Similarly, the terms occurring in the theory are divided into those which are primitive, or undefined within the theory, and those which are defined in terms of the primitives. Since the primitives are regarded as specifying the content of the theory, it seems to make sense to say that all theories which have the same primitives are about the same subject matter, and so to define the set of theories belonging to a particular science as the set of theories which have certain primitives in common. The problem with this approach, as we have just seen, is that there is no way to connect a given set of primitives to a particular science without invoking some prior criterion which specifies when a term is a term of that science. But other difficulties arise, principally from a confusion between a theory and a science. Axiomatic formulation leads very naturally to a criterion for identity and differentiation of theories: namely, two theories are identical if the axioms of each are derivable logically from those of the other and if the primitives of each are definable in terms of the primitives of the other. If the axioms of one theory are derivable logically from those of the other, but not the converse, and if the primitives of the first theory are definable in terms of those of the other, but not the converse, the first theory is said to be "reduced" to the second, and is in fact a part of the second theory. A number of such reductions have been made and are well known—e.g., the reduction of arithmetic as formulated by Peano to logic as formulated by Whitehead and Russell. In many cases, these reductions are referred to as though they were reductions, not of one theory to another, but of one discipline to another, as, e.g., it is often said that mathematics is reduced (or reducible) to logic. Why, if this be so, we should retain the term "mathematics" is not clear, since mathematics would then *be* logic, and the fact that we do retain the term indicates that there is something wrong with the claim. So does the telltale use of the term "reducible" in such contexts. Reduction is a logical relation: one theory is or is not reduced to another. But when we come to speak of sciences or disciplines as subject to reduction, ambiguity arises. For suppose that every biological theory now known were reduced to theories of physics. Clearly, this would not amount to a reduction of biology to physics, since nothing prevents the introduction tomorrow of a new biological theory which is not reduced to any physical theory. To deny that this is possible—to claim that biology is in principle reducible to physics— is to claim either that the primitives of biological and physical theories will not change, or that however they change the relation of reduction will continue to hold between theories of the two classes. The former claim is either a definition of a *science* by the primitives of a *theory,* which leaves arbitrary the relation of those terms to the science, or a prediction which is contrary to everything the history of science has to teach us about the development of science; while the latter claim is purely speculative. It is particular theories which are axiomatized, reduced, and have primitives, axioms, and theorems, not disciplines, and nothing but confusion results from imputing to disciplines the attributes and relations applying to particular theories. Yet this is just what White does when he claims that history is not distinct from sociology because he can find no terms now in use in history which are not also in use in sociology.

In our ordinary way of speaking, what counts as a "discipline" is a field of study the subject matter, methods, instrumentation, and problems of which are sufficiently different from those found in other fields to require special training, special techniques, special instruments, and a special integration of theory and data. It is in this sense that we usually refer to a field such as physics, or biology, or biochemistry, or astrophysics, as a "science," although no one would suggest in the case of the latter two that the theories currently used are not now reducible to

those of other sciences. White is certainly correct when he argues that
the terms currently used in history (meaning by "history" the history of
human society and culture) are also used in contemporary sociological
theories. This is an interesting and important fact. But it has nothing
to do with the question of whether or not history as a discipline ought
to be distinguished from sociology. History deals, as we have seen, with
the events and objects of the past. Is there any reason why this may
not be an adequate criterion for distinguishing history as a separate
discipline?

In the following pages I shall argue that, although this is not an
adequate criterion as it stands, it can be amended so as to form an
adequate criterion, and that even though history may in a certain sense
be regarded as that portion of the social sciences which deals with the
past, still it is distinctive enough not only to merit separate study but
also to permit one to question on good grounds whether it can be referred to as a social science. These are questions, however, with which
we shall have to deal in detail in later chapters. What is important to
note here is that what is distinctive about history as we have defined it
is neither its separate terminology nor its peculiar explanations, but the
fact that its statements refer to events and objects in the past. It is this
reference to the events and objects of the past which marks off history as
a special subject, and it is the problems which arise from this reference
which require special methods, special techniques, special training, and
a special relation of theory and data.

The second problem raised by the historian's definition of his discipline is the problem of reference: how can historical statements be said
to refer to objects and events which no longer exist? A particularly
interesting formulation of this problem is due to Russell:

> There is no logical impossibility in the hypothesis that the world sprang
> into being five minutes ago, exactly as it then was, with a population that
> "remembered" a wholly unreal past. There is no logically necessary
> connection between events at different times; therefore nothing that
> is happening now or will happen in the future can disprove the hy-
> pothesis that the world began five minutes ago. Hence the occurrences
> which are *called* knowledge of the past are logically independent of the
> past; they are wholly analysable into present contents which might,
> theoretically, be just what they are even if no past had existed.[5]

Thus, according to Russell, we could still have exactly the beliefs about the past which we do have even if there were no past objects to which to refer. This claim of Russell's merits particular attention, not only because it directly contradicts the characterization of history proposed above, but because the answer to it succeeds in showing something very important about the nature of historical knowledge.

In his recent book on the philosophy of history, Arthur Danto has attempted to present an answer to this claim of Russell's.[6] What is really disturbing about Russell's proposal, Danto argues, is rooted in certain characteristics of our language: specifically, in what he calls past-referring terms. Thus Danto argues that we can distinguish in our language between expressions such as "is a whitish shiny mark" and "is a scar." The latter term he regards as a past-referring term because its application implies that a wound was received in the past, while the former term he regards as temporally neutral since its application to the same phenomenon makes no claim about how the mark was produced. It is, Danto argues, because our language is filled with past-referring terms that Russell's proposal is so troubling, for all of the applications of those terms which we habitually make would be false if Russell were right. Thus we could not truthfully use such predicates as "is a father" or even "is a man" if the world were really but five minutes old. These remarks, indeed, show good reasons why Russell's proposal is disturbing, for they show that it attacks the notion of causality which is fundamental to our conception of time and is imbedded in our language; but they offer no reason to reject the proposal. In order to do that, Danto is forced to attack Russell on the ground that the stipulation of a five-minute gap since creation is entirely arbitrary and admits of no more justification than a three-minute gap or no gap at all. Hence Danto argues that Russell's proposal is essentially similar to asserting that nothing exists and, so, to total skepticism. Now Danto's argument is ingenious and interesting, but it is not particularly satisfactory; and it misses what seems to me to be the essentially skeptical point about Russell's proposal.

What is it that is skeptical about Russell's proposal? One might be inclined to say that the skeptical point is this: that he is proposing a situation in which two quite different processes would yield exactly the same effects, so that from those effects we should be completely unable to decide which process had really occurred. It would then seem to follow that the methods of evaluating theories on the basis of empirical evidence, which are the foundations of our sciences, are inadequate to distinguish a true from a false theory, and hence that we can repose no confidence in our knowledge. But the trouble with this argument is that the skeptical conclusion does not appear to follow from the premises. It is now commonly admitted that given any set of data, many theories can be constructed, each of which explains the data as well as any other. What follows from this fact, however, is not skepticism, but rather the conclusion that explaining the empirical evidence is a necessary but not a sufficient condition for the truth of a theory, and that other essentially pragmatic considerations such as simplicity and consistency must be invoked to yield a decision among equally well-confirmed theories. We should, in fact, reject Russell's proposal, not because it is refuted by empirical evidence, but because it is more complex than the alternative. Thus it is not the inadequacy of empirical evidence to distinguish among equally well-confirmed, competing theories which makes Russell's proposal skeptical.

Danto has argued that the proposal that the world was created five minutes ago is equivalent to the proposal that it was created any given number of minutes ago, in the sense that whatever evidence supports the five-minute hypothesis supports the others equally well. Let us then suppose that the world was created in 4004 B.C. The interesting thing about this supposition is, of course, that it not only has been held but is still held by a number of people who would hardly qualify as philosophical skeptics in any ordinary sense of the word. Why, then, is it that the supposition that the world was created in 4004 B.C. is not skeptical if the supposition that it was created five minutes ago is skeptical? The answer is certainly not that it took the Lord six days to do what Russell did in an instant; it will do no harm to assume that what one Lord can do another can, and to make the creation instantaneous in both cases. Nor will it do to hold that there is evidence of a sort for the world being created in 4004 B.C.—namely, the Mosaic account. The existence of that account can be explained by alternative theories just as well as by the fundamentalist one. The difference, then, must lie elsewhere, and it seems to lie here: that when God created Adam and Eve, he did indeed create them as adults, but not with false memories of events which supposedly occurred before they were created. They may have been endowed with certain forms of intuitive knowledge, but they did not remember childhoods they had never had and parents who had never existed. In Russell's proposal, on the other hand, not only were all men created five minutes ago but they were created remembering a lifetime of experience which never occurred. I suggest that it is this difference which makes Russell's proposal skeptical whereas the proposal contained in the book of Genesis is not.

In *An Analysis of Knowledge and Valuation*, Lewis presented a very thoughtful analysis of the problem of memory.[7] He notes that one reason we have confidence in what we remember is the fact that our memories hang together in a consistent fashion. Lewis describes this hanging together as "congruence" of memories, by which he means such a relation among a set of statements that the antecedent probability of any one will be increased if the remainder are taken as premises.[8] This is a stronger relation than coherence, which Lewis takes to mean the sort of logical interrelationships evidenced, for example, by the statement of Euclidean geometry. But, although the congruence of our memories is one reason for our belief that they are true, it is not, Lewis argues, a sufficient reason, for it is possible to find congruent systems—indeed, coherent systems—which are not true. Thus, e.g., Lobatchevsky's geometry is certainly coherent, but it is not, so far as we know, true. Congruence is, therefore, a necessary condition for the truth of memory, but it is not a sufficient condition. One might think that the problem can be solved in just the same way that the problem of the truth of geometry is solved namely, by giving the system an empirical interpretation, and testing its consequences. But this tactic, Lewis points out, will not do, for it assumes that we have true cognitions against which the theorems can be tested, and the critical point is that without veridical memory we can have no true cognition. For what else is cognized in a cognition except the similarity of presented sense data to remembered sensations taken as indices for some thing or character? Without memorial knowledge we could not interpret present sensations as representing a man or a table or a boat, or indeed as being white or shiny—we should simply have certain phenomenal suchnesses with which we should have no way to deal. Any cognition at all thus assumes the truth of some memorial knowledge, so that the truth of memory cannot be established in the same way that the truth of an interpreted geometry can. Accordingly, Lewis holds, we must accept memory as having prima facie credibility.[9] This will provide a sufficient basis for establishing a credible cognitive knowledge, while at the same time making possible the revision and correction of particular memories which turn out to be inaccurate. Thus we may impeach particular memories when we find that they are inconsistent with other memories or with the testimony of others, but we cannot impeach all memory without plunging headlong into skepticism. For without memory which is at least prima facie credible, there would be no knowledge at all. And it is just this prima facie credibility of memory which Russell's proposal attacks, for on this proposal we have come by all our memories of events which occurred more than five minutes ago by a route other than experience, so that no prima facie credibility should attach to them. If that were so, then all our knowledge would be in question. It is not, then, merely past-referring predicates that would turn out to be false, but even what Danto has called temporally neutral predicates such as "whitish shiny mark," for to recognize something as "whitish" or "shiny" or a "mark" is to make use of memorial knowledge which we should on Russell's proposal be forced to regard as dubious. This is why I think Russell's proposal is genuinely skeptical.

But if it is the denial of the truth of memorial knowledge which makes Russell's proposal skeptical, it would seem that memory is in some critical way involved in the truth of historical knowledge. Memorial knowledge is knowledge of past events, and since we must give prima facie credence to memorial knowledge, we have strong reason to believe in the existence of past events. But historical knowledge, too, is about past events, including, in some cases, those of which we also have memorial knowledge. How is our historical knowledge related to our memorial knowledge, or, more exactly—since all knowledge is at least partly memorial knowledge —is the relation of historical knowledge to memorial knowledge any different from the relation of physical or biological knowledge to memorial knowledge? There are two ways in which it might be thought that memorial knowledge is particularly relevant to history: first, it might be thought that the historian relies upon his own memory of the events he writes about; and second, it might be thought that he relies upon other people's memories. Each point requires some comment.

It is true that some historians have written accounts in which they used their own memories of events as a source of knowledge about the past. Perhaps the most obvious example of this is Thucydides, who strove to be a witness to as many of the events of the Peloponnesian War as possible and used his own memory of these events in writing. But this sort of case is rare and is generally suspect. When, for example, Arthur Schlesinger, Jr., wrote his account of the Kennedy administration,[10] he did not regard it as a history of that administration but as a personal memoir based on his own remembered experiences, and in so classifying it he showed very clearly the sort of distinction which a historian makes between memoirs and history. In general, historians write about events which they themselves do not remember; so that having personal memory about the events in question is certainly not regarded as a necessary condition for writing adequate history. When a historian does write about events which he remembers, he faces severe problems. For in order to meet the standards of the trade, he must treat his own recollections of events as neither better nor worse than the recollections of any other witness, and this, since he gives prima facie credibility to his own memories but not to the memories of others, is a very difficult thing to do. In fact, many historians would not undertake to write an account under these conditions, feeling that they could not be "objective"—that is, feeling that they would give undue emphasis to their own recollections. Thus, although it is true that some historians do use personal memory as a source of knowledge about the past, this is not the usual practice, and when it is done it is clearly recognized that the practice raises serious difficulties which only the most rigorous controls can overcome. Specifically, the historian must, if he is to follow the standards of the trade, weigh his own recollections in just the same way that he weighs those of other witnesses of equal qualifications, so that the condition upon which the use of personal memory is legitimate is that it be regarded just as if it were someone else's memorial evidence.

Historians certainly make use of what other people remember. In fact, all records—including the laboratory records of the physicist—involve some degree of reliance on memory, and standard historical records such as the census, business records, the *Congressional Record*, etc., do not involve memory in any sense in which it is not involved in other fields. The class of historical evidence where memory is peculiarly present is testimonial evidence, meaning an account (oral or written) of an event or object recalled. Such evidence is never taken as prima facie true—it is always examined more or less in the way testimonial evidence is examined in court to determine bias, opportunity, competence, and consistency with other accounts. In short, memorial accounts of other persons, when used as testimonial evidence of the historial past, are not accepted in the same way that one accepts one's own memories as evidence of the past: they are not regarded as prima facie true but as data to be explained, one possible explanation being that they are true accounts of that of which they purport to be accounts.

Our knowledge of the historical past, therefore, must be sharply distinguished from our knowledge of the memorial past, even in those cases where they refer to the same object or event. Both may be knowledge of the past, but they are different sorts of knowledge based on different evidences and derived by different methods. I must trust my memory, at least to the extent of according prima facie credibility to it, or else I can have no knowledge at all: to deny the credibility of all memory is tantamount to total skepticism. But nothing stops me from denying the truth of the historical past, except the empirical evidence which makes it reasonable for me to believe in it, just as nothing stops me from denying the existence of electrons except the difficulty of accounting for certain empirical facts if I do. That the memorial past existed we know, because we have no choice but to believe it. That the immemorial past existed we believe, on the basis of empirical evidence which could conceivably admit of an alternative explanation. Thus even if one believes that memory provides direct "acquaintance"[11] with the objects and events of the past, one cannot hold that this "acquaintance" is in any sense essential, or even relevant, to historical knowledge. For, so far as what is past is concerned, historical knowledge is knowledge about objects and events with which the historian has no acquaintance, and in those rare cases where he does have such acquaintance, he can use it only as if it were a record of someone else's experience. This is not to deny, of course, that history, too, is based upon sensory experience, but only that it is based upon sensory experience of past objects and events.

The reflections offered above indicate that the relation between history and memory is not different in kind from that between other fields of learning and memory. History is about events in the past and memory is also about events in the past, but the basis for knowledge of the past is different in the two cases; moreover, they are not usually about the same past. It is an obvious but important fact that history deals for the most part with a past which no man now remembers. All men have a knowledge of the memorial past, since all men have memories, and all men appear to have at least some concept of an immemorial past, but the content of that concept varies widely from society to society. Thus to the aborigines of Australia, the past is a dreamtime, peopled by culture heroes whose deeds account for the present condition of the world. For these people, even the distant past is not wholly gone: the heroes of old still exist and can be contacted and induced to intervene in the present world through rituals at appropriate sites, so that the past is a source of creative powers still functioning in the world.[12] But it is hardly necessary to turn to the original myths of primitive peoples to exhibit the extraordinary variability which exists among human accounts of the immemorial past. In our own western cultures, from the triumph of Christianity until the nineteenth century, virtually every educated man believed that the world was created according to the Mosaic account. Knowledge of the immemorial past, then, is not something given but something won; and how extraordinarily difficult that winning really is, is strikingly evident from the fact that, until Darwin published, mankind as a whole was grossly in error about its own origin. It was Darwin's incomparable achievement—surely the greatest feat of historical scholarship ever accomplished—to discover the origin of our own species. Indeed, even the extent of the human past is something that had to be discovered—not recovered, for no one had known the history of mankind before Darwin. History tells us many things about the past which were not known to those who lived in the past. History is thus a discipline which seeks to discover new phenomena and to create new knowledge, including even the fact that there was an immemorial past to be known.

What justifies our statements about the past? If we look, for example, at our statements about the history of the earth, it is clear that our conclusions are based upon findings of the physical sciences—especially of physics, chemistry, and geology. That is to say, those sciences, applied to the current state of the earth, justify certain conclusions about the length of time the earth has existed and about the sequence of events which has transpired since it came into existence. Similarly, our conclusions about man's antiquity are based upon biological, anatomical, and geological theories, upon radioactive and other physical dating methods, and upon the physical remains of human and prehuman creatures, such as the bones and teeth found by the Leakys in the Olduvai Gorge. Again our conclusions rest upon evidence which can be seen and examined now, such as the skull of Zinjanthropos Boesi and the results of the radioactive dating tests done on that skull. And so it must be for every historical statement. Nothing can serve as evidence for an historical statement which is not in existence at the present time. This point may seem obvious, but it is sufficiently fundamental to bear emphasis. History refers to past events and objects, but the evidence which justifies these references must always be present.

If we turn the matter around and ask why we should ever have done history, the same point can be made in a somewhat different but illuminating way. We find in our environment numerous objects about which we can ask the question, why is this thing as it is? We see, for example, houses, monuments, pieces of paper bearing inscriptions, tools, etc. To ask why these things are as they are is often to ask about the origins of the objects or about processes occurring in the past by which these objects came to be as they are. In these cases, an explanation of the state of the present object requires the postulation of events in the past. In fact, all historical inquiry arises from the attempt to provide explanations of some present phenomena, just as all inquiries in physics arise ultimately from the attempt to explain some present phenomena. Were we not motivated to ask about the origins and past of such phenomena (as some people in some cultures are not), we should have no history at all. Thus history, like science, arises from man's attempt to understand the environment in which he now lives, and although it is about things or events which have occurred in the past, it is the phenomena of the present which it seeks to explain.

It follows that the question of whether we can know the *whole* past is a pseudoquestion. We can know what we have evidence for; what we have no evidence for we have no reason to believe ever existed. It is, of course, true that we can have what we usually call "incomplete knowledge." For example, we are sure that there were Indians in the northeast woodlands of the United States before the coming of Europeans. We are sure of this fact because we have evidence for it: we have archaeological evidence, and we may also infer it from our biological and sociological theories and from the fact that there were large numbers of Indians there when the Europeans landed. About these Indians we know very little: we do not know the identities of individuals or the particulars of their lives, although from our general knowledge of human societies, and our knowledge of the state of Indian culture when the Europeans arrived, we can infer that various types of events must have occurred. But the fact that our knowledge in such cases is and must probably remain incomplete does not in any sense call into question the truth of the historical knowledge that we do have. It is one thing for our knowledge to be partial and quite another for our knowledge to be false. There is no inconsistency involved in knowing some things about a subject while not knowing other things. Our knowledge of the past may be true, even though it is also a true inference that there must have been events about which we know little more than that they existed.

Historical statements are about past events or objects, even though all the evidence for these statements consists of phenomena presently in existence. But if this is so, we must face the third of the problems raised by our definition—what is the ontological status of such objects? If I believe that George Washington existed and did the things he is generally reputed to have done, it cannot be because I observe Washington doing these things. It is, rather, because I have now a great many objects of which I can make sense only on the supposition that such a person did exist and did do these things. These objects presently before me range from pieces of paper bearing inscriptions to portraits to objects of clothing to Mount Vernon—they are extremely heterogeneous in kind. What they all have in common, besides present observability, is that I can "explain" (in a sense to be discussed later) these data if I assume the existence and actions of Washington. The confirmation of my statements about Washington must therefore be indirect, in the sense that he, himself, is never observed by me. But this should not pose any insuperable problem, since we believe in the existence of many entities which we do not actually experience. I am not aware that anyone has ever had sensory experience of subatomic particles such as electrons, yet the existence of such entities is widely accepted. Indeed, theoretical constructs of this sort are very common in contemporary physics and are accepted as a legitimate and necessary component of our more advanced scientific theories. What I wish to maintain is that George Washington enjoys at present the epistemological status of an electron: each is an entity postulated for the purpose of giving coherence to our present experience, and each is unobservable by us.

In the philosophy of science, various theses have been advanced regarding the status of theoretical constructs.[13] It has been maintained, for example, that such terms involve no ontological commitment and that the portions of the theory which involve constructs can be instrumentally interpreted as mere calculating devices for producing statements having observational interpretations. Such a view has even been proposed for historical constructs by Danto, although it is difficult to know how seriously he intends this proposal to be taken. But it is equally possible to give a realistic interpretation to constructs, so that when one speaks of electrons in physics one is speaking of real entities and when one speaks of George Washington one is speaking of a real person. Neither the realist nor the instrumentalist view can be proven correct or incorrect, so the choice between them is arbitrary; as the realistic view appears to me the more natural, it is the one I shall adopt here. Thus to say that there really are electrons means that the theory in which electrons are postulated is well confirmed by observational evidence, and to say that there really was such a person as George Washington means that our "theory" about Washington (which for the moment may be taken to mean the set of statements we assert which refer to Washington) is well confirmed by observational evidence. In this sense, the whole of our historical knowledge is a theoretical construction created for the purpose of explaining observational evidence.

To this claim it may be objected that historical entities are not constructs because they are on the same "level" as entities of daily experience. That is, when we postulate an entity such as a gene or an electron, we are postulating something which cannot in principle be observed, whereas to postulate George Washington is to assert the existence of something which is of the same sort as the men we observe every day. But unobservability in principle can be construed in two different ways. If to "observe" an electron means to determine simultaneously its position and its velocity, we know from the Heisenberg principle that this cannot be done. To assert that electrons are observable in this sense would, therefore, involve a logical inconsistency with the axioms of quantum mechanics. On the other hand, the unobservability of a gene is due to the grossness of our senses: it is physically impossible for us to observe genes but not logically impossible. If our senses were different from what they in fact are, it might well be possible for us to observe genes. It is in the latter sense that historical entities such as George Washington may be said to be unobservable in principle. If free mobility in time is impossible, that is a contingent fact about the world—there is nothing logically impossible about such mobility. But since, in fact, it is physically impossible for us to observe past objects such as Washington, we must interpret such objects as theoretical constructs.

The fourth problem which is raised by the historian's characterization of his discipline is the question of how historical statements can be said to be true or false. We must accordingly specify the truth conditions for such statements—i.e., those conditions the satisfaction of which enables us to say that a statement is true or false, or, more accurately, highly confirmed or highly disconfirmed. And since what distinguishes historical statements from nonhistorical statements is reference to events and objects of the past, we may begin our consideration by asking whether or not the pastness of what is referred to in such statements affects their truth conditions. The natural way to discuss events and objects of the past, at least in English, is to use the past tense, and any perusal of historical writings will show at once that this is the standard historical practice. At first glance, one is inclined to think that the use of the past tense is purely a matter of style, and that no issue of significance is involved. Surely, it would seem, to say "Caesar is murdered" (tenselessly) is equivalent in meaning to saying "Caesar was murdered," and the difference reflects merely the aesthetic preference of the historian. But a second glance shows that something important is involved here, for if I change a tenseless statement into a tensed one by simply adding tense to the verb, I change both the meaning of the statement and its truth conditions. Thus if I am told that "Caesar was murdered," I know something which I would not have known from the tenseless statement "Caesar is murdered"—namely, I know that the event referred to is past. Moreover, the former statement would be false if it were uttered in 45 B.C., while the latter is true no matter when it is uttered. Whether or not there exists a tenseless equivalent of "Caesar was murdered" which preserves all the information which that statement gives is another question; it suffices that the statement with the verb tensed conveys to us information which is not conveyed by a statement which differs only in having an untensed verb. Since the truth of a tensed statement varies with the time of its utterance while that of a tenseless statement does not, it would seem that the tenseless statement is in some sense the simpler of the two; and so it should be easier to begin with the question of the truth conditions of such a tenseless statement.

Arguments over the truth conditions of historical statements have generally been phrased as arguments over the meaning of historical statements, since most of those who have argued the issue have been either proponents or opponents of a truth condition theory of meaning. Here, as in so many other questions relating to historical knowledge, the interest has been less in history than in a philosophic issue—in this case the theory of meaning—and the utility of the historical case has been that it appeared to be one to which it was difficult to apply such truth condition theories as pragmatism and positivism. Since I do not subscribe to a truth condition theory of meaning, I am not concerned here with the question of what historical sentences mean; nevertheless, insofar as pragmatism and positivism have developed clear formulations of the notion of truth conditions, we may profit by their labors and so define the truth conditions of a sentence s as all the conditional statements relating operations or conditions of observation to experienced effects which are logically derivable from s. I shall refer to these conditional statements which compose the truth conditions of a statement s as the *consequences* of s. The statement "Caesar is murdered" has among its consequences such statements as that if one is in a particular place in Rome on the Ides of March in 44 B.C., one has certain experiences related to Caesar's death; that if one examines accounts of what occurred in Rome in 44 B.C. written after that date, one finds references to or descriptions of Caesar's death, and so on. It will be observed that the consequences of a statement s which is tenseless may be formulated tenselessly, but the temporal relation *earlier than* (or *later than*) must be used to describe the relation of the operations or observational conditions and experiences referred to in the consequence to the events referred to in s. Some consequences will involve observations made simultaneously with the events referred to in s, some will describe observations made later; and some may involve observations made earlier—e.g., among the consequences of the statement "There will be an eclipse at 4 P.M. on Aug. 3, 1984" are statements concerning what astronomical observations reveal for August 2, 1984. The tenselessness of the consequences is hardly surprising since the statement s is itself tenseless; the important point is not that the consequences are tenseless but that the events referred to in the consequences have various temporal relations to the events referred to in s. What statements occur in later historical records, what archaeological digs at later times reveal, and what Carbon 14 tests made a thousand years later show are as truly consequences of s as what I can observe about the event referred to in s if I am on the spot at the time.

It is obvious from what has been said, but it will perhaps bear repeating, that the operations or observations referred to in the consequences of s need not be operations upon nor observations of any entity in the extension of the terms of s. Thus if s is the statement "Neptune exists," one consequence of this statement is that upon investigation at appropriate times I shall find certain perturbations in the orbit of Uranus. Clearly, this consequence does not involve the observation of Neptune but rather of certain effects of the presence of Neptune. Similarly, the statement "the Battle of Bosworth occurs in 1485" has among its consequences statements about what will be found in records written after that event. We do not in this case observe the event referred to as the Battle of Bosworth but rather certain effects of that event.

If such are the truth conditions of tenseless statements, what happens when we add tense? What is the difference in truth conditions between "the Battle of Bosworth occurs in 1485" and "the Battle of Bosworth occurred in 1485"? It is, I think, not hard to see that the difference consists in the fact that only some consequences of the tenseless statement are in fact testable by me—namely, those which refer to observations made at least four hundred and eighty-seven years after the event. I cannot now go to Bosworth field and witness the death of the last Plantagenet—the only consequences I can directly test are those which refer to effects of that event such as the statements which are contained in certain types of records. What the addition of tense to a statement s does, therefore, is not to alter the consequences of s, but to tell us which consequences of s it is now physically possible to test. But every consequence of s, whether in fact testable now or not, remains part of the truth conditions of s. That the Battle of Bosworth occurred in 1485 implies, among other things,

that had anyone with normal sensory equipment been present on Bosworth field during certain hours of the day of the battle, he would have
seen the battle in progress.

This way of analyzing the significance of tense involves a distinction
between two different meanings of the word "testable." To say that a
consequence is testable is clearly to say that it is possible to test the consequence, but what has usually been meant by possibility in this statement
is logical possibility. Thus a consequence has generally been regarded as
testable if it is logically possible to specify the operations or conditions
of observation and the experienced results in observational terms. All
consequences of s must be testable in this sense. When, however, we add
tense to a statement, questions of physical possibility are introduced.
That I cannot now observe the Battle of Bosworth is a matter of physical
impossibility, not of logical impossibility. The classification of consequences of s into those which are now, once were, or will be testable is a
classification based upon physical possibility and does not at all affect
the logical possibility of these consequences being tested.

In his recent book, Arthur Danto has vigorously attacked the applicability of pragmatic and verificationist theories of meaning to history on
the ground that such theories involve an attempt to eliminate all mention
of the past and so are inherently incapable of dealing with history. But
Danto's objections appear to be based upon an interpretation of the
pragmatic position according to which the meaning of s is limited to
those consequences of s which are either capable of immediate verification now or else can be verified sometime in the future—i.e., those which
are predictions. Thus he remarks:

> What sense can we give to the expression "knowing that the Battle of
> Hastings took place in 1066" if the *whole* of our knowledge consists in
> a set of conditional sentences which refer to future actions and expe-
> riences? How, on such analysis, *can* I know the past, or anything other
> than these conditional sentences?[14]

Danto thus thinks that a pragmatist must deny that those consequences
referring to operations or conditions of observation and experiences
which once could have been, but can no longer be, made are part of the
meaning of s. It must certainly be granted that if Danto is correct in this
claim, the pragmatic view cannot be maintained, for it would lead to
impossible difficulties—e.g., that consequences of s would be eliminated

from its meaning with every passing day. But the view here taken is not open to this objection, for on this analysis every statement which was ever a consequence of s is always a consequence of s, whether it is a prediction, a statement about what can be known now, or a statement about what might once have been the case. Moreover, the term "past" is not eliminated, for the classification of consequences into those testable in the future, those testable in the present, and those testable in the past obviously involves reference to the past.

Danto has also pointed out that the truth value of tensed statements differs from that of tenseless statements, and that it varies with the time of utterance. He has also argued that no theory of meaning which fails to permit this can apply to historical statements. But this result follows directly from the theory here advanced. "The Battle of Bosworth occurred" is false if uttered in 1484 because neither the perusal of relevant records in that year nor interviews with local residents would reveal the occurrence of any such event. Which class of consequences is to be tested is precisely what the tensing of a statement tells us, and since the members of the different classes of consequences refer to operations made and experiences had at different times, the truth value of the tensed statements depends upon matching the right consequences with the temporal order of events. There is thus no problem for this theory of truth conditions in the variation of the truth value of statements with change of tense.

I suspect that what will be found objectionable in this analysis is its heavy reliance on counterfactuals. But it would be quite incorrect to conclude that this position involves some special commitment to counterfactuals. Goodman has shown how inescapably our scientific knowledge involves counterfactuals,[15] and it does not appear that history is any different from physics in this regard. Counterfactuals are a problem for the whole theory of knowledge, not just for history. Furthermore, we must be wary of concluding that consequences referring to past operations or observations are counterfactual. The statement that if anyone had been present on Bosworth field during certain hours of a given day in 1485 he would have witnessed a battle is hardly counterfactual, since many people were present and did witness the battle. The consequences which we can verify only assert that if we examine certain types of records we will find accounts of the battle, and the truth of these consequences alone does not imply the truth of the consequences regarding what an observer so situated would observe, since the document may not be authentic or the witness may have lied. But if the document is authentic, and the testimony of the witness is corroborated, then the fact that we find an account of such experiences as an observer so situated would have had is evidence for the occurrence of the battle. Indeed, if one thinks about the sort of consequences which are relevant to the confirmation of statements about the past, it is obvious that many of these involve the finding of testimony to the effect that some persons did in fact make certain experiments or observations in the past. But how could this be so, if the consequences that an observer so situated would thus observe were not part of the truth conditions of the statement that the battle occurred? How would we recognize the testimony of such witnesses as relevant to the truth of the original statement if that statement did not imply the consequences involved in that testimony? Unless the truth conditions of s contain the full range of consequences of s, the confirmation of s by historical evidence becomes impossible.

The major objection to the view I have developed comes, it seems to me, not from the opponents of pragmatism but from its advocates, notably from Quine. Classical pragmatism implies that, for every sentence s which is meaningful, there exists a set C of statements which relate operations or conditions of observation to experiences, and that this set is so related to s that the verification of members of C confirms s and the falsification of members of C disconfirms s—i.e., C contains the truth conditions of s. But the classical pragmatists, at least from James on, always insisted that other factors in addition to the verification or falsification of members of C could confirm or disconfirm s.[16] This insight has been given a very powerful formulation by Quine which calls into question the dependence of s on the members of C. Quine has made essentially two points. First, consider the relation of members of C to s. S alone does not logically imply most of the sentences in C. To establish a logical relation between s and p ($p \in C$), we must permit s to be conjoined with other sentences. Hence for p to be a member of C, there must exist a set A of sentences $a_1 \ldots a_n$ such that the conjunction $a_1 \& \ldots \& a_n \& s \rightarrow p$. If we define the membership of C in this manner, it is then simply not true that $\sim p \rightarrow \sim s$; rather $\sim p \rightarrow \sim a_1 v \ldots v \sim a_n v \sim s$, so that the rejection of any a_i is a sufficient adjustment to account for $\sim p$. Hence we cannot say that the falsification of members of C determines the disconfirmation of s, since the decision as to which member of the conjunction used as a premise should be rejected is wholly arbitrary.

Second, Quine has pointed out that every member of C may be verified and yet s may be rejected. For there are many cases which show that the choice among competing theories depends not only upon empirical verification but also upon criteria such as simplicity, elegance, and consistency with accepted principles. To achieve a simpler theory or a more elegant one, a sentence s may be dropped from a theory, even though every member of C is verified. Similarly, if s is inconsistent with principles already accepted, we may refuse to accept s even though every sentence in C is verified. Hence the confirmation or disconfirmation of s is not solely dependent upon what happens to members of C: members of C may be falsified without s being disconfirmed, and members of C may be verified without s being confirmed. Accordingly, the attempt to specify as the truth conditions of s some set C of testable consequences of s, upon which the confirmation or disconfirmation of s depends, breaks down, for no such set can be identified.[17]

Faced with difficulties of this magnitude, one is tempted to try to evade them by distinguishing what pertains to a specific system from what pertains to a given component of the system. Thus simplicity, elegance, and consistency are properties of specific systems of sentences, not of sentences individually, and they can hardly be said to be truth conditions of individual sentences. On the other hand, it might be argued that there is still a sense in which individual sentences have consequences, even though auxiliary hypotheses are required for the derivation of those consequences. Thus one might define the consequences of a sentence s as all those testable sentences which are implied by s conjoined with *any* consistent set of auxiliary hypotheses but which are not implied by the conjunction of auxiliary hypotheses alone—i.e., p is a consequence of s if and only if there exists $a_1 \ldots a_n$ such that $a_1 \& \ldots \& a_n \& s \rightarrow p$, and $a_1 \& \ldots \& a_n$ does not imply p. Unfortunately, there are two reflections which show that this move will not do. First, consider any sentence s, and any testable sentence whatever, say q. Then the conjunction of s with $s \rightarrow q$ implies q, and so q is a consequence of s. Hence every sentence is a consequence of any sentence you please, and so all sentences have identical consequences. Clearly, then, there must be some limitation placed upon the range of possible auxiliary hypotheses if we are to avoid talking nonsense. Second, to talk of consequences as sentences logically derivable from certain hypotheses is to assume a particular logic with which the derivation is made, for with different logical systems different sets of consequences would be obtained. Thus a sentence can have consequences and so truth conditions only relative to a given logic. These considerations show that testable consequences are relative to theories, i.e., to sets of statements, and to the logical systems which provide the rules of inference. Thus truth, like simplicity, elegance, and consistency, turns out to be a characteristic of particular systems, not of individual sentences.[18]

Nevertheless, it is still possible to retain a weakened notion of the truth conditions of an individual sentence, at least relative to a given theory. Thus one may define the set of consequences of a sentence s relative to a theory T (including a logic) as the set of testable consequences implied by s conjoined with any consistent set of auxiliary hypotheses in T, but not implied by the conjunction of those auxiliary hypotheses alone. That is, recognizing that the theory (with its logic) constitutes, as it were, the frame of reference of the individual sentence, we must specify the theory before we can talk meaningfully about the individual sentence. But once the theory is specified, then, relative to that theory, it is possible to define the truth conditions of given sentences. Nor is this procedure open to the objection which led to the rejection of the nonrelative concept of consequences, for here the range of auxiliary hypotheses is limited to those of a particular theory.

But this tactic still leaves unanswered the question of how the verification or falsification of consequences of s affect the confirmation or disconfirmation of s, for, as we saw above, the falsification of a given consequence only implies that some one of the hypotheses used in deriving it is false, not that s is false. Which hypothesis we will change in this situation is to some extent arbitrary, but it is not completely arbitrary—one would not, for example, think of settling the matter by rolling a die. Rather, what appears to happen is that one preserves those hypotheses in which he has the most confidence and sacrifices those hypotheses in which he has the least confidence. But this implies that for any set of sentences in T and any given investigator, there exists an ordering, based on degree of confidence, for the elimination of hypotheses. We may, therefore, conceive the theory T as a set of sentences over which a function B is defined which assigns to each sentence t in T a subjective probability. Assuming that the usual coherence constraints are satisfied, it is reasonable to assume that the member of a given set of hypotheses used in deriving a testable consequence which will be rejected first is that which has the lowest subjective probability. If this is so, then s is actually in jeopardy only when consequences of s are tested with respect to the premises of which s has the lowest subjective probability. For convenience, we may speak of consequences which meet this condition as the *crucial consequences* of s. Clearly, the crucial consequences of s may be used to confirm or disconfirm s, since s is, so to speak, the weakest member of the conjunction so that the test outcomes will have most effect upon the subjective probability reposed in it. Noncrucial consequences of s, on the other hand, are not useful in testing s, since a negative outcome will not lead to a rejection of s.

Given this formulation, it would seem that the truth conditions of s must be limited to its crucial consequences. But this conclusion involves certain difficulties. For at any given time the subjective probability assigned to s may be such that it has no crucial consequences; it may not be directly testable, so that it is not a crucial consequence of itself, and it may be so firmly established that in no conjunction of statements of the theory which contains it does it have the lowest probability. Yet we know from experience that successive disconfirmation of noncrucial consequences of s will sooner or later cause such a decay of its certainty that it will become vulnerable. Indeed, it is well known that to call into question a fundamental principle of a science usually requires the accumulation of many anomalous results, and that the recognition that a principle, once deemed established, is now vulnerable develops slowly and unequally among the practitioners of the field. Accordingly, it seems better to regard all consequences of s as truth conditions, even though at a given time only some of them are crucial consequences.

This theory corresponds rather closely to what happens in practice. In designing a test for a hypothesis, one simply does not use noncrucial consequences—to do so would show lack of scientific judgment. No one uses an inaccurate instrument to test a prediction which specifies an exact result, or assumes as an auxiliary hypothesis a statement more dubious than the test hypothesis. The crucial consequences are those which are, in fact, chosen in designing tests. Moreover, it is obvious that the assignment of subjective probabilities varies from person to person and from time to time even for one person. The set of crucial consequences is not immutably decreed by logical relations alone. Yet the person-to-person variance is apt at any given time during the periods of normal scientific activity to be relatively small, since one may on good grounds believe that during such periods most practitioners of the trade have roughly similar distributions of subjective probabilities over the sentences of T. Radical divergences are unlikely except in periods of scientific crisis and revolution, and certainly a part of what is meant by crisis is the very fact that such divergences in distributions of subjective probabilities become prominent. Paradigm change in the sense described by Kuhn is preceded by radical readjustments in the distributions of subjective probabilities of just this sort.[19]

For the purposes of the following analysis, then, we shall employ the concept of truth conditions outlined above. It is theories as wholes which have empirical consequences, but relative to a given theory it is possible to talk meaningfully about the testable consequences and so about the truth conditions of individual sentences, even though such talk is meaningless in absolute terms. We may, furthermore, test individual sentences by testing their crucial consequences, relative to a given theory, even though there are systematic factors such as simplicity, elegance, etc., which might lead to the rejection of such sentences in spite of the verification of their crucial consequences. In the advanced sciences, where theories are formalized and more precisely defined, the theoretical context in which a particular sentence is being used is usually quite clear. In fields such as history, where formalized theory hardly exists, the theoretical context is generally extremely vague. Nevertheless, such a context is always implicit, for in deriving consequences there are auxiliary hypotheses which no historian will employ, e.g., the absolute is perfect. The limited domain of auxiliary hypotheses which are actually acceptable for use marks out the theoretical context in question.

If the truth conditions of historical statements are construed as I have proposed, it seems clear that historical theories must include not only statements referring to objects and events in the past but the consequences of these statements as well. And since those consequences which are now testable refer to evidences which exist in the present, some statements of history are statements about presently existing objects and events.

It is these objects and events which can be observed by us, and it is these observations which provide the sensory experience upon which all historical knowledge rests. Accordingly, the characterization of history proposed above must be amended so as to hold that history is a discipline the theories of which consist of statements referring to past objects and events and of the consequences of those statements.

This characterization of history is broader than that usually in use, and permits the term "history" to be used meaningfully in such statements as "the history of the solar system" or "the history of the universe." In the common use, however, and the one which I shall adopt hereafter, the term "history" is restricted to mean human history—that is, its statements refer to those objects and events which pertain to the past of human societies and cultures. But whether we use the broad or the narrow sense, the past entities referred to are to be interpreted as theoretical constructs postulated to explain present data. This formulation, as we have just seen, leads very naturally to a notion of truth conditions for historical statements which connects past objects and events to present data, and so appears to provide an adequate basis for their confirmation. Yet this account of the nature of historical knowledge is sharply at variance with the traditional account, and it is, therefore, necessary to examine the traditional account from the perspective here advanced.

NOTES

1. Morton White, "Historical Explanation" in *Theories of History*, ed. Patrick Gardiner (Glencoe, Ill.: Free Press, 1959), p. 357.

2. White, "Explanation," p. 360.

3. White, "Explanation," p. 363.

4. White, "Explanation," p. 370.

5. Bertrand Russell, *The Analysis of Mind* (London: George Allen and Unwin, 1921), pp. 159–60.

6. Arthur C. Danto, *Analytical Philosophy of History* (Cambridge: Cambridge University Press, 1968), ch. 5.

7. Clarence I. Lewis, *An Analysis of Knowledge and Valuation* (La Salle, Ill.: Open Court Publishing Co., 1946), ch. 11.

8. Lewis, *Analysis*, p. 338.

9. Lewis, *Analysis*, p. 356.

10. Arthur Schlesinger, Jr., *A Thousand Days* (Greenwich, Conn.: Fawcett Co., 1965), p. ix.

11. Bertrand Russell, *Our Knowledge of the External World* (London: George Allen and Unwin, 1914), p. 151.

12. A. P. Elkin, *The Australian Aborigines: How to Understand Them* (Sydney: Angus and Robertson, 1954); W. E. H. Stanner, *On Aboriginal Religion* (Sydney: Australian National Research Council, 1963).

13. Ernest Nagel, *The Structure of Science* (New York: Harcourt, Brace & World, 1961), ch. 6.

14. Danto, *History*, p. 37.

15. Nelson Goodman, *Fact, Fiction, and Forecast* (Cambridge: Harvard University Press, 1955).

16. Murray G. Murphey, "Kant's Children: The Cambridge Pragmatists," *Transactions* of the Charles S. Peirce Society 4 (1968): 3–33.

17. Willard V. Quine, "Two Dogmas of Empiricism" in *From a Logical Point of View* (Cambridge: Harvard University Press, 1953), pp. 20–46.

18. Carl G. Hempel, "Aspects of Scientific Explanation" in *Aspects of Scientific Explanation and Other Essays in the Philosophy of Science* (New York: Free Press, 1965), pp. 101–22.

19. Thomas S. Kuhn, *The Structure of Scientific Revolutions* (Chicago: University of Chicago Press, 1962), ch. 8.

II

Traditional Historiography

In spite of the fact that history as a field of knowledge has been particularly attractive to idealistic philosophers, practicing historians have generally been thoroughgoing empiricists. The methods which have governed historical research during the past century reflect this staunch empiricism. But is has been a relatively naive empiricism, and many of the problems with which historiography has been preoccupied are as much a result of an excessively Baconian formulation as of the intrinsic difficulties of history. One can distinguish two major views in the historiography of the past century: what I shall call the "classical view," which is particularly associated with the scientific history movement, and what I shall call the "revisionist view," which was a reaction against the classical view and which still prevails.[1] These two views, in fact, agree much more than they disagree, but there are some significant differences to be noted. Accordingly, I shall structure this account around the classical methodology, indicating wherever necessary how the revisionists have differed from it.

Classical historiography is strongly Baconian in outlook. In the standard manuals on historiography, this Baconian view is translated into a methodology which has been taught to generations of historians and which has come to dominate even the form in which works on history are written.[2] One begins, it is held, with "external criticism," which establishes the authenticity of the "documents." One then employs "internal criticism" to interpret and evaluate the statements in the document

and so to arrive at a judgment of their trustworthiness. These statements
are then combined to yield the full set of particular facts believed to
obtain. Then, having collected the facts, the historian "synthesizes" from
them his account of the past. One may wonder how, on the basis of this
methodology, anyone ever wrote good history; but good history was
written, in part by ignoring the limitations of this methodology, but in
part also because classical historiographic method was better than the
naive Baconianism upon which it was based. I would like, therefore, to
examine this classical methodology, and the emendations which the revisionists have introduced, from the constructionist perspective I have
advanced, and to try to show both its strengths and its weaknesses. Moreover, by looking at what historians have traditionally thought they ought
to do, we shall, I think, gain some insight into the nature of historical
knowledge.

External criticism is the examination of the physical object which
it is proposed to use as evidence: traditionally, of the "document" itself
as opposed to its "content," or the "statements" which it contains. In
Hockett's words, external criticism "examines *documents*—a compre-
hensive term which here includes not only manuscripts but books,
pamphlets, maps, and even ancient inscriptions and monuments—with
the aim of obtaining all possible information of any significance about
their origin, and if need be, of restoring the original form or wording."[3]
Clearly, a "document" here means an object bearing an inscription which
is interpreted as human writing. The assumption of the classical methodology that history deals with "documents" exclusively is surprising in
view of the role which archaeology has long played in the study of
antiquity, and the revisionists have correctly insisted that a broader
meaning should be given to the term. Thus Gottschalk has argued that
"any kind of source, whether written, oral, pictorial, or archaeological,"
should be regarded as a "document"[4] and most modern historians accept
this usage.

Consider, for example, the Piltdown skull and a piece of paper inscribed with the date August 15, 1820, addressed to "John Adams," and
signed "Thomas Jefferson." An external criticism of these objects seeks
to determine when, where, how, under what conditions, and in what form
they were originally produced, and what has happened to them since.
With the skull, the critical questions are its age, the exact location at

which it was found, and what happened to it before and after it was found; with the piece of paper, the questions are when it was written, by whom, to whom, and where it has been since it was written. The objective of external criticism is to establish what the object is, so that a decision can be reached as to whether or not it is historical evidence, and if so, for what. To say what something is, is to classify it as something, and from the point of view taken here, it seems best to regard external criticism as an attempt to test classificatory hypotheses about these objects. Thus what we actually have before us in these two examples are, in the first case, some fragments of bone, and, in the second, a piece of paper bearing certain inscriptions. We do not know *a priori* that the fragments are pieces of a skull, nor that the piece of paper is a letter. What we do is to *classify* these objects, and we do so by making a classificatory hypothesis about them. Thus, on the basis of the shape and color of the bone fragments, and the geological character of the gravel bed in which they were found, we classify them as the remains of the skull of a prehuman anthropoid from the early Pliestocene era. Similarly, when we examine the piece of paper, we discover that it has the formal characteristics of a letter: it is dated, it is addressed to someone, it is signed by someone, and it appears to contain a message which one person wished to communicate to another. Accordingly, we classify the piece of paper as a letter written by Jefferson to Adams on August 15, 1820. And so in all such cases. The initial task in historical research is to classify the data, and the classification is historical insofar as it involves reference to events and persons postulated to have existed in the past.

Now to classify is to bring an object under a general category or term, and so to assert that what is true of all members of the class defined by that term is true of this object. It is a general truth about skulls that if x is the skull of any animal, then the brain case of x cannot be older than the jaw of x. Similarly, it is a general truth about letters that if x is a letter written at time t, then x cannot be written on paper made after t or in ink the manufacture of which did not begin until after t. Furthermore, if x is a letter written by z, then the handwriting in x must be similar to that in other letters written by z, certain words must occur with approximately the same frequency in x as in z's other writings, there must exist an individual for whom the letter is intended, etc. Classification thus involves the assertion of universal principles, and these in turn permit the inference by *modus ponens* of consequences which must be true if the object is correctly classified. It is the business of external criticism to test these consequences. The variety of chemical and physical tests applied to the Piltdown skull showed decisively that the brain case and the jaw were not of the same age, and so led to the reclassification of the object as a hoax generated by combining a human brain case with an orangutan's jaw.[5] External criticism applied to the letter has confirmed the consequences derived from the classification hypothesis; however, had the paper referred to in the consequence turned out to be esparto grass paper and the ink to contain aniline dye, or if the handwriting or word frequencies had turned out to be very different from those in other writings of Jefferson, or if no such person as John Adams ever existed, the classification hypothesis would have had to be rejected and the hypothesis of forgery entertained. Thus it should be clear that the initial steps in historical inquiry are no different from those in any science—namely, the classification of the data, or more precisely, the classification of something as data, since the relevance of something to a discipline is not established until some initial classification is made. Historians have not conceived of external criticism as a method for testing the adequacy of classificatory hypotheses and for overthrowing them if they are incorrect, but in practice that is how they have used it. It is a methodological canon which has thorough justification and it is to the credit of traditional historiography that it should have insisted upon the importance of such a canon.

By "internal criticism," classical historiography meant the evaluation of the statements occurring in documents with respect to their meaning and their trustworthiness. This formulation takes it for granted that we can be certain when a statement occurs. Actually, what one confronts is a physical object upon which some kind of figure is inscribed. One does not know *a priori* that the inscription is writing, and cases exist in which there is disagreement on this point. But even when it is clear that the inscription is writing, that fact does not help us to determine what the writing means, as the case of the still-undeciphered Mayan inscriptions makes all too clear. To interpret an inscription, we must be able to attribute to it both meaning and reference. How is this attribution to be made when we are dealing with an inscription which was produced by the people of another time and place? There are two related problems involved here: can one, in at least some cases, determine the meaning and reference of linguistic expressions used by members of another culture; and, can one do so when one is limited to inscriptional evidence only? We will consider these problems in order.

In his recent writings, Quine has dealt with the problem of cross-cultural knowledge in a very interesting way.[6] He has posed what he calls the problem of radical translation—the problem which, for example, confronts the anthropologist when he first meets a hitherto uncontacted people speaking an unknown language. Even under such extreme circumstances, we know that a translation can be established which will enable the anthropologist to communicate with the members of the new society. But how is this done? Quine argues that the process of constructing such a translation begins with the establishing of indicators of assent and dissent. Once this has been done, it is possible to query the native concerning the application of his terms. Thus the anthropologist may point to a rabbit and receive from the native a reply "gavagai." The anthropologist may thereupon conclude that "gavagai" means "lo, a rabbit." By similar ostensive methods, he can build up a large set of what Quine calls "occasion sentences"—sentences which he can use appropriately in the presence of certain objects and whose use by the natives he can also predict. Nevertheless, Quine comments, the possession of occasion sentences which can be correctly used by both parties does not establish genuine intertranslatability.

A little reflection will show that the anthropologist has no basis for assuming that the natives share his view of the rabbit as an object. In fact, what the anthropologist and the natives actually experience are certain stimulations of the sense organs. The natives may interpret these stimulations as indicating the presense of temporal rabbit slices or of undivided rabbit parts rather than of rabbits as we conceive them. Clearly, there is no occasion when "gavagai" would be used to refer to a rabbit when it might not also be used to refer to slices of rabbits or undivided rabbit parts. Alternatively, the native may conceive "gavagai" as a "mass term" like water or rain—a term which refers to an unindividuated kind of thing rather than to individuated objects. Hence he could interpret "gavagai" as "lo, it rabbbiteth" in analogy to "lo, it raineth." Quine's point is that so long as we are confined to ostention, what we really deal with are stimulus meanings—the sensory stimuli which cue the response "gavagai"—and the stimulus meanings do not determine what sort of ontology the natives have. There is nothing to prevent us from attributing our ontology to the native, but there is no way to prove that the attribution is correct. At the level of ostention, we are limited to stimulus meanings—we cannot deal with reference in our usual sense of the term.

At first glance it must appear that such questions of reference can certainly be settled. The differentiation between "lo, it rabbiteth" and "lo, a rabbit" can obviously be made by asking appropriate questions about individuation. Similarly, temporal slices of rabbits and rabbits are distinguishable by questions respecting temporal duration. But Quine's reply is that such questions are possible only where there exists a background language shared by both speakers in which to pose and answer these questions. In the case of radical translation, there is by definition no such background language, for we have assumed that the anthropologist and the native begin with no shared linguistic equipment. In order for the anthropologist and the native to establish the background language in which these questions can be discussed, they must establish a translation of the appropriate pronouns, endings, identity, etc., necessary to deal with such questions. Such words cannot be defined by ostention; they can only be defined by correlating native terms to English terms in a manner which makes sense *in English*. But there are many alternative ways in which this process of translation can be carried out, all of which fit the data equally well and render the native tongue into English with sufficient success to assure complementary responses between speakers. There is, therefore, in this case no *right* translation; there are only various systems of *analytical hypotheses*, as Quine calls them, which will map one linguistic structure into another. Any such translation is, therefore, arbitrary, in the sense that equally legitimate alternative translations exist. And because of this arbitrariness, it is always possible to find a translation which attributes to the native our English ontology of enduring objects. Such a translation will be for us the simplest way to make sense of the native's speech and so the rendering of his language which we will prefer.

Based on these reflections, Quine draws an analogy between the problem of absolute position and that of absolute reference. Position, as Einstein taught us, is definable only relative to a coordinate system which forms the frame of reference. To ask meaningfully for the position of a body is to ask for a relation of that body to the coordinate system. Just so, Quine argues that a language provides a coordinate system for reference. To ask for the reference of a term is to ask how the reference is specified in a language. "Reference *is* nonsense except relative to a coordinate system," comments Quine.[7] Asking how the ontology of one language is related to that of another is like asking how position in one coordinate system is related to that in another; just as the latter question can only be answered meaningfully by a rule which carries position relative to one system into position relative to another, so the former can only be answered by a rule carrying reference relative to one language into reference relative to another. But the resulting statements about reference will always be statements in terms of the ontology of the language into which the translation is being made. There is, therefore, no more sense to the question of what the absolute reference of a theory is than to the question of what the absolute position of a body is. This is Quine's thesis of ontological relativity.

Quine has given an alternative statement of his thesis which is particularly illuminating. One may think of a language on analogy to a formal system as consisting of a set of signs, formation rules, and deductive rules which specify the syntax of the system. Such systems admit of multiple interpretations in principle, of an infinity of interpretations. But from within the system itself there is no way to specify any interpretation—that must be done in another language in which it is possible to say that "x" in our system "refers" to "rabbit." If we then raise the question of reference in this second language, by asking what "rabbit" refers to, we can only answer in terms of other expressions of this language which we already understand. So long as the reference of some primitive terms of the language is treated as known, we can discuss the reference of other expressions in terms of them. But to ask for the reference of all terms runs us in a circle, for we then have no terms left to define the reference of the primitives except terms already defined by them. The classical view that the reference of the primitives can be

defined by ostention is just what the whole argument about radical translation shows to be false. Hence we never escape the loving embrace of
our mother tongue.

To this argument there would appear to be the following reply. Let
us grant that if the only way to learn the native language were by
translating it into English, Quine's argument would hold. But, in fact,
first languages are never learned in this way: the child learns to speak
his mother tongue without benefit of a background language. If, therefore,
the child acquires the referential system of the language, there must be
a way of learning what the terms refer to which is independent of
language. But if the child does not acquire the referential system of
the language, then no two speakers even of the same language have the
same referential system, and reference is relative, not to the language,
but to each individual. But this is merely a special form of solopsism.
This rejoinder has some plausibility, but I think it misses the point of
Quine's argument. Quine certainly agrees that children learn the language, meaning that their linguistic behavior comes to conform to the
canons of the community. But this fact alone does not prove that they
have a common referential system. For what does it mean to say that
speakers of the same language share the same referential system? We
can be sure that two speakers have the same reference for a term T if,
when one speaker asks the other what T refers to, he receives the expected
answers. But this assumes that the speakers already have common references for the terms used in posing and answering these questions. That
assumption in turn can only be supported by further questions and
answers about the references of these terms, which again assumes that
the speakers share a common referential system for the terms in which
that discussion is carried on. Thus at each step of the process of establishing common reference we must regress to terms whose common
reference is already accepted, and to establish that two speakers have the
same referential system for all words in their language, we must regress
into a background language in which the reference of all terms of the
first language can be discussed. Hence we do not know that the child
who learns a language thereby learns the same reference system which
other speakers have, and we cannot prove that he does without assuming
the very point at issue.

As Quine's examples suggest, the problem of determining the referential system involved in another language is peculiarly germane to anthropology. That fact has not escaped anthropologists, among whom the question has been extensively discussed in terms of componential analysis. The questions involved in this discussion are similar to, but not identical with, those raised by Quine. He is concerned with the kind of ontological posits involved in a language. Componential analysis is concerned with identifying the criteria which determine the applicability of a term. But in both cases the question arises as to whether or not it is possible for an observer to discover how the speaker of another language really thinks.

The method of componential analysis was first applied to kinship terms by Ward Goodenough in 1956 in a now-classic paper on Trukese kin terms.[8] In order to do a componential analysis, it is first necessary to define a domain, such as kinship terms, which is to be analyzed, and to record the complete set of terms applied to that domain by members of the society. These terms should form a complete contrast set—that is, they should be the complete set of mutually exclusive terms applicable to the domain. All terms should then be defined in terms of some concise and accurate notation, such as the traditional kin-type notation (e.g., "Fa" for "father," "FaFa" for "grandfather," etc.). One then seeks for a small number of conceptual dimensions which govern the application of the terms. Each dimension must have two or more contrasting values—e.g., male and female for the dimension sex—and each term must be rendered by some combination of such values, or components, in such a way that whatever is characterized by that combination of components is referred to by that term. As this makes clear, the "meaning" sought in componential analysis is referential meaning; the objective is to determine the criteria which define the application of the term. Finally, when each term has been defined by a set of components, one can state the semantic relations among the terms and the principles governing this terminological system.[9]

The method may be illustrated by reproducing the componential analysis of American kin terms given by Wallace and Atkins. The terms analyzed are *grandfather, grandmother, father, mother, brother, sister, son, daughter, grandson, granddaughter, uncle, aunt, cousin, nephew,* and *niece.* These are rendered in the traditional kin-type notation as follows:

grandfather:	FaFa,MoFa	grandson:	SoSo,DaSo
grandmother:	FaMo,MoMo	granddaughter:	SoDa,DaDa
father:	Fa	uncle:	FaBr,MoBr,FaFaBr,MoFaBr,etc.
mother:	Mo	aunt:	FaSi,MoSi,FaFaSi,MoFaSi,etc.
brother:	Br	cousin:	FaBrSo,FaBrDa,MoBrSo,MoBr-
sister:	Si		Da,FaSiSo,FaSiDa,MoSiSo,Mo-
son:	So		SiDa,FaFaBrSo,FaMoBrSo,Mo-
daughter:	Da		FaSiDa,etc.
		nephew:	BrSo,SiSo,BrSoSo,SiSoSo,etc.
		niece:	BrDa,SiDa,BrDaDa,SiDaDa,etc.

It is clear at once that sex is a basic dimension since every term but cousin specifies sex. Similarly, many terms specify the generational relation to ego. But sex and generation alone will not suffice to distinguish father from uncle or mother from aunt—for this the concept of lineality is necessary. Lineality has three values: lineals are persons who are ancestors or descendents of ego; co-lineals are non-lineals all of whose ancestors include, or are included in, the ancestors of ego; and ablineals are consanguineal relations who are neither lineals nor co-lineals. If we let sex have values a_1 for male and a_2 for female, generation the values b_1 for two generations above ego, b_2 for one generation above ego, b_3 for ego's generation, b_4 for one generation below ego, and b_5 for two generations below ego, and lineality the values c_1 for lineals, c_2 for co-lineals, and c_3 for ablineals, we can render the set of terms as:

grandfather:	$a_1b_1c_1$	grandson:	$a_1b_5c_1$	
grandmother:	$a_2b_1c_1$	granddaughter:	$a_2b_5c_1$	
father:	$a_1b_2c_1$	uncle:	$a_1b_1c_2$ and $a_1b_2c_2$	
mother:	$a_2b_2c_1$	aunt:	$a_2b_1c_2$ and $a_2b_2c_2$	
brother:	$a_1b_3c_2$	cousin:	$a\ b\ c_3$	
sister:	$a_2b_3c_2$	nephew:	$a_1b_4c_2$ and $a_1b_5c_2$	
son:	$a_1b_4c_1$	niece:	$a_2b_4c_2$ and $a_2b_5c_2$	
daughter:	$a_2b_4c_1$			

The omission of the subscript means that the term does not discriminate on that dimension.[10]

The difficulty with componential analysis is not that the underlying dimensions cannot be found, but that more than one set of underlying dimensions can be found for the same set of terms. Burling has pointed out that for any fairly large set of terms, such as the kin terms analyzed above, an enormous number of analyses are logically possible, and the method of componential analysis itself provides no guide in choosing among these alternatives.[11] Thus, for example, Romney has provided an alternative analysis for the set of terms analyzed above in terms of the four dimensions sex, generation, collaterality, and polarity.[12] The first three of these dimensions have their usual meanings; polarity refers to the reciprocity between terms—e.g., one term has the same structure as the other except that the generational sequence of one is the reverse of the other, as grandfather is ego's parent's male parent while grandson is ego's child's male child. Using a_1 for male, a_2 for female, letting generation have the values g_2 for ± 2 generations distant from ego, g_1 for ± 1 generation distant from ego, g_0 for ego's generation, and g^* for an unspecified but nonzero number of generations distant from ego, letting collaterality have the values d_1 for direct and d_2 for collateral, and letting polarity have the values p_1 for ascending generations and p_2 for descending generations, we can render the terms as

grandfather:	$a_1p_1d_1g_2$	uncle:	$a_1p_1d_2g^*$
grandmother:	$a_2p_1d_1g_2$	aunt:	$a_2p_1d_2g^*$
grandson:	$a_1p_2d_1g_2$	nephew:	$a_1p_2d_2g^*$
granddaughter:	$a_2p_2d_1g_2$	niece:	$a_2p_2d_2g^*$
father:	$a_1p_1d_1g_1$	cousin:	$a\ p\ d_2g_0$
mother:	$a_2p_1d_1g_1$		
son:	$a_1p_2d_1g_1$	brother:	$a_1p\ d_1g_0$
daughter:	$a_2p_2d_1g_1$	sister:	$a_2p\ d_1g_0$

The five subgroupings Romney calls "range-sets": the members of a given range-set are so related that, starting with any one, one can by successive changes of only one component, pass through the entire set and return to the origin—e.g., one passes from father to son by change of p_1 to p_2, from son to daughter by change of a_1 to a_2, from daughter to mother by change of p_2 to p_1, and from mother to father by change of a_2 to a_1. Furthermore, where polarity discriminates, the range-set contains the polar of each of its members. Thus the terms belonging to the same range-set appear to be more closely linked than terms belonging to different range-sets.

We have here two different componential analyses of the same set of terms, neither of which can be rejected out-of-hand as implausible. Both appear to have what Wallace and Atkins call "structural reality": they can accurately predict the usage of these terms by users of the language. But is either analysis "psychologically real": that is, does either analysis reveal the dimensions which the language users themselves employ? As Wallace and Atkins point out, componential analysis itself cannot answer that question—something more is required.

Romney and D'Andrade have attempted to provide that something more through a variety of tests of language users. They made two assumptions: (1) that the referential meaning of a term for an individual consists of the components of that term, and (2) that the more components two terms have in common, the more alike their referential meanings are. They, therefore, predicted that the more components two terms have in common, the greater the similarity of response to those terms should be. To test this, they asked subjects to list kin terms in free recall, and examined both the order in which the terms were listed and the frequency of occurrence of the terms. With "overwhelming regularity" they found that terms differing only in the sex component (e.g., father, mother) tended to occur together. Second, they examined the use of the modifiers "step," "in-law," "great," "half," and "second" as applied to these terms. The results are shown below.

Percentage of subjects modifying kin terms with common modifiers (frequencies below 10 excluded)

TERM	STEP	IN-LAW	GREAT	HALF	SECOND
father	55	54			
mother	55	57			
son	20	28			
daughter	20	30			
brother	55	73		28	
sister	50	63		25	
grandfather			78		
grandmother			77		
grandson			33		
granddaughter			33		
uncle			63		
aunt			52		
nephew			10		
niece			10		
cousin					60

Note that if a modifier applies to any term, it applies to every term in the range-set of that term. Thus, although the same modifier can apply to two range-sets, no modifier applies only to a part of a range-set—a finding which strongly supports the psychological significance of the range-sets. Finally, a test using the method of triads was done.* In this test, subjects were given three terms (e.g., father, son, cousin) and were asked to pick the two which were most alike. The frequency with which each pair was chosen as more alike was then computed. The results showed that if the terms were considered to have the components of Romney's analysis, all high-frequency pairings occurred between terms differing in one component only, but if they were considered to have the components of Wallace and Atkins' analysis, some high-frequency pairings occurred between terms which differed in more than one component. With some justice, Romney and D'Andrade argue that these results support the psychological reality of their model.

The issues raised by Quine and by the debate over componential analysis are of profound importance for history, as they are for any discipline which seeks cross-cultural knowledge. It is the avowed objective of historians, as it is of anthropologists interested in subjects such as world view, to see the cultures they are studying "from the inside"—that is, to share the perceptual and conceptual systems of their subjects. Our analysis must, therefore, to use the terminology of Wallace and Atkins, achieve "psychological reality." But it is worth pondering just what psychological reality means and what it is that we are seeking to find out. Wallace and Atkins define the terms "psychological reality" and "structural reality" as follows:

> The psychological reality of an individual is the world as he perceives and knows it, in his own terms; it is his world of meanings. A "psychologically real" description of a culture, thus, is a description which approximately reproduces in an observer the world of meanings of the native users of that culture. "Structural reality," on the other hand, is a world of meanings, as applied to a given society or individual, which is real to the ethnographer, but it is not *necessarily* the world which constitutes the mazeway of any other individual or individuals.[13]

A theory which purports to describe the psychological reality of a person or group is one which includes as determinants of behavior the perceptual and conceptual systems characterizing that person or group; a

---

* They also used a test involving Osgood's semantic differential which is not relevant here.

theory which purports to describe structural reality only is one which does not include such determinants. Thus the componential analyses discussed above can be interpreted as purporting to describe psychological reality if the dimensions they reveal are taken to be those which are used by English speakers in determining reference, but these analyses can also be interpreted as purporting to describe structural reality if these dimensions are regarded merely as yielding a convenient way of predicting the usage of kin terms. A psychologically real description, however, is not an attempt to reproduce the content of consciousness. Thus, in the example above, it was not possible to decide between the two alternative componential analyses of English kin terms simply by asking English speakers which set of dimensions they used, since most English speakers do not know the answer. Patterns of perception and conception are usually at least partly unconscious. Few people in any culture are aware that there are alternatives to their own ways of seeing and thinking, and probably no one is ever fully conscious of his own cognitive structure. Of course, the verbal reports of conscious activity are primary data respecting cognitive structure, but the structure itself is never fully conscious. It follows that the cognitive structure of a group or person is not something which an informant can report to us. It is rather something which we construct on the basis of evidence provided by the behavior of the group or person. It is thus a theoretical construction produced by us to explain their behavior. Nevertheless, if the theory is well confirmed, it is also a description of how those people really perceive and conceive their world, in the only sense of "really" which is meaningful when applied to constructs. Epistemologically, the term "real" means the same thing when applied to perceptual or conceptual systems that it means when applied to electrons. In both cases, what is real is what is postulated to exist in a well-confirmed theory.

The preference which most historians and social scientists have for theories which seek psychological reality is based upon the presumption that the way people behave is at least in part a function of their perceptual and conceptual systems. As Wallace and Atkins note, "structurally real descriptions do not predict certain phenomena so well as psychologically real descriptions."[14] Thus, in seeking to prove the psychological reality of their componential analysis, Romney and D'Andrade used a wide range of behavior including predictions of the actual use of the kin terms, modifier usage, associations of terms in free recall, and similarities choices. As they remark, "the test of the psychological reality of a description seems to involve not only the ability of the description to encompass a wide range of a particular kind of behavior, but also to make predictions about new and different classes of behavior."[15] There are, therefore, sound empirical reasons to seek theories of this sort, and there is behavioral evidence which permits one to discriminate between alternative theories. Here as elsewhere, the wider the range of data that the theory can explain, the greater our confidence in the theory.

Such talk of world view and cognitive structures, however, can be misleading because it takes for granted what may well be false—namely, that there is *one* system characterizing all members of a society. We have no guarantee that all members, or even any two members, of a society have the same cognitive structure. All that is necessary for the functioning of a culture is sufficient complementarity in pattern to permit reciprocal expectations and actions, and this, as Wallace has shown,[16] is a requirement which can be satisfied by quite different patterns. What one is dealing with therefore is a structure which can, and doubtless does, vary from person to person. The most that we can hope to establish from the behavior of members of a society is thus a modal structure, or more likely several modal structures; there is probably no single structure which all members of the society share.

If there is a cognitive structure which is modal for a group, that fact has to be explained in terms of cultural variables. Since current studies indicate that there are significant perceptual and conceptual differences among cultures, it should be possible to relate these differences to cultural variables which affect the process by which these cognitive patterns are learned. Accordingly, one result of this line of inquiry should be a theory about how cognitive patterns of different types are acquired. Thus, for example, Romney and D'Andrade point out that if their components are psychologically real, it must be possible to explain how they became part of the cognitive structure of English speakers; and to this end they argue that these components serve as discriminative stimuli for individuals.[17] This thesis has implications concerning the processes by which the terms were learned which can be empirically checked, and the verification of the fact that the learning process has these features in turn adds confirmation to the claim that these components are psychologically real. In general, any claim that a group has a learned behavior pattern will acquire confirmation if it can be shown that there exist a learning process or processes affecting the group members which should produce that pattern.

This view of the matter is challenged by Quine's thesis, which would seem to imply that efforts to determine at least some aspects of the perceptual-conceptual system of another culture are hopeless. This thesis concerns reference rather than meaning; it is difficult to be sure how the thesis relates to meaning, chiefly because it is unclear what Quine means by meaning. In *Word and Object, Ontological Relativity and Other Essays,* and in other writings, he seems to be on the verge of embracing a behavioral theory of meaning, if indeed the match is not already consummated, and so we are treated to epigrams such as "there is nothing in meaning that is not in behavior."[18] But, although he praises Dewey's behavioral outlook and drops certain sly hints about a new theory of meaning, he has nothing very explicit to say about this behavioral theory of meaning. On the other hand, his enthusiasm for Davidson's recent work may lead one to believe that Quine is looking for a theory of meaning along the lines of Davidson's projected extension of Tarski's work.[19] Such a theory would equate the meaning of a sentence s with its truth conditions, and, since these are relative to the theory containing s, it would of course imply relativity of both meaning and reference. Such a development would be thoroughly in line with Quine's past work, though not, one might have thought, with the turn toward behaviorism he seemed to be making. Indeed, despite his loving references to behaviorism, one cannot avoid the suspicion that Quine's position in both *Word and Object* and *Ontological Relativity and Other Essays* is fundamentally a truth condition theory of meaning. Thus he defines the stimulus meaning of a sentence in terms of the stimuli which lead one to assent to it or dissent from it, but he ignores other types of behavioral responses to sentences which one would have thought should figure in any behavioristic treatment of speech utterances. It is, therefore, worth considering whether or not a satisfactory theory of meaning can be constructed on the basis of truth conditions.

It seems to me doubtful that such a theory can be adequate in any general sense. For even if sentences are the primary units of meaningful discourse, there are sentences which do not seem to admit of truth or falsity and whose meaning therefore cannot be stated in terms of truth conditions. Interrogative and imperative sentences, for example, are admitted by everyone not to be capable of truth or falsity, yet they are surely meaningful. Moreover, it is at least questionable whether all declarative sentences admit of truth or falsity. In *How To Do Things With Words*,[20] Austin pointed out that the relation of truth and falsity to a sentence depended upon the act which that sentence is used to perform: sentences used to perform fact-stating acts (what Austin calls "constatives") admit of truth or falsity, but sentences used for some other sorts of acts, e.g., christening or judging, do not. Hence truth conditions can provide a basis for the meaning of only a very limited portion of the sentences which must be meaningful on any acceptable account of linguistic behavior.

The approach pioneered by Austin seems to open up a promising alternative to the truth condition theory and one which has a significant bearing upon the problem of radical translation. Instead of viewing sentences as eternal objects, Austin viewed them as instruments through which acts are performed, and so turned attention to the nature of the speech acts involved. He analyzed these acts in terms of the important distinction among locutionary acts, illocutionary acts, and perlocutionary acts. By a locutionary act, Austin means "the utterance of certain noises, the utterance of certain words in a certain construction, and the utterance of them with a certain 'meaning' in the favorite philosophical sense of that word, i.e., with a certain sense and with a certain reference."[21] By an illocutionary act, he means the "performance of an act in saying something as opposed to the performance of the act of saying something."[22] Thus, in performing the locutionary act of saying to a person "Don't shoot," one also performs the illocutionary act of urging him not to shoot. A perlocutionary act, on the other hand, involves effects produced *by* the locutionary act. Thus *by* saying to a person "Don't shoot," one performs (hopefully) the perlocutionary act of stopping him from shooting, since this is the effect produced by the locutionary act.[23] Austin regards this trichotomy as presupposing meaning—the sounds uttered must already have meaning or we do not have even a locutionary act. An attempt has been made by Alston to reverse this order of dependence and to define meaning in terms of illocutionary acts,[24] but this attempt has not turned out to be successful since Holdcroft has shown that, in at

least many cases, the semantic content of the locutionary act is necessary to identify the illocutionary act performed.[25]

More recently, Searle has attempted to elaborate Austin's insights
into a general theory of language. Searle is concerned not simply with
English or some particular language, but with *language*—its nature and
functions. The starting point for his analysis is the distinction between
what he calls "brute" and "institutional" facts. Brute facts are those for
the understanding of which a purely physical—one might say physicalist
—description is sufficient. Institutional facts are those which cannot be
understood except in terms of cultural rules. Thus a marriage ceremony,
a trial, and a baseball game are intelligible only in terms of cultural
rather than physical rules and concepts. It is to this latter class of
"institutional" or cultural facts that language belongs, and especially
that illocutionary acts belong. The fact that an utterance of a locution
of the form "I promise that F" in a certain context *counts as* a promise
is only explicable in terms of the rules of the culture which endow that
locution in that context with that significance.[26]

Curiously, Searle does not develop this insight as thoroughly as one
might have expected. When he comes to deal with perlocutionary acts, he
seems to regard them as lying somehow outside the institutional domain.
Thus he writes:

> If we could get an analysis of all (or even most) illocutionary acts
> in terms of perlocutionary effects, the prospects of analysing illocu-
> tionary acts without reference to rules would be greatly increased.
> The reason for this is that language could then be regarded as just
> a conventional means for securing or attempting to secure natural
> responses or effects. The illocutionary act would then not essentially
> involve any rules at all. One could in theory perform the act in or out
> of a language, and to do it in a language would be to do with a con-
> ventional device what could be done without any conventional devices.
> Illocutionary acts would then be (optionally) conventional but not
> rule governed at all.[27]

If one leaves aside those effects of locutionary acts which are due solely
to their physical as distinct from their cultural properties—e.g., the
startle response to a shriek, or the attraction of attention to one lustily
bawling—it is hard to see in what sense perlocutionary acts are any less
due to cultural rules than are illocutionary acts. If by yelling "Bunt" to
a batter, I perform the illocutionary act of ordering him to bunt and the

perlocutionary act of getting him to bunt, it is not easy to see how either act could be intelligibly described in noninstitutional terms. What is true is that perlocutionary acts (usually) require cultural rules beyond those which are purely linguistic, as, e.g., the bunt is constituted by the rules of baseball, but this is a far cry from reducing us to some naive physicalism. Indeed, the importance of perlocutionary acts lies just in the fact that they are one of the points where linguistic behavior joins other types of culturally constituted behavior and various sets of cultural rules interact.

Like Austin, Searle believes that the performance of an illocutionary act presupposes that the components of the expression used to perform that act have meaning and reference. But Searle differs from Austin regarding the relation of meaning and reference to locutionary acts. Searle believes that Austin confused the meaning of an expression with the illocutionary act which that expression is used to perform in a particular case, and so failed adequately to account for the fact that expressions which have the same meaning can be used to perform different illocutionary acts. To avoid these difficulties, Searle seeks to introduce a new distinction between illocutionary acts and propositional acts: thus, in the sentence "I promise that I'll be there," the phrase "I promise" is the illocutionary force indicator while "I'll be there" is a proposition which could occur equally well and with the same meaning in an utterance performing a different illocutionary act, e.g., a threat. A propositional act is the expression of a proposition. It is not the assertion of a proposition, for assertion is an illocutionary act; rather, the propositional act expresses the proposition which is asserted in the illocutionary act of assertion. Thus for Searle the canonical form of utterances which perform illocutionary acts becomes $F(p)$, where F is the illocutionary force indicator and p stands for the proposition expressed in the propositional act. And since Searle believes that "saying something and meaning it is a matter of intending to perform an illocutionary act,"[28] it is clear that he regards this canonical form as applicable to all meaningful speech acts.

Searle's resurrection of the proposition raises difficulties which his theory only imperfectly meets. It is not true that all utterances which perform illocutionary acts can be put into the canonical form. Searle himself points out that utterances such as "Down with Caesar" or "Hurrah for Manchester United" can at best be rendered as $F(n)$, where n is a "referring expression" but not a proposition.[29] Hare notwithstanding, it is not easy to see how the analysis is to be extended to all interrogatives,[30] and to extend it to imperatives such as "Shut the door" requires that the proposition expressed be "The door is shut" and that the illocutionary force be the demand that the world be made to conform to the proposition—a peculiarly awkward rendering.[31] The problems of fitting other types of performatives into the mold appear to be formidable. Yet Searle's formulation does have the happy effect of integrating something like a traditional theory of the proposition into the theory of speech acts, without thereby sacrificing Austin's insight into the performative role of utterances.

If from this viewpoint we return to the case of the anthropologist confronting his hitherto uncontaminated native, and to the question of radical translation, it must be obvious that the point at which the anthropologist, who stands outside the culture of the native, must begin his analysis is the perlocutionary acts performed by native utterances. But this is not equivalent to saying that the anthropologist must seek to explain "institutional" or cultural facts in terms of "brute" or physical facts. We do not begin, for example, by viewing the natives' actions as responses to the physical properties of the sounds emitted by them, but as perlocutionary effects of speech acts which have meaning—even Quine takes it for granted that the natives have a language rather than characteristic cries. In short, we bring to bear upon the natives our general theories about culture, including our general theories about language, in an effort to make sense of their behavior, linguistic and other. From our theories, it follows at once that the perlocutionary acts effected by utterances are functions of the meanings of those utterances and of the illocutionary acts they perform. Quine takes this for granted in focusing on responses of assent and dissent, but clearly these are only two of the many behavioral responses which are perlocutionary effects of speech acts. Indeed, viewed in this perspective, it becomes clear that one reason Quine finds translation so underdetermined by behavior is that his devotion to the truth condition theory of meaning has led him to exclude most of the behavior which might help to make translation determinate. Consider the following situation. In a given room, I observe two speakers, A and B, who converse in a language unknown to me. I note that one speaker, A, looks at the other, B, and says "Ouvrez la fenêtre." I further note that B thereupon walks over to the window and opens it. It seems to me a straightforward inductive inference that A performed the perlocutionary act of getting B to open the window. What can I infer from this about the meaning of the locution "Ouvrez la fenêtre" or about the illocutionary act involved in uttering it? Austin has remarked, "Clearly *any*, or almost any, perlocutionary act is liable to be brought off, in sufficiently special circumstances, by the issuing, with or without calculation, of any utterance whatsoever."[32] Thus "Ouvrez la fenêtre" might mean "Open the window" or "It's hot in here" or "I'm suffocating" or "We need some air" or many other things, and the illocutionary act might be commanding, stating, asking, begging, etc. Yet clearly Austin was a bit too enthusiastic in this statement: the circumstances in which the utterance of "Grass is green" could convince me that I have cholera are, to put it mildly, difficult to imagine. The fact that there are alternative meanings for the locution "Ouvrez la fenêtre" does not mean that any meaning will do. Furthermore, there are ways in which I can bring these alternatives to test. I can utter the expression "Ouvrez la fenêtre" in a variety of circumstances, thus determining experimentally what effects it has. Granting, as is obvious, that such experiments may result in "infelicities" (as when a guest gives an order), the ability to use the utterance experimentally will usually permit a relatively rapid determination of its perlocutionary effects under various circumstances. And from these effects I can begin at once to test out the meaning and reference of individual components of the utterance to see if they have the expected stimulus meaning and use. In short, by observing the effects upon conduct of locutionary acts, I can infer the perlocutionary acts involved, and so sharply limit the possible meanings of the utterance. Austin may be right that in circumstances sufficiently weird an utterance can bring off almost any perlocutionary act; but under the circumstances which usually prevail, the range of locutionary acts which yield a given perlocutionary act is very limited. Thus when speaking is viewed as a component of behavior, there turn out to be more constraints upon translation than Quine's thesis admits.

Not all locutions have immediately observable behavior as consequences. The illocutionary acts of convincing, persuading, and informing, for example, often do not lead to overt actions, or at least not to any immediate, determinate, overt acts. But there are many locutions which do promptly produce determinate behavioral consequences in a wide variety of situations—"Please shut the door," "Please place this object between those two," etc. And once we know the perlocutionary act performed by the locution, we are in a fair way to explore the meanings and reference of its component words. Even if we grant that it is the utterance of sentences which performs acts, given the sentences we can begin to analyze out the role of individual words. Moreover, no one denies that once we know the meaning and reference of some words, we can understand, and frame, new sentences involving these words. Hence, although it is likely to be locutions involving exercitives and behabitives* which will involve perlocutionary consequences of the most easily determinable sort, the constraints so established will ramify throughout the language as a whole, since it would be hard to think of a term which could not be used in such a locution.

Given these added constraints imposed by behavior, it seems to me questionable whether the indeterminacy of reference is as severe as Quine claims. Take, for example, the claim that I can never detect whether the native uses "gavagai" to refer to a rabbit or to rabbit-slices. Let us suppose that the stimuli which evoke "gavagai" also evoke "lo, a rabbit," and that we then seek analytical hypotheses which will carry enough of the native's language into ours to permit us to pursue the question of reference. We shall then want to ask the native if the gavagai here now is identical with the gavagai that was here a minute ago. For this purpose we shall need translations of "now," of some unit of time, of "here," and of course of "identical with." I shall assume for the moment that sufficiently precise equivalents of "now," "here," and a unit of time are established to permit attention to focus on identity. If we then put the question to the native, employing an analyical hypothesis which correlates a native expression "x" to our "identical with," and the native assents to the question, despite the fact that he really uses "gavagai" to refer to rabbit-slices, the problem is whether or not we can find out that the analytical hypothesis is false. If we try to imagine what

---

* Exercitives are illocutionary acts which involve the exercising of powers, rights or influence; behabitives involve social behavior and attitudes (Austin, *Words*, pp. 150–1).

"x" could mean to the native that would permit him to assent, it seems
clear that such a relation as "is a member of the same sequence as"
would do the trick. Could we detect the difference between x, so understood, and identity, or equivalently, between rabbit-slice and rabbit?
I think we can, assuming that we can teach him to count to two. That he
can count is perhaps already assumed in saying that he has a notion of
a sequence; if not, we can certainly teach him to count to two, and verify
that we have done so by asking questions such as "How many are
these?" or "Would you please give me those two?" etc. Note that his
responses to these questions should be the same whether he regards the
objects referred to as object-slices or objects. Now we could find out
whether he thinks a gavagai is a rabbit or a rabbit-slice if we could
present him with two temporal slices of the same rabbit and then ask
him if they are two gavagai or one. But of course we can do this by
filming the rabbit and then slowing down the film to reveal a succession
of "slices." Hence a question can be put which will distinguish between
the analytical hypotheses proposed, using nothing more than the standard
equipment of the field anthropologist.

Again, consider the claim that we cannot tell whether gavagai is a mass
term like water or refers to objects. The same kind of strategy applies
here. If gavagai are portions of unindividuated rabbitstuff, a request for
the *same* gavagai that was here yesterday should mean to our native
merely that we wish some more gavagai. Hence if we can find a native
term "ye" such that the request for "ye gavagai here yesterday" brings
always just that rabbit and no other, even when other rabbits are more
easily available, we have, I think, fair reason to conclude that "gavagai"
is not a mass term. Thus it would appear that when language is viewed
as a component of behavior, there are sufficient behavioral constraints
upon translation to reduce indeterminacy to a trivial level.

Viewed in this perspective, what is to be said of Quine's thesis of
ontological relativity? To say that the members of a particular culture
have a peculiar referential system is to make a hypothesis about a
certain aspect of their cognitive structure. The thesis of ontological relativity would seem to mean that we should never adopt a hypothesis attributing to the members of another culture an ontology different from
our own—i.e., the simplest hypothesis will always be that they share our
ontology. So stated, the thesis looks somewhat less compelling. One is

reminded of Poincaré's claim that whatever the empirical data, we should always find it most convenient to interpret them in a theory employing Euclidean geometry[33]—a thesis hardly propounded before overthrown by the acceptance of a theory employing Reimannian geometry. How is one to prove that we shall always find it simpler to attribute our own ontology to others? Quine remarks:

> The case of the linguist and his newly discovered heathen, finally, differs simply in that the linguist has to grope for a general sentence-to-sentence correlation that will make the public circumstances of the heathen's affirmations and denials match up tolerably with the circumstances of the linguist's own. If the linguist fails in this, or has a hard time of it, or succeeds only by dint of an ugly and complex mass of correlations, then he is entitled to say—in the only sense in which one *can* say it—that his heathens have a very different attitude toward reality from ours; and even so he cannot coherently suggest what their attitude is.[34]

But this comes to saying something very peculiar indeed—that it is impossible for an English speaker to conceive of an ontology other than the one involved in English. This surely is false; as Quine's own elaborate discussion of rabbit-slices, undivided parts of rabbits, and mass terms like rabbiteth makes clear, it is quite possible to talk in English about what an alternative ontology might be. Indeed, developments in physics during the last fifty years have added to our ontology entities of a character so different from any previously hypothesized by English speakers that it is fair to say that their admission has marked a revolution in our concepts of what there is—a revolution which would have been impossible had our ontological imagination been as rigidly constrained as Quine would have us believe. It is one thing to say that position cannot be described except in terms of some frame of reference; it is quite another to say that within a given frame of reference it is impossible to describe how a point is related to another frame of reference. I can see no reason to believe that the simplest theory always attributes our ontology to another language, and I see every reason to believe that we can conceive of other ontologies which might be attributed to those speakers. And if a theory making such an attribution turned out to be simpler than its competitors, consistent with all the known data and with the known principles of human behavior, I am at a loss to know in what sense this theory would not have "psychological reality." For a theory which has psychological reality is simply one which involves as components the perceptual-conceptual system of a society and which is well confirmed. To deny this—to say that there remains some recondite reality beyond our reach—is to talk of an unknowable for the existence of which no rational grounds can be provided.

The problems of cross-cultural knowledge are more severe for the historian than they are for the anthropologist. The anthropologist, after all, has access to living members of the culture which he wishes to understand; he can elicit verbal responses by pointing at objects or providing stimuli of his own, and he can observe nonverbal behavior which can be used as a check on his understanding of their speech. Such avenues are generally closed to the historian, who is, by definition, denied the possibility of behavioral interaction with his subjects. What the historian confronts in the form of linguistic evidence is not the words of a living speaker but a document containing signs in a certain order. From his documents the historian can learn the set of signs used by his subjects, and he may even be able to develop formation rules which accurately describe the ways in which these signs are combined. But what he cannot learn from his documents is the meaning and reference of signs. Lacking the ability to interact with his subjects, the historian can only enter the charmed circle of another language if he can find a translation of some portion of that language into one which he already knows. Thus until the discovery of the Rosetta stone, the writings of ancient Egypt were lost to modern scholars, and the lack of any similar key has left the writings of the Mayas a closed book. The historian, therefore, is always dependent upon existing translations of one tongue into another. Even when he develops a new translation for some hitherto unknown inscription or for an inscription which he believes to have been incorrectly translated, he can do so only by relying upon a background knowledge gained from other translations.

It might seem that, with respect to languages which are spoken by living subjects, the historian is in the same position as the anthropologist, for he can certainly learn the language from the living subjects and then use it to interpret the documents. But this assumes that the language which is spoken now is the same as that which was spoken in the past. Unfortunately, this assumption is false; language, like any cultural phenomenon, changes over time, and a given sign sequence may now have a meaning which is quite different from what it had several centuries ago. Thus, for example, in the Liberties of Massachusetts in 1641[35] there occurs the sentence "It is the libertie of the freemen to choose such deputies for the Generall Court out of themselves, either in their owne Townes or elsewhere as they judge fitest." The meaning of this sentence seems quite clear, but if one were to conclude from it that every nonslave was entitled to vote for the deputies in Massachusetts in 1641, one would be in error. In fact, the term "freemen" in this sentence has a special meaning: it refers to a legal status which was occupied by only a fraction of the inhabitants of the colony. Changes of this sort are very common and fairly straightforward—less obvious are the changes which obscure what were once puns or double meanings. In fact, the historian often finds that his knowledge of the modern form of a language is as much a hindrance as a help, for it is extremely difficult to remember that familiar signs may not have their familiar meanings when they occur in historical contexts.

That a given series of signs has a particular meaning is a hypothesis which must be confirmed by empirical data. So far, the historian's problem is identical with the social scientist's. The difference lies in the data available. Tests based on behavioral interaction are by definition excluded for historical purposes. The nearest analogue to pointing that the historian has is the use of pictorial or artifactual data which have inscriptions reasonably interpretable as naming either the object depicted or the object upon which they are inscribed, and there are far too few data of this description to provide a significant set of ostensively defined terms. For the most part, the meaning of terms occurring in historical documents must be inferred from their use, and the nearest that one can come to establishing what a given term means is to find a meaning which makes sense of the term in all the contexts in which it appears. This is, in fact, the procedure which historians follow, although the comparison of the contexts in which a given term occurs has rarely been systematically and rigorously carried out. The advent of computer technology and the application of content analysis, however, are beginning to make such systematic analysis possible.

When by such means a hypothetical construction of the meaning of the terms used at a given time and place has been reached, are we entitled

to say that this construction is psychologically real? Suppose, for example, that one had, from a study of their use, come to a hypothesis
about the meaning of kin terms in Massachusetts in 1640. On what basis
could one accept this hypothesis as a description of psychological reality? Clearly, from the data afforded by usage, it would be possible to
do a componential analysis of this lexicon, so the question may be put
in the form of whether or not historical data are adequate to permit us
to accept a given set of components as those used by Puritan speakers.
If one follows the argument of Romney and D'Andrade that this decision
must be based upon a range of tests which go beyond the componential
analysis itself, one must ask whether or not such tests can be performed
on historical subjects. To make this decision, Romney and D'Andrade
used an experiment in which kin terms were listed by free recall, a
modifiers test, and a similarities test. It is very difficult to see how the
data for the first and third tests could be recovered from historical
sources. There is no doubt, however, that the data for the modifiers test
could be obtained from documentary sources, since this involves only the
determination of the use of certain modifiers. We have here a situation
which is fairly standard in attempts to apply contemporary data-gathering
devices to historical data—the limitations of the data permit only some of
the tests used by Romney and D'Andrade to be applied to the historical
case. But the important point is that some of the tests can be applied,
and it is not hard to see how more tests might be developed which would
also be applicable. Thus, e.g., if the approach taken by Romney and
D'Andrade is the correct one, one would expect that when kin terms are
generalized along a given dimension—say, collaterality—the range-set
as a whole is generalized. Thus the generalization which yields godfather
also yields godmother, godson, and goddaughter, but not goduncle or
godbrother. Here again, historical data are adequate for the testing of
hypotheses of this sort. It would appear, therefore, that with respect to
the problem of developing psychologically real descriptions, the historian
is not in an essentially different position from the social scientist, although he is more limited in the kinds of tests he can apply—*provided*
that he has some knowledge of the historical language to begin with. But
in those cases where the historian confronts an entirely unknown language and has not even a partial translation to start with, the case is
quite different. The historian is then in the position of having to deal

with a wholly uninterpreted formal system and any interpretation which he places upon its symbols will be purely speculative. It is perhaps fortunate for the historian's peace of mind that most of the languages of the world for which there are no translations have never been written down.

Once the meaning of the statements in the documents has been established, internal criticism is supposed to establish their trustworthiness. If one examines the standard manuals, such as Langlois and Seignobos or Gottschalk, what one finds is an attempt to formulate guidelines for assessing the author's bias (i.e., his reasons for distorting) and accuracy (i.e., whether or not he had the opportunity and capacity to serve as a good witness). Obviously, in this process the document is interpreted as testimonial evidence or record evidence (i.e., the document is regarded as containing descriptive statements about events or objects) or as expressive evidence (i.e., the document is conceived as yielding statements about the author's thoughts and feelings). In either case, the statements derived from the document are regarded as true or false, or rather as having greater or less probability of being true or false. What the guidelines offered by classical historiography really amount to are an attempt to develop rules for assigning degrees of belief or subjective probabilities to these statements. The rules given do not actually suffice to establish a genuine assignment of probabilities; they amount, rather, to admonitions to trust or distrust certain classes of statements, as, e.g., "we must, therefore, always distrust a statement which attributes to the author or his group a high place in the world"[36] or "because the testimony of a schooled or experienced observer and reporter . . . is generally superior to that of the untrained and casual observer and reporter, the greater the *expertness* of the author in the matter he is reporting, the more reliable his report."[37] No attempt has been made in the more recent literature to develop these rules to the point where they could be used for the purpose of introducing actual subjective probabilities or even of producing a rank order of kinds of statements in terms of degrees of warrant, although examples of this sort can be found in the older historiographic literature.[38] But this reticence is apparently due more to doubt as to whether or not the procedure can be successfully formalized than to lack of the desire to do so, for the manuals certainly require the historian to make such judgments intuitively.

As classical historiography conceived its method, internal criticism was to yield the historian a set of statements weighted according to their probability of being true, on the basis of which the "synthetic" task of the historian was to be carried out. The first synthetic step was the comparison of these discrete statements to determine particular facts. The basic questions asked about the relations of statements were independence or dependence, and agreement or disagreement. Where independent observers who are individually credible witnesses agree as to what occurred, that upon which they agree is regarded as fact, and the more independent witnesses there are, the higher the certainty is supposed to be. Conversely, the testimony of a single witness, however credible, is never regarded as sufficient to establish a matter of "fact," and the matter in question may be referred to only as the witness's opinion. Thus by a process of comparing and combining the descriptive statements furnished by criticism, each appropriately weighted according to its probability, it is supposed that we can establish a set of particular facts which then furnish the raw material—the chronicle, as it were—upon the basis of which the historian may attempt the second synthetic step —the "interpretation" of the facts. This "interpretation" is regarded as categorically distinct from the "facts," and as something added to them after they have been established. Nothing illustrates this view more accurately than the form of the standard historical work. Whatever is necessary to establish the "facts"—e.g., the citation of evidence, etc.—is consigned to the footnotes, while the main text elaborates, almost always in narrative form, the author's "interpretation" of his "facts." Nor is it merely the form of the standard work that is governed by this method. History students are taught to compose their works according to these canons. The standard working procedure for a historian is first to read all the documents relevant to his subject, dutifully transcribing in his notes the statements he will use to establish "facts," and then, when he has finished his research in the documents, to decide what the "facts" were and what his "interpretation" is.

Revisionist historians have sharply criticized this classical view, but the differences between the revisionists and the classical writers are much less important than the former have generally believed. The revisionists accept fully the importance of external and internal criticism of the sources, although some are inclined to regard these as the work of

auxiliary sciences rather than as belonging to history per se.[39] They also
accept with little if any modification the procedures for establishing
facts from the documents.[40] But they have differed very sharply from
classical writers over the question of the relation of the interpretation to
the facts. Whereas the classical writers, in true Baconian style, believed
that from the study of "all" the facts the true interpretation would emerge,
revisionists have argued that the historian never uses all the facts: he
selects a certain set of facts and builds his account around these. It has
been particularly this selective process which has preoccupied the revisionists, because they have seen it as determined by the biases, interests,
and beliefs of the historian, and therefore as leading to interpretations
which represent only a particular and partial perspective. Not all revisionists have gone as far as Beard and Becker in claiming that objectivity in
history is impossible, but most now accept the claim that the historian's
selection of the facts with which he will deal introduces an inescapable
element of relativity.[41] It is interesting that these criticisms have been
directed, not to the process of establishing facts, but to the selection of
establishable facts with which the historian will deal. The latter is a problem to which we will turn in Chapter IV; the former concerns us here,
and upon this matter there is very little real difference between the
classical writers and the revisionists.

The limitations of both the classical and revisionist views are obvious
and serious. First, the categories of historical evidence considered are
limited almost exclusively to testimonial or record evidence and to expressive evidence. But documents are often instruments through which
an individual sought to accomplish something, and their value as evidence
may lie, not in the testimony they offer, but in the act they perform. Thus
what appears to be testimony may turn out to be nothing of the sort when
we understand the purposes of the document, but may nevertheless be
vitally important evidence. Second, the attempt to distill the "facts" by a
critical analysis of documentary materials without the use of any conceptualization is naively Baconian and is, in fact, violated at every step
by the very critical procedures used. The initial classifications tested by
external criticism are theory-laden from the beginning, and the attribution of reference and meaning to the inscriptions of a document involves
a complex hypothetical construction replete with theoretical assumptions.
Third, the same naive demand for pure, uncontaminated "fact" leads to a

misuse even of testimonial evidence. To regard the differences between testimony as due to "bias" or "competence" or "opportunity" is to say that those differences are of negative value and must be eliminated to get at the "pure fact." But those differences are themselves parts of the data and must be accounted for, not ruled out of court as disturbing influences. It is a fact of great importance about a society that people occupying different social positions perceive the same things in different ways. These differences are not "errors" to be eliminated, but functions of the social and cultural characteristics of the observers. Any feature of an artifact produced by a past society, including its differences from other artifacts, is evidence for some hypothesis about that society and to write off such features as disturbing influences is to throw away the baby with the bath.

The limitations of the classical methodology were less important in actual practice than might have been expected because the classical methodology was often abandoned when it led to results which seemed unreasonable. Perhaps the most striking example of this is the case of the synoptic gospels a case which, curiously enough, is often cited as exemplifying the classical methods.[42] The problem of the synoptic gospels is well known. The originals of these documents no longer exist, so physical methods for determining their time and place of composition are useless—the earliest copies extant date from the third century. Originally, it was believed that we had in the synoptic gospels three independent accounts of the career of Jesus, at least one of which was by an eyewitness. Scholarship, however, has led to the conclusion that Mark was written at about 70 A.D., and Matthew and Luke between 80 and 100 A.D.,—dates which make it doubtful, to say the least, that any of their authors were eyewitnesses to the events they describe. But the problems involved in these documents concern more than dates, for these accounts are neither consistent nor independent. It is true that the most flagrant contradictions are between the synoptic gospels and the fourth gospel; nevertheless, there are a number of significant inconsistencies among the synoptic gospels themselves. Thus, for example, Matthew contradicts Mark and Luke as to what the voice from heaven said at the baptism of Jesus and to whom it spoke; Luke contradicts Mark and Matthew regarding the last words of Jesus; and all three disagree in their account of the healing of the blind at Jericho.[43] Additional examples could be cited. But the most surprising aspect of the problem is the clear-cut dependence of the documents. Careful study shows verbal similarities among them of a sort which cannot be credibly attributed to chance. In fact, both Matthew and Luke used Mark, not only as a source, but as the framework upon which their accounts are built. Mark has 661 verses, of which Matthew reproduces the substance of over 600, using fifty-one percent of the actual words in Mark. Luke omits about forty-five percent of the Marcan material, replacing it with similar material evidently from another account, but where he agrees with Mark the language of the two is very similar. As one would expect, therefore, there are many passages where all three gospels are virtually identical, many where Mark and Matthew agree but Luke does not, and some where Mark and Luke agree but Matthew does not. But there are also about two hundred verses where Matthew and Luke are too similar for the agreement to be accidental, but which are not in Mark. The logical inference from this fact would seem to be that either Matthew was the source for Luke, or Luke was the source for Matthew, and some so interpret the data.[44] There is, however, a further fact which is very difficult to explain on this supposition: after the temptation story there is no case where Luke and Matthew put the same non-Marcan material into the same Marcan context. That is to say, each of these authors combines the verses which he shares with the other with different material from Mark. If, then, either Luke or Matthew used the other as a source, he would have had to pick out these two-hundred-odd verses from their context in the other's story and put them in a different order and context, all the while following the general story line in Mark. Such a procedure seems so unlikely that an alternative explanation is clearly needed.

The alternative which is generally accepted today is that there existed a source, which has been named Q, which was used by Matthew and Luke but which has since disappeared. This source contained the two hundred verses common to Matthew and Luke but not in Mark, and very likely a good deal more. It evidently consisted chiefly of sayings of Jesus and of accounts of his actions which pointed a moral, but it contained no chronology which could guide Matthew and Luke in working the material into the Marcan story—hence the lack of agreement as to where that material fitted. Such a document would then explain the relations among the synoptic gospels revealed by textual criticism.[45]

I am less concerned with the truth of this argument than with the structure of it. Surely, it must be obvious that Q is a theoretical construct —one for which we do not have any direct evidence at all. No copy of Q is known; no reference to Q can be definitely identified, unless the remark of Papias about the document compiled by Matthew is taken as referring to Q, and that, while certainly possible, cannot be empirically supported at present. The sole function of Q is to resolve the anomalous situation with which the analysis of the synoptic gospels presents us. By postulating the existence of Q, it becomes possible to give coherence to the data and so to remove some of the anomalies which would otherwise render the accounts questionable.

As is usually the case, given the postulate of Q, further indirect evidence can be found. Q is a source which has some remarkable characteristics, notably its freedom from chronology. It must have consisted of relatively isolated units embodying sayings and acts of Jesus. We know that, during the years immediately after the death of Jesus, the main thrust of the church was toward the Jews, and the central objective of Christian preaching was to establish the messiahship of Jesus by proving that he fulfilled the Old Testament prophecies. Any collection of sayings and deeds of Jesus used for this purpose would thus be ordered topically by prophecy rather than chronologically. Furthermore, since one incident can be used for multiple purposes, variant accounts of the same event could easily be included in such a document. This would account for the celebrated doublets of the gospels, since the evangelists would not have been able to tell the variants from true accounts of two different, but similar, events and so would have included them both. There is, in short, a variety of indirect evidence to support the hypothesis of Q.

The postulation of Q solves the problem of dependence, but not that of consistency. Different sources may account for some of the inconsistencies but certainly not for all of them—one must also look to the purposes of the evangelists. As Enslin has emphasized, the evangelists were not historians: each wrote for a specific purpose and adapted his material to that end. Thus, for Mark, whose objective was to explain the death of Jesus, it was essential that his messianic claim should have remained a secret until the very end—hence the voice from heaven could speak only to Jesus without betraying the great secret. Matthew, however, saw Jesus as the announcer of the New Law, and for that role it was essential that his claim to be the messiah should be explicit—hence

Matthew has the voice from heaven speak so all may hear. While there are contradictions among the synoptic gospels which this strategy will not remove, it is successful in removing a number of them. But note that the strategy consists in denying that the gospels are to be treated as record or testimony, as the classical approach required—rather, they are reclassified as instruments through which the evangelists sought to achieve certain objectives. Statements occurring in these documents must now be interpreted in terms of these objectives, and contradictions become clues to the purposes of the evangelists rather than grounds for impeaching the evidential value of the documents.[46]

The importance of the synoptic problem for the theory of historical knowledge lies in the fact that these documents do not fit the categories of valid evidence provided by the classical methodology. Faced with this difficulty, what scholars did, in fact, was to try to explain the characteristics of the data in front of them. Thus the dependence, the contradictions, the doublets—all the features which made the documents so unsatisfactory as evidence—became themselves problems to be explained. The justification for the postulation of Q is that this postulate, together with the hypothesis of the priority of Mark and the recognition that the gospels are not records or testimony but instruments, does bring coherence to the data. It is just because the problems presented by the data are so severe that the postulational character of the explanation is so obvious. When, however, one turns to what are called "historical facts," the postulational character of the "facts" is less obvious because documents which agree seem to establish them beyond question. But take, for example, the baptism of Jesus by John. Enough has already been said about the gospels to make it clear that they must be used as evidence only with extreme caution. But many scholars accept as fact Jesus' baptism by John. The basis for this acceptance is (1) the occurrence of the story in all the synoptic gospels, (2) the differences among the gospels respecting the incident. In Mark it is simply recounted in a matter-of-fact way. In Matthew the incident is elaborated to include a protest by John that it is Jesus who should baptize him, and a reply by Jesus which amounts to a command to John to perform the baptism. Thus the subordination of Jesus to John which is implied by the baptism is here reversed. In Luke an elaborate history of the relation of John and Jesus is introduced, which again has the effect of reversing the subordination implicit in the act.

And in John, the baptism is eliminated entirely, and John proclaims Jesus without baptizing him. From these differences it is generally inferred that the relation of Jesus and John, with the subordination implied by the baptism, was an embarrassment to the evangelists which they tried to explain away. The fact that the incident is preserved, despite its interference with the purposes of the evangelists, leads many scholars to accept it. In this case, then, the argument for the historicity of the incident is quite clearly that it seems to explain the data better than any alternative. What makes the postulational character of the "fact" stand out is the questionable character of the documents and the fact that the documents differ in ways which, given the purposes of their authors to glorify Jesus, the historicity of the event would explain.

What is true of the baptism of Jesus is no less true of so mundane a fact as the birth of Charles Peirce on September 10, 1839. We have for this event a variety of evidence, ranging from formal records to casual comments in letters, all of which agree. To say that by "postulating" the event we "explain" the data may seem forced, for the consistency of the data makes it appear that there is nothing there to explain. But the same argument holds even more strongly with respect to physical objects. We seem to *see* a table with a circular top. It is only upon reflection that we recognize that we have never seen the top as circular but always as oval, that the vision could have been an illusion—in short, that the table is a posit to explain sense experience. Historical "facts" are much further removed from observation than tables. We account for the consistency of the data by postulating the fact. Having made the posit, we forget its hypothetical status, just as we do with tables, unless disturbing data turn up. But in the case of tables, we can, and usually do, proceed to act in ways which quickly bring us new data to confirm or disconfirm our postulate. In the case of historical facts, the obtaining of such new data is far less automatic or easy, and it is therefore particularly important to keep the postulational nature of the facts in mind.

The historical methodology which we have reviewed above is an expression of the forthright empiricism which has generally prevailed in the historical trade. Its objectives are laudable, but its view of the process by which historical knowledge is attained is naive. In holding that external and internal criticism yield statements from which facts are determined, and that the function of interpretation is to account for all, or a preselected few, of these facts, it badly distorts the actual practice of historians. In fact, interpretation enters at every step along the way. External criticism is really a process of testing classificatory hypotheses about objects and so depends upon such interpretative hypotheses being made. Similarly, the attribution of meaning and reference to an inscription is an interpretative or hypothetical process. Historical facts are not established from pure data—they are postulated to explain characteristics of the data. Thus the sharp division between fact and interpretation upon which the classical view insisted, and which the revisionists have accepted, does not exist. The function of historical theory is to explain the evidence; and the facts are hypotheses introduced into that theory because they have explanatory value. But if this be so, we must come to a clearer understanding of what constitutes explanation in history.

NOTES

1. John Higham et al., *History* (Englewood Cliffs, N.J.: Prentice-Hall, 1965), ch. 2.

2. Charles V. Langlois and M.J.C. Seignobos, *Introduction to the Study of History*, trans. Berry (London: Duckworth, 1912); Homer Hockett, *The Critical Method in Historical Research and Writing* (New York: Macmillan Co., 1958).

3. Hockett, *Critical Method*, p. 14.

4. Louis Gottschalk, *Understanding History* (New York: Alfred A. Knopf, 1965), p. 57.

5. J. S. Weiner, *The Piltdown Forgery* (London: Oxford University Press, 1955).

6. Willard V. Quine, *Word and Object* (Cambridge: Harvard University Press, 1960); *Ontological Relativity and Other Essays* (New York: Columbia University Press, 1969).

7. Quine, *Ontological Relativity*, p. 48.

8. Ward Goodenough, "Componential Analysis and the Study of Meaning," *Language* 32 (1956): 195–216.

9. Anthony F. C. Wallace and J. Atkins, "The Meaning of Kinship Terms," *American Anthropologist* 62 (1960): 58–79; William Sturtevant, "Studies in Ethnoscience," *American Anthropologist* 66 (1964): 99–131.

10. Wallace and Atkins attributed their usage to Goodenough, but this is incorrect. Goodenough defined lineals as ancestors or descendents of ego, co-lineals as non-lineals having the same ancestors as ego, ablineals as non-lineals and non-co-lineals all of whose ancestors include or are included in ego's, and collaterals as all other consanguineals.

11. Robbins Burling, "Cognition and Componential Analysis: God's Truth or Hocus-Pocus?," *American Anthropologist* 66 (1964) : 20–28.

12. A. Kimball Romney and Roy G. D'Andrade, "Cognitive Aspects of English Kin Terms," *American Anthropologist* 66 (1964) : 146–70.

13. Wallace and Atkins, "Kinship Terms," p. 75.

14. Wallace and Atkins, "Kinship Terms," p. 79.

15. A. Kimball Romney and Roy G. D'Andrade, "Summary of Participants' Discussion," *American Anthropologist* 66 (1964) : 238.

16. Anthony F.C. Wallace, *Culture and Personality* (New York: Random House, 1969), Introduction.

17. Romney and D'Andrade, "Cognitive Aspects," p. 168.

18. Willard V. Quine, "Philosophical Progress in Language Theory," *Metaphilosophy* 1 (1970) : 6 ff., 14; *Ontological Relativity*, p. 26 ff.

19. Willard V. Quine, "Replies" in *Words and Objections*, ed. Davidson and Hintikka (Dordrecht, Holland: D. Reidel Co., 1969), p. 333 ff.; Donald Davidson, "Truth and Meaning," *Syntheses* 17 (1967) : 304–23.

20. J. L. Austin, *How To Do Things With Words* (New York: Oxford University Press, 1965).

21. Austin, *Words*, p. 94.

22. Austin, *Words*, p. 99.

23. Austin, *Words*, pp. 101–2.

24. William P. Alston, "Meaning and Use," *Philosophical Quarterly* 13 (1963) : 107–24.

25. David Holdcroft, "Meaning and Illocutionary Acts," *Ratio* 6 (1964) : 128–43.

26. John Searle, *Speech Acts* (Cambridge: Cambridge University Press, 1969), p. 51 ff.

27. Searle, *Speech Acts*, p. 71.

28. Searle, *Speech Acts*, p. 46.

29. Searle, *Speech Acts*, p. 31, n. 1.

30. R. M. Hare, "Meaning and Speech Acts," *Philosophical Review* 79 (1970) : 3–24.

31. Searle, *Speech Acts*, p. 124.

32. Austin, *Words*, p. 109.

33. Henri Poincaré, "Science and Hypothesis" in *The Foundations of*

Science, trans. Halsted (Lancaster, Pa.: Science Press, 1946), p. 65. First published as *La Science et l'Hypothèse* (Paris, 1902).

34. Quine, *Ontological Relativity*, pp. 5–6.

35. *Massachusetts Historical Society, Collections of* (Boston: Charles Little and James Brown, 1843), ser. 3, vol. 8, p. 227.

36. Langlois and Seignobos, *Introduction*, pp. 168–69.

37. Gottschalk, *History*, pp. 90–91.

38. Joannis Craig, *Craig's Rules of Historical Evidence. History and Theory*, Beiheft 4 (The Hague: Mouton and Co., 1964).

39. Gottschalk, *History*, p. 126 ff.

40. Gottschalk, *History*, chs. 6, 7.

41. Gottschalk, *History*, chs. 9, 10, 11; Edward Hallett Carr, *What is History?* (New York: Alfred A. Knopf, 1962), ch. 1.

42. Hockett, *Critical Method*, p. 34.

43. Morton Enslin, *Christian Beginnings* (New York: Harper and Brothers, 1938), p. 428.

44. Enslin, *Beginnings*, p. 433 ff.

45. Burnett H. Streeter, *The Four Gospels* (London: Macmillan & Co., 1964), pt. II.

46. Enslin, *Beginnings*, chs. 39, 40.

III

Historical Explanation

No question in the philosophy of history has received more detailed and persistent attention in recent years than the nature of historical explanation. On this issue there are now established positions, "classic" formulations, and even the beginnings of a special vocabulary. Nor is this attention surprising once it is recognized that the fight is less about history than about the claims of competing theories of the nature of empirical knowledge. The interest which history has had for philosophers has usually come, not from any deep commitment to history as a field of learning, but from the fact that historical knowledge is admittedly a type of empirical knowledge, yet one which is not easily fitted into the mold of scientific knowledge. This was its great attraction to idealists, who thought they saw in it a kind of empirical knowledge which could not be accounted for by the methods empiricists were willing to allow. And it was just this claim of the Idealists such as Collingwood[1] which made it necessary for Hempel to argue that insofar as history was really knowledge—that is, insofar as history ever explained anything—it was really a kind of rudimentary science.[2] Hempel's claim was so extreme that it provoked counterattacks by humanists such as Dray,[3] and required even those who fundamentally agreed with Hempel's basic position to offer more moderate formulations, e.g., White.[4] In fact, Hempel himself has retreated somewhat from the extremist position which he advanced in 1942.[5] The argument over historical explanation, therefore, has been philosophically important because it concerns the nature of a field of knowledge which seems to be an anomaly when viewed in terms of the

67

various theories of knowledge. But the argument has importance for
history, too, for historians seek to explain something in some way, and
it is worth examining just what that something and that way are. Accordingly, I shall first review briefly the status of the debate currently in
progress, looking at Hempel's "classic" formulation of the "covering law"
thesis, then at the major criticisms which have been leveled at this thesis,
and finally at some of the attempts of the covering law theorists to meet
these criticisms. I shall then attempt to show that these writers have generally been unclear about what historians explain and how they explain
it, and that clarity on these matters leads to a view of the historian's task
which is different from the one which they have generally entertained.

Hempel opens his polemic by giving a definition of what constitutes
an explanation in science. To explain the occurrence of an event of a
given kind E at a specific time and place, he argues that we must have two
elements: a set of conditions $C_1 \ldots C_n$ which are taken to be the causes of
E, and at least one "universal hypothesis" or law, such as the statement
that, for every case, if C_1 & $\ldots$ & C_n occur at certain times and places,
then E occurs at a specific time and place. These universal statements
must be "reasonably well confirmed" and such that from them, together
with the statements that $C_1 \ldots C_n$ occurred, the statement that E occurred
can be logically deduced. It is the fact that the occurrence of E is logically
deducible from the laws and the statements of initial conditions that yields
an explanation of the occurrence of E. There may be any number of conditions $C_1 \ldots C_n$, and any number of laws, so long as those laws and the
statements that the initial conditions are fulfilled, taken as premises, yield
the occurrence of E as a conclusion.

Hempel was not as clear in 1942 about the nature of law as he has
since become, but the problems involved in the notion of law were less
clear then than they have since become. Nevertheless, it is quite clear
that by a "universal hypothesis," Hempel did not mean to include merely
summatory generalizations reporting the results of enumerating finite
collections. Specifically, he would exclude any general statement which
is equivalent to a finite conjunction of singular statements. He also requires that such a law, or law-like statement, permit prediction and support counterfactuals. Moreover, he believed in 1942 that a law could
contain no uneliminable reference to particular individuals—i.e., the law
had to be wholly general in form, holding for all individuals of a given

type. Similarly, he insisted that the causes and effects must be instances of events rather than wholly unique, particular events themselves—unique individuals Hempel regarded as simply inexplicable. He also considered briefly the possibility of using statistical laws and noted that from such laws only the probability of the occurrence of an event of type E could be deduced, but he did not in this paper pursue that subject.

Hempel further claims that the logic of an explanation so defined differs in no particular from that of a prediction. The difference between the two is solely a question of whether E has occurred already, in which case the premises yield an explanation, or will occur, in which case the same premises yield a prediction. Any explanation which is "complete"— i.e., contains all the causes and laws required for the deduction of the occurrence of the event E—is thus logically indistinguishable from a prediction of the occurrence of E, and the predictability of E from the laws and initial conditions stated is a sufficient proof that the explanation of the occurrence of E is complete. Thus, from Hempel's point of view, the classic claim that history differs from the sciences in that the latter make predictions while the former does not loses most of its point. If explanations and predictions are logically identical, and differ only "pragmatically," the difference between a science which predicts and a science which explains is not so serious.

Now it is obvious that if explanation is defined as Hempel defines it, explanations in history are, to put it mildly, rare. He therefore introduces a second concept—that of explanation sketch. "Such a sketch consists of a more or less vague indication of the laws and initial conditions considered as relevant, and it needs 'filling out' in order to turn into a full-fledged explanation."[6] It is explanation sketches, often presented in singular causal statements, which Hempel thinks characterize history— "The interpretations which are actually offered in history consist either in subsuming the phenomena in question under a scientific explanation or explanation sketch; or in an attempt to subsume them under some general idea which is not amenable to any empirical test."[7] Thus the claim is that all historical explanations which really explain are scientific explanations or explanation sketches.

Hempel's formulation of his position was certainly abrasively strong, and it has provoked numerous criticisms and proposals for modification from proponents of the covering law model as well as from its opponents.

William Dray, among others, has pointed out that the model must be readjusted to include statistical laws if it is to be at all realistic and that this requires dropping the deducibility requirement: from a statistical generalization connecting the C's with E, only the probability of the occurrence of E can be deduced, not the actual occurrence.[8] Hempel has, however, accepted this criticism and in his most recent formulation has extended the term "covering law" to include statistical or probabilistic laws. Thus if $P(G,F) = r$ is the statement that the probability is r that, if x is an F, then it is also a G, and if i is an individual variable, so that Fi means i is an F, then Hempel proposes to count as an explanation the argument

$$P(G,F) = r$$
$$Fi$$
$$\overline{\qquad\qquad} \ /r/$$
$$Gi$$

where the double line indicates the nondeductive character of the argument and /r/ indicates the probability with which the conclusion is asserted. The argument is not deductive, since Gi does not logically follow from the premises: on the other hand, the argument does make the occurrence of Gi highly probable, and in this sense has explanatory force. Hempel is unwilling to set a lower bound to r, since obviously any such bound must be arbitrary, but the lower r is, the less the explanatory force of the argument.[9]

A second common criticism of Hempel's position has been that the term "explanation" has multiple meanings, only one of which is captured by him, and that to pick this as the "true" one, while dismissing others as "pseudo" explanations, is at best arbitrary. Dray has insisted that to classify x "as a revolution" is to "explain" x without using a covering law,[10] and Scriven has emphasized that when we "explain" the rules of the Hanoverian succession, or the significance of an event in terms of its consequences, we are "explaining" in a sense quite different from that used by Hempel.[11] Yet these criticisms seem wide of the mark. Hempel was concerned with explanations of the occurrence of a given type of event and his point was that only covering law explanations perform that function. He would be the first to concede that classification and exposition of the rules of the Hanoverian succession are important historical enterprises, but he would insist—I think rightly—that they should be clearly distinguished from explanations of the occurrence of events. It is only when classification and exposition are presented as if they accounted for the occurrence of events that Hempel would regard them as "pseudo" explanations.

A third criticism which has been frequently advanced is that historical explanations do not offer sufficient conditions for the occurrence of E but, rather, necessary conditions. This is a covering law claim, for the necessary conditions are related to the occurrence of E by a general law, but it is weaker than Hempel's claim, since such an explanation would not allow prediction. Gallie particularly has argued that "characteristically historical explanations" are a type of genetic explanation that cites for the event E a necessary condition which is somehow continuously related to E.[12] Here, as in other examples of the claim that a "continuous" series is involved, the difficulty is in knowing what "continuous" means. When, for example, a motive is said to cause an act, it is certainly not clear in what the continuity of the motive and the act consists. One suspects, in fact, that the motive is viewed as somehow continuous with the act just because it is causally related to it, for there would appear to be nothing else which would justify the claim of continuity in this case which would not also justify saying that a frown was continuous with the act. The real question appears, rather, to be one of whether explanations which cite only necessary conditions for E are to be regarded as incomplete, following Hempel, or as normal and complete in themselves. White, however, has pointed out that to call C a necessary condition for E is equivalent to saying that in every covering law argument explaining E, C is a cause of E.[13] But to prove that there is no alternative explanatory argument for E, containing, say, C* but not C, is extremely difficult if not impossible, and the concept of a necessary condition for E is therefore not a particularly useful one, since it can rarely if ever be applied.

A fourth criticism which has been urged particularly by Dray concerns Hempel's claim that prediction and explanation have an identical logical structure. As Dray has argued, one may predict rain from observing a red sky in the morning, yet one would certainly hesitate to accept the statement "always a red sky in the morning is followed by rain" as being an explanatory law.[14] In such cases, the prediction is based upon the observation of what Dray calls "inductive signs" of the event rather than causes, yet the prediction may be perfectly confirmed. Hempel has noted this criticism, and in his latest formulation admits that some predictions may be made from inductive signs which are not causes, so that his earlier claim that explanation and prediction have the same logical structure becomes at least questionable. But he continues to hold the thesis that the logical structure of explanation always justifies a prediction, although he now admits that the truth of the converse is an open question.[15]

A fifth criticism raised by Dray is that historical explanations are often not of the covering law form but rather of what he calls the "rational type." "The goal of such explanation is to show that what was done was the thing to have done for the reasons given, rather than merely the thing that is done on such occasions, perhaps in accordance with certain laws (loose or otherwise)."[16] Dray's argument is that we understand why x did ϕ when we see that, given x's reasons for doing ϕ, ϕ was the thing to do. Reasons in this sense are not causes—they are rather the justifications for the act—those things which made the act appropriate or rational for x. To understand x's reasons is thus to be able to appraise the act as rational for x, and to empathize with x in the sense that "the historian must be able to 'work the agent's calculation.' "[17] Thus Dray argues that "history is logically continuous with literature rather than social science."[18] For, as Dray sees it, the humane studies differ from the scientific ones in the criteria of what constitutes an explanation: the humane studies seek an appreciation of the agent's reasons for an action, the scientific studies seek to describe his action in terms of regularities.

Both Hempel and White have addressed themselves to this claim of Dray. Hempel's answer is that, even if in a given situation one could show that E was the rational thing to do, this would give us no reason for believing that E was done, and hence no explanation of the occurrence of E. In order to produce such an explanation, one would need an argument of the following sort:

> A was in a situation of type C.
> A was a rational agent.
> In a situation of type C, any rational agent will do E.
> Therefore, A did E.

But Hempel points out that the generalization here involved is not what Dray calls a principle of action—that is, a statement of what the thing to do was—it is a general law stating what occurs under certain conditions, and without this law the explanation fails.[19]

White makes a somewhat different argument, stressing the distinction between asserting a statement and asserting that A believes a statement. A may argue that

> I am in a situation of type C.
> When in a C type situation, one ought to do E.
> Therefore, I ought to do E.

But the historian explaining A's action must argue that

> A believed himself to be in a C-type situation.
> A believed that when in a C-type situation, one ought to do E.
> A believed that he ought to do E.
> Partly because A believed he ought to do E, he tried to do E.
> Partly because A tried to do E, he did E.

As White notes, the connection asserted among A's beliefs in the second argument is not logical, for even if a proposition q follows from a proposition p, A may not believe that q follows from p. All the statements in the argument are factual statements: they are either statements of initial conditions or singular causal statements. In no case does the explanation depend upon Dray's principles of behavior.[20]

A sixth criticism, urged particularly by Dray,[21] is that if one searches for the covering law which is alleged to be implicit in historical explanations, one is driven in either of two directions. Either one retreats to more and more general hypotheses, until one reaches a level of generality at which the relation between the supposed law and that which it is supposed to explain becomes at best obscure, or one is driven to add so many and so restrictive initial conditions that there is but one thing in the universe to which the law applies. In either case, Dray argues, the alleged explanatory argument becomes a travesty and the whole case is reduced to absurdity. This point has also bothered Danto, who argues at length that in most historical cases the covering law can "cover" the event E only if E is described so vaguely that an explanatory deductive argument would not serve to predict E.[22] Danto has here illustrated some of the difficulties involved in the pursuit of law by retreat to increased generality, and his argument explores in an imaginative way one horn of the dilemma posed by Dray. This argument is a powerful one, and it is not fully answered by the introduction of probability laws, or by any other considerations which the covering law theorists have yet adduced.

This summary of the state of the debate over historical explanation is far from complete—there are, for example, several important doctrines, particularly those advanced by Morton White, to which we will return below—but it will serve to give some general notion of the state of the argument today. In general, Hempel's classic article has been the focus of both attack and defense, and practically all the writing on the subject has been either an attempt to refute Hempel, as, e.g., that of Dray, or an attempt to modify Hempel's doctrine so as to bring it more into line with actual historical practice. Perhaps just because the argument has been so focused on Hempel's thesis, there are significant points which have been overlooked and which require examination. Specifically, I should like to examine the question of the nature of the laws used in historical explanations, the logical structure of historical explanations, and what it is that such explanations explain.

The concept of law is clearly one of the crucial concepts in the debate over historical explanation; it is also one of the most complex notions in contemporary philosophy, and, I shall argue, one the application of which to history has been critically misunderstood. It is not my interest here to enter into the question of the explication of the notion of law-likeness. That notion has thus far resisted a full explication, but sufficient progress has been made so that there is general agreement upon at least some criteria for something being a law-like statement. Thus, everyone agrees that a law-like statement cannot be merely a summatory generalization, such as "all chairs in this room are made of wood." It appears also to be agreed that all law-like statements must support predictions and must furthermore support contrary-to-fact conditionals. Clearly any statement which is to qualify as a law must satisfy these three criteria.

Nevertheless, these criteria are not enough to distinguish explanatory general statements from nonexplanatory ones. We noted above that predictions of an event of type E may be made either from what were termed "inductive signs" or from causes, but that the general statement connecting "inductive signs" to E would not be explanatory whereas that connecting the C's to E would. Yet if these inductive signs are constantly conjoined to E in nature, they would certainly satisfy the Humean definition of cause, and the statement of their relations to E may well be nonsummatory and support counterfactuals. On what ground, then, do we deny explanatory force to such statements? So long as we know only of the relations between the inductive signs—let us call them the I's— and E, there would be no reason to regard a proposition of the form

$$(1) \quad \text{Always } I_1 \ \& \ \ldots \ \& \ I_m \text{ then } E$$

as not being an explanatory law. If, however, further research brings to light the laws

$$(2) \quad \text{Always } C_1 \ \& \ \ldots \ \& \ C_n \text{ then } E$$

and

$$(3) \quad \text{Always } C_1 \ \& \ \ldots \ \& \ C_n \text{ then } I_1 \ \& \ \ldots \ \& \ I_m,$$

we may attribute the relation of $I_1 \ldots I_m$ to E to the fact that they are both effects of $C_1 \ \& \ \ldots \ \& \ C_n$ rather than to any causal relation between the I's and E. Under these circumstances, the general statement (1) may be said to have been *eviscerated*, and the status of the I's reduced to that of inductive signs.

This formulation has some interesting implications. First, it is clear that we cannot distinguish inductive signs from causes merely by inspecting the general statement which connects them to E, for the difference lies in the relation between the I's and the C's, and that relation does not appear in the original statement. The decision as to which factors are C's and which are I's, and so which statements are law-like, is a decision which depends upon the systematic connections within the theory in which these statements are imbedded. Hence factors which at one time are believed to be causes of a given type of event may subsequently come to be viewed as inductive signs as the development of the theory reveals new interconnections among its elements. But, second, it is important to distinguish the process of evisceration from that of reduction. A statement of the form

$$(4) \quad \text{Always } X_1 \ \& \ \ldots \ \& \ X_k \text{ then } Y$$

may be said to be reduced to a statement of the form (2) if Y is shown to be a special case of E and $X_1 \ \& \ \ldots \ \& \ X_k$ is shown to be a special case of $C_1 \ \& \ \ldots \ \& \ C_n$. But a reduced law is still a law, for it formulates a genuine causal connection between antecedent conditions and consequent effects.

Thus Galileo's law of falling bodies remains a law, even though it is derivable from Newtonian mechanics, for the antecedent conditions of Galileo's law are specifications of the antecedent conditions of Newtonian laws. But an eviscerated law is no longer a law, for what had been supposed to be antecedent conditions are shown by the process of evisceration to be effects of those factors of which E is also an effect. Hence they are not specifications of a more general set of antecedent conditions— they are not antecedent conditions at all.

In the discussion which follows, I shall take it for granted that general statements which are not summatory, which support predictions and counterfactuals, and which are not eviscerated are law-like, without thereby suggesting that these four criteria are sufficient to explicate the concept of law-likeness, as they manifestly are not. There is, however, another criterion which has frequently been proposed for law-likeness— namely, that a law-like statement can contain no uneliminable reference to individual things or to particular times and places. This criterion has been proposed by, among others, Hempel and Oppenheim,[23] and has been used repeatedly in writings about history. But it was attacked by Ryle,[24] who showed that there are explanatory principles which violate this criterion. More recently, Hempel has retreated from this position, impressed by the fact that Galileo's law of falling bodies contains uneliminable reference to the earth.[25] But White has gone much further than this, asserting that "there are laws about individuals."[26] Thus White argues that a statement such as "whenever John eats spinach, John breaks out in a rash" is a law in every legitimate sense of the term. Even though the statement contains uneliminable reference to John, it is still a universal statement as its logical formulation shows: "for every time t, if John eats spinach at time t, then John breaks out in a rash at $t+24$ hours."[27] Such statements are predictive, support counterfactuals, and have explanatory power.

The usual way of eliminating reference to individuals from a general law is to absorb them into the statement of initial conditions. Thus it could be argued that John is eliminable from the above statement, since the reference to John can be replaced by "a person allergic to spinach." It is not clear that such an emendation is acceptable, even if it were the case that allergic reactions always take the form of rashes. It might still be argued that the statement about John is a law and that the elimination of the reference to the individual is pointless and arbitrary. But the case can be made more strongly than this, for it is possible to find law-like statements about individuals where it is not possible to absorb reference to particulars into general conditions, and this is particularly obvious in the case of customary behavior.

Let us begin by considering a society S. As a minimal characterization, we may consider S simply as a set of people having some number of members n. It is then obvious that there are $2^n - 1$ nonnull subsets of S. Now it will turn out that the members of some of these subsets perform no distinctive behaviors while members of some other subsets perform quite distinctive behaviors. Among the former are usually the set of red-haired people, the set of people between $5'6''$ and $5'7''$, and the set of people with gray eyes. Among the latter one finds always the set of women and the set of fathers, and (sometimes) the set of eldest sons. But we shall be on the wrong track if we think of the distinguishing feature of this latter class of subsets as some inherent characteristic of its members— the difference lies rather in the structural relations which its members bear to other subsets. Let us call those subsets of S to which distinctive behaviors attach "positions." If we ask how these distinctive behaviors come to attach to a position, we shall find that the position is always related to certain other subsets. For any position A whose members are characterized by the performance of a behavior B not performed by members of other positions, there exists a subset of S, call it C, such that members of C expect B of members of A, and there exists at least one (and usually more than one) subset of S, call it D, whose members sanction the members of A according as they do or do not perform B. Thus if A is the position of department store clerk, certain behavior is expected of members of A by the set of expecters C, and there exists at least one set of sanctioners—namely, the department store supervisors D— who will sanction the members of A as they do or do not perform the expected behavior. We may speak of behavior of this sort as "customary." Clearly, custom encompasses a wide range of behavior, from the single habit pattern (e.g., the handshake greeting) to complex role behavior (e.g., the role of a doctor), and from ascribed behavior (e.g., the role of a woman) to achieved (e.g., the role of a senator), but all are maintained by structural relations of the sort briefly described here.[28]

Now when we know the customary behavior associated with a given position, what do we know? We know what is expected of members of that position, i.e., what is appropriate for such persons; hence we know the norms governing performance and the sanctions that are applied. What we do not know from the custom alone is how closely actual performance conforms to the custom. But this is a feature of the social system which itself receives detailed analysis in studies of deviance. Where our knowledge of the social system is adequate, we know not only the structure of customary behavior which constitutes the social system but the deviance from these rules as well. We are, therefore, in a position to say something about the probability that a member of a given social position will perform in a certain way in specified circumstances. And the question I would now like to pose is, are such customary patterns properly regarded as laws?

If I know that a man is a professor in the United States, I am certainly in a position to make a good many accurate predictions about how that man will act. I know that he will meet classes, that he will attempt to teach them something, that his methods will conform to a fairly narrow range of practices, and that his interaction with his classes will have certain characteristics—e.g., that he will assume direction of the group, that he will respond to certain types of cues (e.g., a raised hand) and not to others (e.g., a sneeze), and so on. Not only does knowledge of his position permit prediction—it also supports counterfactuals. I know that if x were a professor he would act this way, I know that if professor x had met his Monday class, he would have behaved in certain appropriate ways. And this knowledge is certainly not summatory—it is not because I have observed every professor and seen him so act (for there are deviants here, too, who do not so act) but because I know how *professors* act that I can predict and support my counterfactuals. In short, these customs are law-like and they both can and do serve as the generalizations upon which explanations of human behavior are based. If anyone doubts this, let him reflect upon the possible explanations he might offer for the fact that he sees a car being driven on the right side of a two-way street. Surely, the explaining generalization would be that, in the United States, all drivers drive on the right side of two-way streets. What other generalization could be offered which would answer to the occasion? But this generalization is a statement of a custom. American drivers behave this way because they are expected to behave this way and are sanctioned positively for doing so and negatively for not doing so. As the English custom of driving on the left makes clear, there is nothing necessary about our practice. Nevertheless, our custom has explanatory force. We can predict with high probability that the next driver we meet on a two-way street will drive on the right. (Indeed, we do predict this every time we drive down a two-way street). Furthermore, few will question the truth of the subjunctive conditional that, had any American driven down a two-way street in Colorado Springs yesterday, he would have driven on the right. Thus the generalization has the properties and functions of a law, and should be treated accordingly.

The domain of behavioral regularities is by no means exhausted by customary behavior. But customary patterns are often sufficiently strong to yield very high levels of probability and they are, therefore, particularly good examples of law-like social patterns. Where the sort of structural supports which enforce custom are lacking, regularities in behavior are often much less marked. The literature of the social sciences is filled with findings of "significant" relations among variables, meaning associations too strong to be due to chance only, but that yield quite low probabilities of prediction. Nevertheless, even in these cases, we are dealing with genuine associations which reflect an underlying structure of causal relations governing behavior. The point I wish to stress is not the difference between customary and other behavior patterns, but the fact that behavioral regularities are often law-like, and this is probably most obvious in the case of customary behavior.

But if the argument thus far be granted, a most important consequence should be at once apparent. Custom is specific to a particular society at a given time. The behavior customary for a given position—say, adolescent, unmarried females— varies from one society to another so radically that behavior prescribed in one society is often proscribed in another. Accordingly, laws governing social behavior must often be formulated with reference to a particular society at a given time, just as Galileo's law of falling bodies had to be formulated with reference to a particular entity: the earth. This does not mean, let it be clear, that *all* laws of social behavior require such formulation. It appears clear, for example, that the laws of learning hold for all men, independently of race or culture, and very likely hold over a domain considerably larger than the human race. But the laws of learning are one thing—what is learned is quite another. Even if the learning process is universal, the patterns of behavior learned vary from time to time, and from place to place, and these learned patterns of behavior are law-like too. These are not mere summaries of what people in fact do, nor are they eviscerated, and they support prediction and counterfactuals. They are, therefore, as thoroughly laws for purposes of explaining behavior as are the more universal laws of learning.

It may be held, and is held as a matter of faith by most social scientists, that the fact that there are different customs in different societies is itself explainable. The thrust of recent cross-cultural research has been to establish laws of behavior holding for all cultures. For example, Whiting and Child[29] tried to show that the prevalence of certain types of explanations for and treatments of disease in a culture were functions of the child-rearing patterns which prevailed in that culture. It may, therefore, become possible to develop laws of human behavior where the temporal and spatial restrictions can be absorbed into antecedent conditions, as Galileo's law was absorbed into Newtonian mechanics. Indeed, a great deal of contemporary research in the social sciences is devoted to this very objective. For example, many of the generalizations of economics and sociology are about industrial societies having a particular sort of exchange system. Historians, too, have felt the lure of comparative studies, and some have attempted to propound theses that would apply to any culture satisfying certain initial conditions.[30] But we are talking here about a program barely begun—the hoped-for outcome of research still largely undone—not something presently complete and available for use. Furthermore, even if the objectives of cross-cultural research are achieved, as I do not doubt that someday they will be, it will remain true that the localized customary pattern, complete with its temporal and spatial restrictions, is a law-like principle, just as Galileo's law remains a law, mauger its derivability from Newtonian mechanics. For reduction in such cases would not amount to evisceration; the spatio-temporal restrictions would amount to limiting the domain of application of the more general law to one in which certain specific values of the antecedent conditions obtained, but the antecedent conditions of the particular custom would remain antecedent conditions and the customary response would remain a consequent. It is, then, at present true that many laws—i.e., general statements regarding behavior which meet the criteria we have specified for being law-like—do contain restrictions regarding time and place, and such statements will remain law-like, and, therefore, principles legitimately employed in explanation, whether or not they are someday shown to be derivable from broader theories.

It is in the fact that law-like statements may legitimately contain un-eliminable reference to particulars that one finds the reply to the argument of Dray that covering laws must either become so general as to be trivial or so specific as to admit but one case. As Danto has perceived,[31] the flight into generality is required by the edict that laws cannot refer to particulars. Thus, Danto holds that to explain why Monegasques flew the American flag side by side with their own, we must ascend to the principle that:

> Whenever a nation has a sovereign of a different national origin than its own citizens, those citizens will, on the appropriate occasions, honour that sovereign in some acceptable fashion.[32]

But, of course, from this principle nothing follows regarding flag-flying: cannon-firing might be an equally acceptable method of doing the honors. To get a law-like statement which would permit a prediction of flag-flying, even on a probability basis, one would have to refer to the customs of the Monegasques, and this Danto, Dray, and Hempel regard as contrary to the nature of law. But once it is seen that reference to particulars in no way compromises the law-like character of a generalization, this entire problem vanishes. All laws are general, but there are different degrees of generality; and what may be a fact about a particular society may also be a law governing the behavior of members of that society.

The bearing of these remarks on the philosophy of history should be obvious. No statement has been more often repeated in philosophic dis-cussions of history than the one that historians only apply laws to explain particular facts: they do not discover laws. The result is a view that the historian is something like an applied scientist: he draws upon a stock of laws furnished by other disciplines in order to explain particular facts or events, but he never encroaches upon the prerogatives of these theo-retical fields by trying to discover a law or to formulate a theory him-self. And where, I would fain know, are these laws he uses to come from? We have, according to the philosophers, two sources: the social sciences, and "truisms of common sense." Now this view is not only false, it is pernicious as well, for if any historian were so naive as to believe that he ought to do what the philosophers have claimed he ought to do, he would quickly come to grief. To make this clear, let us examine the consequences of the philosophers' views.

On one view, the historian is an applied social scientist who borrows from sociology, anthropology, political science, economics, psychology, etc., a set of principles which he then applies to his data. Now, as I have argued above, many of the findings of the social sciences, e.g., many of the law-like regularities used to account for human behavior, are specific to certain societies at certain times. Anthropologists have normally understood this fact very clearly, but their sophistication about the nature of culture has not always been shared by workers in other fields. Suppose, then, we accept contemporary "laws" from sociology and apply them to the study of the past. In considerable part, we are adopting generalizations established as true for our own culture at the present time, and applying them to another society at another time or to our own society at a different time. To see how utterly misleading such an approach can be, consider the following relatively simple example. In contemporary sociology, studies of socio-economic mobility very often use occupation as an index of status. This practice is justified by the fact that there exists a very strong association between occupation and income in our society—strong enough so that a rank order with respect to income can be inferred from an ordering of occupations. Now it is virtually impossible to obtain income data for large segments of the U. S. population in the early nineteenth century, but it is possible to obtain occupational data—at least for large segments of the urban population. It might be thought, therefore, that socio-economic mobility in the early nineteenth century could be studied by using occupation as an index of status. In a recent study, Blumin examined this possibility,[33] but rather than make so naive an assumption, he tried to test the strength of the relation between occupation and income for his early-nineteenth-century Philadelphia data. Unable to acquire income data, he used data on wealth and occupation. The result was an η^2 of .17, showing clearly that most of the variation in wealth was *within* the occupational groups, not between them. (As Blumin notes, the use of wealth as a variable probably underestimates the relation of occupation and income, but this can hardly account for so low a statistic.) This fact is less surprising once it is recognized that the occupational structure in question is that of a society not yet fully industrialized; whereas the strong relation between income and occupation is probably particularly characteristic of industrial societies. Hence the attempt to apply findings validated on contemporary American society to one of the early nineteenth century would yield a seriously distorted picture. History cannot simply borrow the "laws" of social science to explain its data, for the very obvious reason that those laws may not apply under the conditions that prevailed at the time in question.

On the second view, the generalizations used by historians to explain their data are the product of "common sense": they are the "truisms" which are obvious to everyone. It should not be necessary to pursue so naive a proposal at great length. Consider, for example, the Puritan customs regarding engagement which Morgan detailed in *The Puritan Family*.[34] That people who are not in love should become engaged in order to see if they can fall in love does not, I rather think, strike most people as a "truism of common sense." It was, no doubt, a "truism of common sense" to John and Margaret Winthrop since it was the customary pattern of their society, but it was no "truism" to historians of our time since it is not a custom of our society. In fact, reliance on "truisms" or "common sense" always means reliance upon what is customary for us. But to the extent that the culture we are studying is different from our own, such reliance must, of course, be misleading, and the greater the difference, the more misleading it must be. No more somber proof of this sad truth can be imagined than the fate of Charles Beard's *An Economic Interpretation of the Constitution*[35]—a book which was once regarded as a classic of American history but is now regarded as a model of what not to do. Writing in 1912 and deeply imbued with the progressive ideology, Beard set out to muckrake the constitution, taking it for granted that the same sorts of "interests" and the same patterns of corruption and greed which, as a progressive, he believed to be dominant in American politics in his day must have operated in the 1780's. As Robert Brown and a host of others have shown all too clearly,[36] Beard transposed a model of social "reality" from his own time to an earlier period to which it had very little if any application. Doubtless it was a "truism" to Beard that the interests of personalty and agriculture must be opposed—unfortunately for Beard, it was false for America in 1787. To rely upon "truisms of common sense" is to abandon the attempt to write responsible history.

Once it is recognized that the learned patterns of behavior character-istic of a society are law-like and possess explanatory force, it must surely be apparent that history cannot rely upon either common sense or other sciences to provide the laws required for explanation. The his-torian deals with societies which those sciences have not examined and whose common sense is common no longer. It cannot be assumed that what is true now was true in the past. It is therefore the task of the his-torian not only to explain particular facts but also to discover true law-like generalizations in terms of which those explanations can be given. And this is necessarily the historian's task, for there is no one else who can do it. Of course he may rely upon findings of other sciences, as for example he relies upon the laws of learning in those cases where there is good reason to believe that laws are culture-free. And he may also rely upon comparisons with contemporary cultures similar in known respects to that upon which he is working. More than this, he should and must rely upon conceptual schemes which appear to hold promise of revealing significant aspects of any social structure. But, when all this is said, it remains his inescapable problem to try to determine what law-like generalizations are true of the society he studies. That is pre-eminently the task of the historian.

But do historians in fact attempt to discover such generalizations? It is hard to see how anyone familiar with recent writing in American history could doubt that they do. It is now generally agreed that the greatest historian of the last generation in the American field was Perry Miller. And I think it can hardly be denied that what Miller was chiefly concerned with was the patterns of thought and action charac-terizing New England society. Volume I of *The New England Mind*[37] could scarcely be described in any other terms. It is the most striking example in American historiography of a work devoted entirely to the delineation of the patterns of belief characterizing a single society. Indeed, the change in attitude toward seventeenth-century New England which has occurred since 1939 is almost entirely due to Miller's work, for he provided the structure of patterns which made the behavior of New Englanders of that period intelligible. Nor is Miller's work the only example. Edmund Morgan's *Puritan Family*[38] is a study of the customs characterizing the family in Puritan Massachussetts. The explicit purpose of the book is to provide a set of generalizations about the family as an institution in this society which would explain the behavior of its members. Examples could be multiplied, but these will perhaps suffice to show that historians of the first rank have been and are concerned, not with particular facts alone, but with discovering the law-like generalizations which give coherence and sense to such facts.

If historians have in fact been involved in the search for generalizations having explanatory power, how are we to account for the fact that they have generally been regarded as doing something else? There are three classes of generalizations to which a historian can appeal to explain his data: those which are true of the members of a given society at a given time, those which are true of the members of all societies of a given type, and those which are true for the members of all societies. Only laws of the latter two classes can be stated without uneliminable reference to particulars, and since it has long been held, particularly by philosophers, that explanatory laws cannot contain such references, this has led to the denial that generalizations of the first class were laws at all. But it is generalizations of the first class that have been chiefly used in history, and to the discovery of which the field is oriented. Thus the specialities in history are usually culture areas, or are limited to aspects of culture areas—e.g., American colonial history or American political history (rather than political history)—in contrast to the specialities in sociology or economics. In fact, of the social sciences, history has been closest to anthropology, where the emphasis on particular culture areas has remained strong due to the importance of ethnography. Only to a very limited degree have historians employed generalizations of the second and third classes, and this fact has led philosophers and others who deny the law-like character of the generalizations of the first class to claim that historians never seek laws at all. Why history as a discipline should have followed this course is a question which we cannot pursue here. What needs to be emphasized is that once the law-like character of the generalizations of the first class is understood, it becomes clear that historians are and have been fundamentally concerned with discovering laws.

It remains to comment on the question of whether or not there are distinctively "historical laws." I have emphasized already that history depends upon law-like statements characterizing past societies, but these are not the sorts of statements which are usually meant when the question of historical laws is raised. What is usually called a "historical law" is some law of change or sequence defining a succession of events or states such that, given certain initial conditions, and the occurrence of the first event or state, the entire sequence follows. At the risk of being obvious, it might be remarked that, at least at the macrosocial level, any such law would almost have to be historical, since the earlier members of the sequence would have passed into history before the later ones occurred. The question, therefore, is really whether there are such laws of social change covering temporally extended intervals of moderately long duration—say, greater than a generation. So put, the answer is almost certainly "yes," although we seem to have very little knowledge as to what they are. Attempts to formulate such laws, however, are not difficult to cite. Murdock's attempt[39] to define the possible sequences of kin structures is one example, and the theory of critical elections marks a start, at least, toward long-term generalizations in political science,[40] though hardly yet in a form which could be stated as a law. An extremely interesting example of this sort is the theory of scientific revolutions advanced by Thomas Kuhn.[41] That his generalization is a brilliant description of what has been the case is generally agreed by historians of science, but whether the theory is law-like is another matter on which even Kuhn's own position is unclear. Many historians regard his thesis as summatory only—the claim that it should be considered law-like, and so predictive of the future of science, is one which will exercise both scientists and philosophers of science. There are, then, examples of generalizations of this sort which are often called "historical laws," but there are few examples which have significant confirmation.

Having considered at some length the question of the nature of the laws used in historical explanation, I would like to turn now to the question of the logical structure of that explanation. The Hempelian view of explanation holds that it is always in the form of an argument, whether deductive or inductive. This claim has been challenged by Scriven and by White, both of whom assert that an explanation may be given by a singular statement. As White's argument seems to be the stronger of the two, I shall examine it first. He distinguishes between a contributory cause of E and the whole cause of E. The whole cause of E consists of the total set of causes which are sufficient for the occurrence of E; any subset of this total set may be regarded as a contributory cause of E. He then notes that historians typically present explanations in terms of singular statements of the form "A happened because of B." On Hempel's analysis, this statement is an explanation sketch, and must be "filled in" before it becomes an explanation—that is, the statement is elliptical for an argument which is the true explanation. But as White remarks, the statement cannot be equivalent to the argument because the statement is true or false while the argument is valid or invalid. Furthermore, if under duress a historian were to supply an argument justifying a singular causal statement and a philosopher were to point out that the general law of the argument was false, it is not true that the historian would at once abandon the singular causal statement—rather, as White points out, he would look for another argument which would stand up. Combining these two facts, White arrives at what he calls the thesis of Existential Regularism.

> A statement of the form "A is a contributory cause of C" is true if and only if there is an explanatory deductive argument containing "A" as a premise and "C" as its conclusion.[42]

By an "explanatory deductive argument" here White means a deductive explanatory argument of the Hempelian type with a well-confirmed general law. That is, what the historian is committed to is the existence of such an argument—the singular causal statement itself, however, is not equivalent to such an argument.

The plausibility of White's thesis is obvious—it is in line with historical practice, and historians do defend themselves in the way he asserts. But if the truth of any singular causal statement depends upon the existence of an explanatory argument, it would seem that the historian would have to support his singular statement by exhibiting the argument, so that the difference between White's and Hempel's positions might not be so great. But White denies this, for he believes that the historian can offer inductive reasons for believing that such an argument exists even when he cannot exhibit the argument itself. To show that a's being a P is a contributory cause of a's being a Q, the historian might first try the law-like statement that all P's are Q's. However, suppose he finds that this law is not strictly true, but that it is only mildly probable that P's are Q's. Upon consideration, suppose he can formulate a further law-like statement, whatever is P and R is Q. Suppose again that this law fails to hold strictly but the probability that what is P and R is Q is greater than the probability that what is P is Q. Again, the historian searches the treasury of his wisdom, and proposes the further law—whatever is P and R and S is Q, which again holds only with probability, but a higher probability than its predecessor. Then White remarks:

> This investigator, I suggest, has good inductive reasons for thinking that there is a strict explanatory law and that there are true singular statements about *a* which, together with "a is P," logically imply "a is Q" and hence make up a deductive argument of the kind required.[43]

Several remarks are in order on this claim. First, White refuses to admit probability hypotheses as covering laws, preferring to opt for a strictly deterministic situation. Hence for him the probability hypothesis discovered by his hypothetical investigator cannot be the covering law itself but must be regarded as an approximation of it. But this position is utterly arbitrary. So far as explanatory theories are concerned, we appear to face the following situation. An explanatory law or theory may be formulated either probabilistically or in absolute terms. If the former course is chosen, the most that can be deduced is the probability of the occurrence of E. But if the latter alternative is chosen, observation invariably disconfirms the theory. There are no generalizations about human behavior which hold with absolute generality—exceptions always exist. These exceptions may indeed be explained away as due to errors of observation or the disturbing influence of factors not included in the model—hence it is always necessary to supplement such absolute theories with a probabilistic error theory—but the point is that the most that can ever be verified empirically is a high degree of statistical regularity. Whichever formulation is chosen, if by successive additions of variables a generalization has been achieved which makes the event E highly probable given certain antecedent conditions, there is no ground for not accepting this generalization as the covering law operative in the case. Second, if one takes literally the procedure outlined by White, the inference that there exists a strict explanatory law from the fact that, by adding variables, the degree of probability of the consequent can be increased is certainly incorrect. Consider, for example, a standard regression problem, where we seek to explain x_1 by x_2, using the linear model

$$x_1 = a + bx_2$$

Suppose that the coefficient of determination is .2. Now we add further variables to obtain the equations

$$x_1 = a + b_{12.3} x_2 + b_{13.2} x_3$$
$$x_1 = a + b_{12.34} x_2 + b_{13.24} x_3 + b_{14.23} x_4$$

and so on. Suppose that the coefficient of determination of the second equation is .3 and that of the third equation is .4. Certainly from such evidence the inference that by successive additions of variables we can reach a coefficient of determination of 1 is completely unjustified, either mathematically or empirically. Either we do succeed in constructing a linear model which explains most of the variance of x_1, in which case there is no reasonable ground for refusing to say that we have exhibited the covering law, or we do not succeed in constructing such a model, in which case we certainly cannot infer that such a model exists. In order, then, to demonstrate that there exists a deductive argument, or an inductive argument, explaining the phenomenon in question, we must in fact exhibit the law. That is, White's thesis that the singular causal statement is equivalent, not to an argument, but to the statement that an argument exists, does not avoid the necessity of providing the argument, because the only way in which the existence of the argument can be demonstrated, and so the only way in which the singular causal statement can be supported, is by exhibiting the argument. White's point is a valuable one, because it does make clear that the historian very often does not have a specific explanatory argument in mind but merely believes that such an argument can be found. But if the historian is to present a justification for his singular causal statement—and certainly he is called upon to do so—it must be by exhibiting the argument in question. Existential Regularism, therefore, does not legitimize the current practice of presenting singular causal statements only and ignoring general laws. The historian is responsible for the truth of the statements which his history contains. No historian would hazard a noncausal factual statement without citing evidence to support it. Similarly, he must present evidence to support his causal statements, and the only way he can present such evidence is to exhibit the covering law in question.

A rather different defense of singular causal statements has been made by Scriven. Like White, he wants to regard singular causal statements as explanations. But he notes that there are three ways in which explanations may be said to be defective: they may be inaccurate, meaning that the factual statements of initial conditions are false; they may be inadequate, meaning that there is no generalization which will justify the asserted connection of antecedent conditions and consequent event; or they may be irrelevant, meaning that they do not explain what needs explaining or answer the question asked. Therefore, to justify an explanation we must adduce three types of grounds for it: factual grounds confirming the accuracy of the explanation, a general hypothesis confirming the adequacy of the explanation, and evidence of relevance to the question asked. But these grounds, so Scriven claims, are not part of the explanation: the explanation itself is the singular causal statement. To this argument, it may of course be replied that whether the term "explanation" is limited to the singular causal statement or extended to the statement plus its grounds, it is nevertheless the business of the historian to present not only explanations but also justifications of them. Historians clearly must and do present evidence of the accuracy and relevance of their explanations, and would be called to account if they did not; similarly, they should and must present evidence of the adequacy of their explanations, so that the generalizations must be exhibited in any case.

But Scriven goes on to argue that the generalizations which uphold an explanation need not be general laws in the Hempelian sense. Thus he argues that to explain the fact that the ink tipped over when I bumped the table with my knee, the only generalization I could furnish would be of the form "if I hit the table hard enough with my knee and the ink is unstable enough, then the ink upsets." This is not a general law, Scriven avers, because the terms "hard enough" and "unstable enough" do not permit of precise stipulation; the statement is, rather, a "truism of common sense." Scriven then goes on to argue that the sort of generalization needed in explanation is what he calls a "normic" generalization —a generalization which states what happens in a certain type of case, except when exceptional circumstances exist. Such generalizations involve terms like "usually," "ordinarily," "naturally," "normally," and range, so Scriven holds, from seemingly statistical generalizations to normative statements of ethics.[44]

Now the usual criticism of Scriven's view is that the class of normic statements is so heterogeneous that one does not know what is to be found there. But the problem seems deeper than this. Scriven's preference for normic statements is apparently an attempt to maintain at once that the justification of the adequacy of an explanation must involve a deductive argument, and that the generalizations occurring in this deductive argument must somehow be immune to the countercases which they will inevitably face. Instead, then, of admitting statistical laws, which would require the dropping of deductivity, or holding to absolute laws, which would be disconfirmed by countercases, he proposes normic statements which are not probabilistic, but are selectively immune from countercases, and leaves it to the judgment of the historian to determine whether or not the exceptional circumstances mentioned obtain. But such a procedure hardly seems defensible. A statement to the effect that "A is normally B, except in exceptional circumstances" admits of two analyses: on the one hand, we can formulate the statement as a statistical generalization that "A is B in r percent of the cases"; on the other hand, we can demand to know what these circumstances are and can reformulate the statement as "whatever is A and not C (where C defines the exceptional circumstances) is B." Either formulation appears to be clearer than Scriven's, and preferable since it eliminates the rather vague appeal to "judgment."

On the basis of these reflections, it appears clear that whether we extend the meaning of the term "explanation" to include both arguments and singular causal statements, or restrict it to arguments alone, the task of the historian is very much the same. In either case, he is obliged to justify his assertion that a's being P causes a's being Q by citing a generalization of the covering law type, and unless such a generalization is forthcoming the putative explanation remains conjectural only.

Having looked in some detail at the notion of law in history and at the structure of historical explanation, I would like now to turn to the question of what history explains. The almost universal verdict of philosophers who have written on history has been that it explains particular events. Thus to give only some conspicuous examples, Nagel writes:

> Even a cursory examination of treatises in theoretical natural science and of books on history reveals the prima facie difference between them, that by and large the statements of the former are general in form, and contain few if any references to specific objects, places, and times, whereas the statements of the latter are almost without exception singular and replete with proper names, dates, and geographic specifications.[45]

Gallie is equally clear-cut:

> Thus no one denies that history is concerned with particular facts, with what actually happened on this or that particular occasion . . .[46]

So is Frankel:

> Although books on history usually contain at least a few explicit generalizations about human behavior or the relations of social institutions to one another, they contain for the most part singular statements asserting the occurrence of unique events at specific places and times.[47]

White regards a historical narrative as implying a chronicle which contains all of the noncausal factual statements of the narrative, and remarks that all of these statements are logically singular, whether they are about specific events or "conditions of life,"[48] such as how the people make a living. These are for White equally particular statements. These citations could be multiplied easily, but the point is, I trust, sufficiently clear. Now it cannot be denied that history seeks to explain particular events. What must be denied is that that is an adequate characterization of what history explains. For, in fact, history seeks to explain at least four rather different sorts of things—changes, laws, data, and facts. Let us examine these in order.

I should like first to consider the suggestion of Arthur Danto that what history explains is always a change: "the explanandum describes not simply an event—something that happens—but a *change*."[49] Now Danto's thesis that what is explained is *always* a change appears to me either trivial or false. It is, I think, trivial if what it means is that the occurrence of E is always a case of a change from not-E to E. This is certainly true; but it is a truth adequately handled by incorporating among the initial conditions used to explain the occurrence of E at t_1 the statement that E does not occur at t_0. It does not follow that in explaining E we are explaining a change, except in this trivial sense in which

to speak of anything at all as occurring is to speak of going from not-E
to E. But Danto does not mean the thesis to be trivial. What he wants
to point out is that what we want explained is a change from F to E,
where F is not the same as not-E, and that here it is not just the occurrence
of E but the change itself that is the explanandum. This is certainly
true in some, indeed many, cases, but not in all. For example, a historian may reasonably ask (1) why did the Republicans win in 1896?;
or he may ask (2) why did the Republican percentage of the presidential
vote increase between 1892 and 1896? These two questions involve the
same event—McKinley winning—but the questions are not the same.
The answer to (1) would certainly involve an analysis of the vote in
1896; the answer to (2) would involve an analysis of the difference
between the vote in 1892 and that in 1896. These are different questions
which require different answers. (1) is a question about the occurrence
of a particular event, while (2) is a question about a change. Both
questions are equally legitimate, and both are frequently asked. Neither
type can be said to have exclusive claims.

But even if we grant this emendation due to Danto, we would still
appear to hold that history deals with particular *facts*, whether events
or changes. But what would one do with a book such as Woodward's
Strange Career Of Jim Crow?[50] Certainly what Woodward seeks to.
explain in this book is how a pattern of race relations came to be characteristic of a society. This pattern is a general fact: it is instanced indeed
in numerous particulars, but the pattern which we understand as the
Jim Crow code of race relations is a law-like pattern in the sense we have
discussed above. If historians write books to "explain" the existence
of such patterns, then they are certainly trying to explain the existence
of laws. Now to explain a law means, in the physical sciences, to deduce
that law from some other law or laws. But this is not what Woodward
is trying to do—he does not seek the logical deduction of the Jim
Crow system from some general theory, but rather he tries to explain what
caused the code to be adopted in the South at a particular time. His
explanation has to do essentially with the changes in the relative power
of sanctioning groups—changes which led to the ascendency of particular groups who wished the Jim Crow code enforced, and who were
ready and able to enforce it. Now this sort of explanation of a law does
not exist in physics, for it makes no sense in physics to talk of subatomic

particles "learning" to behave in a certain way (at least one would be
very surprised if it did make sense), or of laws changing over time.
But in respect to human society, behavior patterns do change, as the
structural features of the social system which support them change, and
people do learn to behave in ways different from those which their
fathers followed. There is then nothing surprising about a historian such
as Woodward addressing himself to the problem of explaining why such
a law-like pattern should have come to prevail at a particular time and
place—this is pre-eminently the task of the historian, and especially of
the superior historian. Historians then seek to explain more than particular facts—they also seek to explain general facts or laws.

When a historian seeks to explain how a given pattern of behavior
became characteristic of a society, the explanation involved is still of
the covering law type. Such an explanation is couched in terms either
of laws of learning or of a theory of social structure which attributes
the formation and maintenance of custom to the characteristics and
behaviors of actors, expecters, and sanctioners. Thus, to take the simplest
example, a habit of an individual may have sufficient strength so that
his behavior in the presence of the appropriate antecedent conditions
is very highly predictable. Such a habit then is a law-like principle for
purposes of explaining his behavior. If we ask for an explanation of this
habit, an answer can be formulated in terms of learning theory which
explains the formation and strength of the habit as due to repeated
reinforcement over a series of trials. Such an explanation is fully consistent with the covering law model. Thus the fact that explanations of
laws in history are often of a different type from those found in physics
does not serve to introduce any new type of explanation; rather, what
it shows is that principles which are general with respect to some
phenomena may appear as particular facts when viewed in relation to
still more general principles.

It should also be pointed out that historians seek to explain statistical
regularities of a non-law-like character in the sense that any social
scientist does. There are many examples of this—fluctuations in prices
and wages in economic history, patterns of voting behavior in Congress
or in county election returns in political history, changes in age of first
marriage in social history, and so on. The explanations here consist
essentially in showing that the variance of the dependent variable can

be largely accounted for by some relatively small set of independent variables. In the simplest sort of case, the dependent variable which defines the series to be explained is shown to be a linear function of n independent variables by fitting a regression equation to the data. Such methods are, of course, standard in all social sciences and require no particular comment.

Thirdly, history seeks to explain the data. As we saw in Chapter I, these data consist of things now in existence, whether they are inscriptions on objects, oral traditions, or artifactual remains. It is observations of these presently existing items which constitute the sensory basis upon which all historical construction ultimately rests. It is, therefore, in an ultimate sense the function of historical theory as a whole to account for these data. Philosophers of history have been so convinced that history explained particular facts that they have often failed to note that these "facts" themselves are postulated to explain observational evidence.

That the facts are postulates to account for the data may be most easily illustrated from the familiar example of the detective story. In such stories, if the victim was murdered, it is a fact that some person murdered him; yet in the usual case that person in unknown and must be discovered. The story hangs upon the attempt of the detective to decide among various alternative hypotheses attributing the deed to different suspects, and this decision has to be made on the basis of which hypothesis explains the data best. Since the actual crime was not observed, or if observed, the witnesses are unavailable, the confirmation has always to be indirect, and the more artful the story, the more indirect the confirmation. Only when one of the hypotheses has been proven beyond reasonable doubt are we treated to the confession and/or desperate attempt at escape which adds absolute certainty to the conclusion.

The analogy between the historian and the detective has been noted by various writers[51] and rests on more than the occasional interest of historians in past murders. The historian cannot observe the historical fact any more than the detective can observe the crime; he must infer it from data which are often more fragmentary than the detective's clues. In both cases, the objective is to establish a particular factual hypothesis, and in both the confirmation of the hypothesis must be indirect. The search for evidence, and particularly for missing witnesses, often takes a somewhat different form for the historian than it does for the detective, but the objectives of the search are very much the same in both cases. And if the historian is denied the final dramatic scene in which the villain's behavior shows the detective's reasoning to have been flawless, that is all the more reason why he must make the most of all the clues he does have.

A factual hypothesis, if true, is confirmed by the data, and it also explains those data. To do this it must, of course, be conjoined with other statements, some of which are general. Thus, consider the alleged fact that George Washington was President of the United States from 1789 to 1797. From the point of view I have adopted, this is a postulate, and an extremely complicated one which involves several constructs. Before anything can be deduced from it, we shall require some further statements—we need to know what the United States was in 1789, and particularly we need to know what the presidency was. Now the presidency is a social position; there is a role assigned to members of that position, and to say that we need to know what the presidency was between 1789 and 1797 is to say we need to know what behavior was assigned to that position. Any such statement is general:

$$(x) (x \text{ is president at } T_1 \text{ then } F_x)$$

for some appropriate values of F. This statement supports both prediction and counterfactuals and is neither summatory nor eviscerated; it is therefore a law-like statement about the past. Let F be "signs most bills passed by Congress which become laws." It then follows that if we can find documents which were bills passed by Congress and which became laws between 1789 and 1797, we shall find most of them bearing the inscription "G. Washington." This is at once an explanation of a characteristic of such documents if they are before us and a prediction as to what we shall find true of them if they have not yet been inspected.

Historical "facts" are asserted in particular statements which involve either the attribution of a characteristic to an entity (e.g., George Washington was president from 1789 to 1797) or the claim that an event occurred (e.g., a slave revolt occurred in Hanover County, Virginia, in 1832). In either case, the entity referred to (Washington or the slaves) is a theoretical construct and the statement itself is a hypothesis about a construct. As is usually the case with hypotheses, little or nothing follows from the hypothesis alone: consequences can only be derived when law-like statements are also invoked. Some of these, as in the case just examined, will be role-defining statements; others may be laws true of all men independently of culture, or of men in certain types of cultures, and still others may be statistical generalizations relating the occurrence of a particular sort of event (e.g., a slave revolt) to a given type of record (e.g., newspaper accounts). But whether the law-like statements are customary, universal, or statistical, they are essential to the derivation of the consequences. And it is through these consequences that the original hypothesis is related to the actual data, so as to provide an explanation of those data. That it is in fact the role, and the justification, of the hypothesis to explain the data is clear if one considers what would happen to the hypothesis if an alternative explanation of the data were adopted. Thus if it could be shown that all newspaper and other accounts of this slave revolt appeared in papers printed outside of Virginia, while no records exist in Virginia which refer to it, the alleged "fact" would look much less certain, since the hypothesis that the revolt occurred would lead us to expect the contrary. But this new characteristic of the data could be accounted for by hypotheses regarding the degree of anxiety about slave revolts in the South in the wake of the Turner uprising and the resulting credence given to rumor. The fact that our alleged "fact" can thus be displaced by alternatives which account for added features of the data shows very clearly that it is an explanatory hypothesis. When historical theory is viewed as a whole, it is clear that what it seeks to explain is observations made by us at the present time.

The fact that, in an ultimate sense, historical theories serve to explain present observations does not mean that the philosophers have been wrong in claiming that these theories serve to explain particular facts. Historical theories serve to explain both data and fact at once, for any generalization which explains the behavior of past objects must yield consequences which are supported by, and so explain, present observations. One may, for analytic purposes, regard explaining the facts and explaining the data as two different "levels" of explanation. Thus one can talk of explanations offered for the behavior of certain particles in quantum theory without simultaneously discussing the way in which that part of the theory explains observational evidence, and one can discuss explanations for Washington's economic policies without referring to the data which support them. The temptation to make such a division is particularly great in history, where the approved style of presentation relegates reference to the data to the footnotes, and reserves the text for the account of the facts. Yet such a division is artificial and is apt to be highly misleading, for it obscures the ever-present reciprocal relations between theory and data. The whole structure of law and "fact" is a single hypothetical construction the purpose of which is to make sense of the observational data, and the explanations of the facts are fully as constrained by the data as are the factual hypotheses themselves. To propose an explanatory generalization for past facts from which no consequences follow which are testable against presently existing data is to indulge in speculation rather than history. It is perhaps just because this fact has not been kept in mind by philosophers that they have been so willing to think of history as applied social science, as if the data of sociology were the same as the data of history.

NOTES

1. R.G. Collingwood, *The Idea of History* (Oxford: Clarendon Press, 1946).

2. Carl G. Hempel, "The Function of General Laws in History" in *Theories of History*, ed. Patrick Gardiner (Glencoe, Ill.: Free Press, 1959), pp. 344–56.

3. William Dray, *Laws and Explanation in History* (Oxford: Clarendon Press, 1957).

4. Morton White, *Foundations of Historical Knowledge* (New York: Harper and Row, 1965).

5. Carl G. Hempel, "Aspects of Scientific Explanation" in *Aspects of Scientific Explanation and Other Essays in the Philosophy of Science* (New York: Free Press, 1965).

6. Hempel, "General Laws," p. 351.

7. Hempel, "General Laws," p. 353.

8. Dray, *Explanation*, p. 31.

9. Hempel, "Aspects of Scientific Explanations."

10. William Dray, "Explaining What" in *Theories of History*, ed. Gardiner, pp. 403–8.

11. Michael Scriven, "Truisms as Grounds for Historical Explanations" in *Theories of History*, ed. Gardiner., pp. 443–75.

12. W. B. Gallie, "Explanations in History and the Genetic Sciences" in *Theories of History*, ed. Gardiner, pp. 386–402.

13. White, *Foundations*, p. 151 ff.

14. Dray, *Explanation*, p. 61 ff.

15. Hempel, "Aspects of Scientific Explanation," pp. 374–76.

16. Dray, *Explanation*, p. 124.

17. Dray, *Explanation*, p. 126.

18. Dray, *Explanation*, p. 139.

19. Hempel, "Aspects of Scientific Explanation," pp. 463–86.

20. White, *Foundations*, ch. 5.

21. Dray, *Explanation*, ch. 2.

22. Arthur C. Danto, *Analytical Philosophy of History* (Cambridge: Cambridge University Press, 1968), ch. 10.

23. Carl G. Hempel and Paul Oppenheim, "Studies in the Logic of Explanation," *Philosophy of Science* 15 (1948): 135–75.

24. Gilbert Ryle, *The Concept of Mind* (New York: Barnes and Noble, 1949), p. 120 ff.

25. Hempel, "Aspects of Scientific Explanation," p. 342.

26. White, *Foundations*, p. 48.

27. White, *Foundations*, p. 49.

28. S. F. Nadel, *The Theory of Social Structure* (Glencoe, Ill.: Free Press, 1957); John W. M. Whiting and Irvin L. Child, *Child Training and Personality* (New Haven: Yale University Press, 1953), chs. 1 and 2; Murray G. Murphey, "Culture, Character, and Personality" in *American Character and Culture*, ed. John A. Hague (Deland, Fla.: Edwards Press, 1964).

29. Whiting and Child, *Child Training*.

30. Lee Benson, *The Concept of Jacksonian Democracy* (Princeton: Princeton University Press, 1961), p. 276.

31. Danto, *History*, p. 219 ff.

32. Danto, *History*, p. 221.

33. Stuart Blumin, "Mobility in a Nineteenth Century American City: Philadelphia, 1820–1860" (Ph.D. diss., University of Pennsylvania, 1968).

34. Edmund S. Morgan, *The Puritan Family* (Boston: Boston Public Library, 1956).

35. Charles A. Beard, *An Economic Interpretation of the Constitution of the United States* (New York: Macmillan Co., 1913).

36. Robert E. Brown, *Charles Beard and the Constitution* (Princeton: Princeton University Press, 1956). Cf. Forrest McDonald, *We, The People* (Chicago: University of Chicago Press, 1958).

37. Perry Miller, *The New England Mind: The Seventeenth Century* (New York: Macmillan Co., 1939).

38. Morgan, *Family*.

39. George P. Murdock, *Social Structure* (New York: Macmillan Co., 1949).

40. V. O. Key, "A Theory of Critical Elections," *Journal of Politics* 17 (1955): 3–18.

41. Thomas S. Kuhn, *The Structure of Scientific Revolutions* (Chicago: University of Chicago Press, 1962).

42. White, *Foundations*, p. 60.

43. White, *Foundations*, p. 86.

44. Scriven, "Truisms."

45. Ernest Nagel, "Some Issues in the Logic of Historical Analysis" in *Theories of History*, ed. Gardiner, p. 374.

46. Gallie, "Explanations," p. 386.

47. Charles Frankel, "Explanation and Interpretation in History" in *Theories of History*, ed. Gardiner, p. 409.

48. White, *Foundations*, pp. 222–23.

49. Danto, *History*, p. 233.

50. C. Vann Woodward, *The Strange Career of Jim Crow* (New York: Oxford University Press, 1966).

51. Robin Winks, ed., *The Historian as Detective* (New York: Harper and Row, 1968); Josephine Tey, *The Daughter of Time* (New York: Berkley, 1959).

IV

Historical Interpretation
and Historical Theory

I would like to turn now to the question of whether or not there are such things as historical theories, and, if so, what sort of theories they are. Such an investigation is particularly necessary since I have talked of historical entities as "theoretical constructs," thus suggesting the existence of some type of historical theory, and because the existence of such theories, at least in any sense of the term "theory" used in the sciences, has been denied. Indeed, it is certainly true that historical writing is oriented to a subject matter localized in time and space rather than to general principles applying universally. Historians usually write about a specific socio-cultural unit or subunit—the United States, Massachusetts in the seventeenth century, the Methodist church in the antebellum South—and rarely about revolutions in general or civil wars in general. But as I have argued, the historian has excellent reasons for limiting his subject in this way, for many of the explanatory generalizations which he uses apply only within a specific spatio-temporal domain. The historian who does not hesitate to attempt to "explain" certain features of the behavior of the Connecticut churches in the late eighteenth century may justly doubt that his thesis can be transposed to German churches of the twentieth century, for the simple reason that the cultural contexts are so different that patterns obtaining in one society very likely do not obtain in the other. There are, to be sure, attempts at broad comparative studies, but these are relatively rare—the emphasis has been on particular social units over particular time periods, and, given the state of the discipline at present, it is hard to see how it could have been on anything else. This concentration on particular social units, however, is not necessarily a weakness, and is not opposed to the explanatory character of historical writing—it merely expresses the fact that the generalizations used in such explanations are often limited to particular socio-cultural systems.

If one examines what historians do, one quickly finds that they do not propose theories: they propose what they call "interpretations." What is such an interpretation, and what is it supposed to do? First, an interpretation always contains a causal model—whatever else it may tell us, it always claims to tell us why certain events or sequences of events occurred. Second, interpretations are generally proposed, not as interpretations of evidence, but of "facts" antecedently established from evidence. Third, an interpretation tells us the "significance" or "meaning" of the events which it purports to explain. Fourth, interpretations are generally presented in narrative form, particularly when the subject dealt with is a change of some sort. And fifth, the interpretation is alleged not to be exclusive of other and equally legitimate interpretations. Each of these points requires some discussion.

The causal character of an interpretation is usually quite explicit, and is indicated by the use of terms such as "because," "thus," "hence," "therefore," etc. Sometimes it is said that an interpretation merely seeks to describe what "really happened," but when this is said it is understood that part of what is being described is the causal connections among the events. Unless an interpretation does tell us why something happened, it is regarded either as a bad interpretation or as no interpretation at all. Now, as covering law theorists have urged, such explanatory claims require for their justification the use of law-like generalizations, and it is notorious that in historical writing such generalizations are usually not stated. Thus we are usually told that x did A because of B, without being told that whenever B, x's do A— that is, we are presented with what White calls singular causal statements. Why this is the case is one of the problems before us; and we shall, I think, begin to make some progress toward its solution if we look at some concrete cases of historical interpretations. For purposes of illustration, I shall therefore discuss three interpretations of a well-known event in American history—Bacon's Rebellion. This revolt occurred in Virginia in 1676. At that time, Virginia was a royal colony governed by a royal governor, an appointed council, and an elected assembly called the House of Burgesses. Nathaniel Bacon, who led the revolt, was a young man of high social standing in England who had come to Virginia in 1674, and had established a plantation on the James River near the western edge of settlement. When the revolt erupted, Bacon became the leader of a large revolutionary movement which succeeded in driving the governor, Sir William Berkeley, off the mainland. However, Berkeley retained naval control of the Bay and military control of the outer shore, and, after Bacon's sudden death on October 26, 1676, demoralized the revolutionaries, he was able to counterattack with such success that the revolt was quickly crushed. This event has remained one of the most famous puzzles in American history and has been the subject of conflicting historical interpretations. In what follows, I shall discuss those of Wertenbaker, Washburn, and Bailyn.

Wertenbaker has written several works which deal with Bacon's Rebellion, but essentially the same interpretation appears in all of them.[1] Briefly, Wertenbaker interprets the rebellion as a prefiguration of the American Revolution in which the "common people" of Virginia rose in defense of their rights against the corrupt and despotic rule of the royal governor. As he writes:

> With the staple crop of the colony a drug on the market because of the Navigation Acts, with tax piled on tax to buy back the liberties of the people from favorites of the King, with self-government made a mockery by the corruption of the Burgesses, with the small farmers in rags, the people were ready to rise in arms at the least excuse.[2]

These factors—the low tobacco prices, the high taxes, the corruption and oppression which characterized the rule of Berkeley—Wertenbaker regards as the "underlying" or basic causes of the revolt; the precipitating cause he sees in the Indian troubles which brought Bacon and Berkeley into conflict. But the Indian War is for Wertenbaker merely the occasion for the revolt, as the firing upon Sumter was for the Civil War:[3] the Indian troubles alone cannot account for the fact that the whole colony, tidewater as well as frontier, rose against the governor, nor for what Wertenbaker regards as the democratic legislation passed by the revolutionary assembly and known as Bacon's Laws. It is only when one recognizes that the "real" causes of the revolt were the economic and

political oppression visited upon Virginia by England and the determination of the Virginians to defend their rights that the course of the
revolt becomes intelligible.

Several comments are in order respecting this interpretation. First,
it is impossible to read Wertenbaker's account without recognizing that
he is interpreting Bacon's Rebellion in terms of the American Revolution.
He is perfectly explicit on this point:

> The more one examines the movement which Bacon headed, the more
> its kinship with the American Revolution becomes apparent, for both
> had as the main principle the defense of American rights.[4]

Thus he is not dealing with a unique event, but with one of two events
which have the same causes and are governed by the same principle,
and the significance of the rebellion lies for him in its relation to that
principle. Second, his interpretation is implemented throughout by a
narrative account of events which reads like an adventure novel. Bacon
is portrayed as a hero, Berkeley as a rogue; even Bacon's most dubious
actions, such as the attack on the Occaneechees,[5] become for Wertenbaker
glorious victories, while Berkeley's actions are uniformly portrayed as
despicable. The selection and treatment of the facts all reflect this bias.
Third, although Wertenbaker clearly believes that he is explaining
Bacon's Rebellion in a causal sense, the most that he could be said to
present is a chronological narrative account containing singular causal
statements: he does not attempt to present deductive or inductive explanatory arguments involving law-like statements. But it is worth asking
what kind of law-like statements he could advance. Since he regards the
fundamental causes of the revolt as English tyranny and the determination of Virginians to defend their rights against that tyranny, he requires
a statement something like this:

> In all cases, the more Virginians believe their rights violated by
> authority, the more likely they are to seek to overthrow that
> authority.

This statement would be too strong for Wertenbaker: he would insist
that other conditions must also be present—e.g., the presence of adequate leadership and perhaps a precipitating cause such as the Indian
troubles. But with such modifications, it is clear that Wertenbaker does

accept essentially this principle—thus he says of Bacon and his men that "the roar of their cannon proclaimed to the world that Virginians would resist to the end all attempts to deprive them of their heritage of English liberty."[6] Beneath the resounding rhetoric, what Wertenbaker is saying here is that English oppression always evokes opposition from the Virginia colonists; hence, given the Stamp Act and all that, the American Revolution, or at least Virginia's part in it, is perfectly predictable. But there are several points which need to be observed about this generalization. First, it cannot be stated in universal form, for it is not all men, or all colonists, or even all English colonists in the New World who so respond to oppression: it is Virginians, or at most Americans. What underlies Wertenbaker's interpretation is a generalization about the behavioral dispositions of a particular group of people, and the reference to the particular group is uneliminable. Second, although the generalization is implicit throughout the narrative, it is only explicitly stated after the narrative has been completed, and is then presented more as a conclusion derived from the narrative than as a principle which accounts for the narrative. Now it is a commonplace that every explanation of an event E by a law L provides a confirming instance of L, so that logically explanation and confirmation have a reciprocal relation. But where the law is doubtful, the relation of E to L is likely to be presented as one of confirmation rather than of explanation. Wertenbaker, I am sure, was personally convinced of his principle, but his mode of presenting it suggests that he was worried about its acceptance. Thus he presents it as a conclusion derived from the narrative and employs literary devices with great skill to make the events appear to illustrate the principle.

The second interpretation of Bacon's Rebellion to which I should like to turn is due to Wilcomb Washburn,[7] and is aimed directly at Wertenbaker's. Washburn is fully aware of the economic difficulties which plagued Virginia and he regards these as contributing causes of the revolt. But he denies that Berkeley was either corrupt or oppressive or that he in any way violated the rights of Virginians. He also denies both that Bacon was a hero or a champion of the people and that he was interested in social or political reform. Indeed, Washburn's book presents Berkeley as the hero and Bacon as the rogue, for Bacon emerges as a hot-tempered, avaricious man chiefly interested in destroying the Indians so that he could claim their land. Whereas for Wertenbaker the Indian troubles were merely the occasion for the rebellion while the real causes were political and economic, for Washburn the Indian troubles are the "real" cause of the whole uprising, and the political and economic issues are secondary. We have here a complete reversal of Wertenbaker's interpretation: heroes become villains and villains, heroes; minor causes become major, and major causes become minor. There is no relation for Washburn between Bacon's Rebellion and the American Revolution, and the rights of Virginians play no role at all.

The explanation which Washburn offers for Bacon's Rebellion is a more complex and less naive one than Wertenbaker's. The most important cause he holds to be the "aggressiveness of the frontiersman."[8] But this is not simply a matter of land hunger, however important that element may be. Washburn paraphrases with approval Beverley's* explanation.

> He [Beverley] cites the misfortunes suffered by the colony because of the low price of tobacco, the tyranny of the English merchants, the great taxes necessary to throw off the proprietary grants, the restraints on trade caused by the Navigation Acts, and the Indian disturbances. But more important, he relates Virginia's depressed condition to the psychology of the planters and shows how this condition affected their attitude toward the Indians, Governor Berkeley, and the rebel Bacon. It was the Indian disturbances, he finds, which tipped the balance and caused men whose minds were "already full of Discontent" to imagine there was an easy way out by "vent[ing] all their Resentment against the poor *Indians*."
>
> Beverley probably came as close to a successful interpretation of the rebellion as anyone since his time.[9]

To formulate this discursive account as explanatory generalizations would require a set of statements somewhat like this:

(1) If a condition of economic threat is perceived as induced by the action of an agent x, anger is aroused against x.

(2) If a condition of physical threat is perceived as induced by the action of an agent x, anger is aroused against x.

---

* Robert Beverley's account of the rebellion appeared in his *History and Present State of Virginia* in 1705. He was the son of Major Robert Beverley, one of Berkeley's chief aides.

(3) If the expression of anger against an agent x is blocked by strong loyalty to x, the anger may be displaced to another threatening stimulus y.

(4) Violence against a threatening stimulus y has cathartic value— i.e., reduces anger—whether the anger is originally aroused by y or displaced from x.

(5) For any person, the higher the level of anger against an object w, the greater the probability of violence against w.

Giving the variables appropriate values, one has, I suspect, a representation of the kind of explanation that Washburn has in mind. The generalizations involved are universal psychological principles applied to a particular context—there is no Spirit of '76, no peculiar destiny of America marching through Washburn's pages. Moreover, such an explanation can meet Wertenbaker's chief argument against the importance of the Indian troubles namely, that the Indian troubles cannot account for the rallying of so large a part of the colony to Bacon's standard. By making the Indians the common scapegoats for the varying angers of the Virginians, the startling unanimity of the Virginians can be accounted for. But what cannot be accounted for are the political-reform aspects of the rebellion, evident for example in Bacon's Laws. Whereas Wertenbaker saw these laws as expressing the democratic ideology of Bacon and his men, Washburn is at great pains to show that Bacon had little to do with them, cared less about them, and would have been adversely affected by some of them. This argument may indeed show that most of Bacon's Laws were not, in fact, Bacon's, but it leaves unexplained the fact that they were passed at all.[10]

Like Wertenbaker, Washburn presents his explanation as a conclusion drawn from the narrative rather than using it to account for the progress of the narrative itself. Thus one sees again the reticence of the historian respecting generalizations and explicit explanations; even though the generalizations may be implicit in the narrative, they must appear to be a conclusion derived from the course of the events narrated.

The third interpretation of Bacon's Rebellion which I would like to examine is due to Bailyn.[11] He remarks that Bacon's Rebellion is not a unique event, but one of a series of revolts which occurred at approximately the same time in Carolina, Virginia, Maryland, New York, and New England. Although Bailyn deals exclusively with Virginia, this

comparative perspective is never absent from his mind and it determines
the kind of explanation which he offers. Thus, for example, questions of
Bacon's or Berkeley's personality are irrelevant to an explanation which
views the revolt in this perspective. Bailyn's interpretation is in terms
of the relation between power and social structure in Virginia. He points
out that in seventeenth-century England society was hierarchically conceived, and it was taken for granted that political office and power be-
longed in the hands of those who held high social status. This view of
the relation of power and status was transferred intact to Virginia. Thus
Bailyn notes that, during the existence of the Virginia Company, the
political power in Virginia was held by an elite group who came from
the English upper class. But after the dissolution of the Virginia Company, this elite vanished from Virginia and political power passed to
those planters of obscure origin who had been most successful in amass-
ing wealth. This situation—an anomaly in terms of the accepted relations of power and status—lasted until the Commonwealth period. But
during the period from 1645 to 1665 a new wave of people arrived in
Virginia, among them many younger sons of upper-middle-class families
which had held stock in the Virginia Company and so acquired claims in
Virginia. These men, aided by resources and connections in England,
their determination to acquire power and position in Virginia, and the
deference due them because of their status, rapidly became a new planter
elite, engrossing positions of authority at the local level. Meanwhile,
Charles II took the throne and began to gather the reins of power into
his hands, including control over the colonies. To do this, he sought to
build up in each colony a coterie of men who would be dependent upon
royal favor rather than upon their local holdings. This policy, applied
in Virginia through Governor Berkeley, divided the elite into a faction
around him, which reaped rich rewards in patronage and profit, and
the remainder, whose power was based upon their local wealth and
leadership. Berkeley used the powers of his office to enrich his faction
and increase its power, while following policies, especially regarding the
Indians, which were unfavorable to the local leaders. Thus the agitation
over the Indian lands involved more than "frontier aggressiveness"—it
involved differential access to wealth in the form of land. As Bailyn sees
it, then, two processes of transfer of power were taking place simultaneously: the transfer of local power into the hands of the rising elite,

and the aggregation of colonial power into the hands of the governor's faction. But neither the new local elite nor the governor's faction had yet been able to establish itself sufficiently to acquire legitimacy. Thus, when the rebellion erupted, it embodied both the protest of the local leadership against the concentration of power in the hands of the governor's faction, and of the small farmers against the whole developing elite, the local leaders as well as the governor's men—hence the seemingly contradictory character of the laws passed by the revolutionary assembly, which in fact represented two conflicting interests.

Bailyn's interpretation, unlike Wertenbaker's or Washburn's, is not a narrative of events—rather it is a description of social processes. But it is, like the others, an attempt to give a causal explanation. Note that at least one of the important generalizations involved is specific to a time and place—namely, the relation between power and social status accepted in England and America is a customary belief governing behavior. Other implicit generalizations may be universal in scope—e.g., that perceived loss of power is a cause of hostility against those to whom the power is perceived to go. As is true for the other interpretations, the law-like generalizations are for the most part left implicit, and even when stated are not stated *as* laws to explain events. Nevertheless, the interpretation is conceived as a causal explanation of the occurrence and characteristics of the rebellion.

It should be clear from this brief discussion of three alternative interpretations of Bacon's Rebellion that all of them seek to provide a causal explanation of events. Although the generalizations underlying these explanations are left implicit, and the explanation is presented through singular causal statements, these generalizations can be made explicit to support the argument. And, as would be expected in the light of Chapter III, these generalizations are of several sorts, ranging from universal psychological principles to customary patterns specific to one or to a few societies. Yet these three interpretations of the same event are strikingly different: they differ in their use of narrative, the significance which they attribute to events, and even the facts which they discuss.

The view that interpretations deal with "facts" antecedently established is derived from the classical historiography which we have discussed at some length above. This view has become the basis for a number of philosophic discussions of historical interpretations. Thus, for example, White draws a distinction between what he calls a "chronicle" and a "narrative."[12] The chronicle contains the complete set of singular, factual, noncausal statements which occur in the history; the narrative consists of the chronicle together with singular, causal statements which relate the statements of the chronicle to each other. On White's view, the chronicle gives all the "facts"; the narrative gives the interpretation of these facts. White does not say, as the classical historiography does, that the chronicle is temporally prior to the narrative— only that it is logically implied by the narrative; but, in making the distinction, he is accepting the classical view of the nonexplanatory character of the "facts." Of course, this position finds substantial justification in historical practice, where evidence is consigned to the footnotes and the text deals (usually) with the interpretation of the so-called facts; but, as we have seen, it is fundamentally misleading to think of facts as free of interpretation. There is no radical discontinuity between the level of interpretation and the level of facts: the facts are explanatory too, and what is a fact, and what facts are significant, depends upon interpretation.

The point can be illustrated by reference to the three interpretations of Bacon's Rebellion discussed above. Among the evidence of that affair is a document embodying Bacon's Laws*—the laws passed by the House of Burgesses during June of 1676, when the rebellion was at its height. These twenty laws are extremely heterogeneous in character. Some of them appear to have nothing to do with the revolt—e.g., the law concerning mischief due to unruly horses, or the one regarding the bounty for killing wolves. Others clearly are related to the revolt—e.g., the general pardon act, which granted complete pardon to all involved in the revolt. Three laws deal with the Indian problems, and eight with questions of office, office holding, and debt. All of the laws in this latter class can be read as "democratic" reforms—that is, they involve a widening of the franchise, limitations on the exemptions granted councilors, limitations on the number of local offices which could be held

---

* The Peyton Randolph MS, Jefferson Collection, Rare Book Room, Library of Congress.

simultaneously and on consecutive tenure in the sheriff's office, and the election of vestrymen.[13] This fact led Wertenbaker to explain these laws as the embodiment of the democratic ideology which he supposed Bacon and his followers to hold. That is, Wertenbaker regarded the rebellion as a conflict between two parties, one representing democracy and the other, autocracy. The June assembly represents the triumph of the democratic faction, and Bacon's Laws the success of this group in enacting its program. Note here that the explanation of these laws involves factual assumptions about the parties in the revolt and about the composition of the June assembly, and these assumptions, in turn, are supported by the evidence furnished by the laws. Washburn, however, has pointed out that Wertenbaker's explanation will not do. In addition to collateral evidence regarding Bacon's manifest lack of interest in the reform legislation, there are characteristics of the laws themselves which Wertenbaker's thesis does not explain. Thus one of the acts of the June assembly provides that no one could hold any office who had not been a resident of Virginia for at least three years—an act which would have disqualified Bacon himself, since he had been in Virginia for only two years. Moreover, of the eight laws which might be interpreted as "democratic," six were re-enacted by the assembly of February, 1677, after the revolt had been put down and the forces of "tyranny" had presumably regained control. It is difficult, therefore, to accept Wertenbaker's analysis as adequate when it leaves such salient questions unanswered.[14]

If one compares Bailyn's interpretation with Wertenbaker's, what is most striking is the factual differences between them. Most of the events described by Wertenbaker are not mentioned by Bailyn; most of the events discussed by Bailyn are not mentioned by Wertenbaker. Yet both interpretations seek to account for Bacon's Laws. Bailyn's analysis in terms of the dual transfer of power going on in Virginia shows Bacon's "party" to be, in fact, a heterogeneous collection of interests, some of which were as opposed to Bacon's objectives as to Berkeley's, and which acted together only because Bacon's actions provided a means to diverse ends. The reform laws of the June assembly can then be viewed as representing these divergent interests; e.g., the acts limiting the powers of councilors embodied the hostility of local leaders to the governor's faction, while the act providing for the election of vestrymen was an attack on the power of the local elite. And it is just those acts which limited the power of the local elite that the February assembly did not re-enact.

These interpretations, of course, rest upon much documentary evidence in addition to the acts of the June assembly. But, by focusing on these acts, it is possible to indicate both how the facts function to explain these manuscript remains and that alternative explanations involving alternative choices of "facts" are possible. The difference in the facts discussed by Wertenbaker and Bailyn is part of the differences in their interpretations. They did not each first establish a set of facts, and then come to different interpretations because they had chosen different facts to start with. They started with certain documentary remains, and, in seeking to account for them, they elaborated a structure of fact *and* hypothesis which, taken as a whole, made sense of the documentary remains. What is being accounted for is the character of these remains; what accounts for that character is the whole structure of "fact" and "law." It is as arbitrary to separate historical "fact" and historical "interpretation" as it would be to separate physical constructs and physical theories. Interpretations explain facts in just the way physical theories explain the behavior of subatomic particles. The particles are not something given which the theory then explains, and historical "facts" are not something given which is then interpreted. Subatomic particles are constructs which are part of physical theories, and historical facts are constructs which are part of historical interpretations. In both cases, what is ultimately explained are the observations which we make here and now through our sense organs.

A third characteristic of historical interpretations upon which there is general agreement is that they attempt to state the "significance" or "meaning" of the events with which they deal. But just what is meant by the "significance" or "meaning" of historical events remains far from clear. Frankel has argued that such events have significance in terms of the terminal consequences to which they lead. Thus he writes:

> Broadly, when an historian provides an "interpretation" of an age or a culture or an institution, he is doing something like the following. He is telling a story of a sequence of causally related events that have consequences of value or dis-value; in other words, he is showing that certain events are causally related to what I shall call "terminal con-

sequences." To state the "meaning" of an historical process is to state these terminal consequences.[15]

A similar position is taken by Danto:

> To ask for the significance of an event, in the *historical* sense of the term, is to ask a question which can be answered only in the context of a *story*. The identical event will have a different significance in accordance with the story in which it is located or, in other words, in accordance with what different sets of *later* events it may be connected.[16]

More specifically, Danto believes that significance is attributed to historical events by what he calls "narrative sentences"—sentences which relate an event x to a later event y and describe x in terms of y. Thus, for example, "Petrarch opened the Renaissance," "Aristarchus anticipated Copernicus," and "The defeat at Gettysburg caused Lee's retreat" are narrative sentences. Clearly, all causal sentences in which the cause is conceived as temporally prior to the effect are narrative sentences, so Danto's account does not contradict the causal character of historical interpretations, but there are many narrative sentences which are not causal—e.g., Aristarchus did not cause Copernicus to develop a heleocentric theory. In these cases, narrative sentences serve to relate earlier and later events noncausally and to integrate them into a unified *story*. The significance of a historical event therefore lies in its role in the story or narrative, and this role is defined by its relation to later events.[17]

A crucial question for this thesis is how the later events to which a given event is related are to be chosen. Frankel argues that four criteria are operative: the interest of the later event as judged by the historian, the importance of the later event as a cause of further events, the significance of the later event for policy, and its relation to some scheme of human good to which the historian subscribes.[18] Although in all four cases, as Frankel carefully notes, factual and causal considerations enter in, it is obvious that this view makes the choice of terminal consequences largely relative to the values and interests of the historian and so is essentially relativistic. An even stronger conclusion follows from Danto's argument, for he holds, not only that the choice of future events to which past or present events will be related by narrative sentences is relative to the interests of the historian, but also that narrative sentences, the later event of which lies in the future, are neither true nor false. It follows, not only that the future contingent propositions either have no truth value or have an indeterminate one, but also that there are past contingencies which depend upon what will occur, since the significance of past events depends upon what narrative sentences are true, and what narrative sentences are true cannot be known until the later of the events referred to in the narrative sentence occurs.[19] These arguments are both complex and important and require some analysis.

I should first like to consider Danto's claim that future contingent propositions are neither true nor false. He presents this argument as an answer to logical determinism, which he regards as a form of fatalism, and his discussion is based explicitly upon Aristotle's discussion of future contingency in the *De Interpretatione*. In brief, Danto regards the logical determinist as asserting that not only is the disjunction p v ∼p necessarily true, but that necessarily p or necessarily not∼p.[20] It must follow then, as Danto understands the logical determinist, that whatever happens, or will happen, happens necessarily, so that there can be no such thing as freedom. As against this, Danto interprets Aristotle as arguing that, with respect to past and present contingents, it is indeed true that whatever happens, happens necessarily, but that, with respect to future contingents, there is real indeterminacy—a future contingent such as "There will be a sea battle tomorrow" is neither true nor false. It is not clear whether Danto thinks that such propositions simply do not have a truth value or he thinks they have a truth value such as indeterminate, but what is clear is that he thinks they do not have either of the two truth values "true" or "false." Danto develops his position in the following form. Consider these six sentences:

(1) s is F   (2) s is not F   (3) s was F
(4) s was not F   (5) s will be F   (6) s will not be F

Danto defines the notion of time-truth as follows: if (3), (4), (5), and (6) are false, (1) and (2) are time-true; if (1), (2), (5), and (6) are false, (3) and (4) are time-true; and if (1), (2), (3), and (4) are all false, (5) and (6) are time-true. Statements not time-true are time-false and also false. Now if (1) and (2) are time-true, one of them is true and the other false; if (3) and (4) are time-true, one of them is true and the other false; but if (5) and (6) are time-true, they are neither true nor false. (5) and (6) are in fact never true, unless by their becoming true one means that at some time (1) and (2) become time-true and one of them true while (5) and (6) become time-false and also false. From this analysis Danto then argues as follows:

> But if the future cannot be known, the past cannot be known completely. In so far as we are logically prohibited from having knowledge of the future, we are, again logically, prohibited from knowing whatever is expressed in sentences which express *past contingencies*. We can only know narrative sentences when these are time-true and true, and they are not this when they contain a singular time-true, future-referring proposition. But since it is by means of narrative sentences that we ascribe historical significance to events, God, even if omniscient, cannot *know* what the significance of events is before they in fact *have* this significance.[21]

It follows that the past is not irrevocably fixed, as one might have thought, but that there are real past contingencies. For to know an event is, for Danto, to know that event under some description; and the descriptions which narrative sentences furnish of past events depend upon the later of the events mentioned in the narrative sentences. Hence if the narrative sentence refers to a future event, and any past event may be connected to some later event in a narrative sentence, and that narrative sentence is neither true nor false, there is a real contingency about the past event which will not be eliminated until the narrative sentence "becomes" true. The significance of past events, therefore, cannot be fully known now; and future historians will ever rewrite the history, not of *the* past, for there is no such thing, but of their past.

Danto's argument is an interesting one, but one which seems to me to be fundamentally in error on at least three major points. First, he misconstrues the position of those who hold that future contingent propositions have a truth value—indeed, as Rescher has pointed out, it is possible to interpret Aristotle as holding that such propositions have truth values.[22] For while it is certain that Aristotle did hold that, with respect to past and present contingents, what is true is necessarily true, it is possible to construe his argument respecting future contingents as holding that such propositions are either true or false, but not either necessarily true or necessarily false. Whether the future contingent is true or false on this view depends on how things happen to turn out— hence upon the outcome of real future contingencies; but, however they will turn out, the future contingent proposition has one of the two ordinary truth values. More recently, Gale has developed this point of view in a way which appears to avoid most of the difficulties which Danto has raised. We may define an *A-statement* as a statement whose truth value depends upon when it is used. More exactly, Gale defines it as follows:

> Any statement which is not necessarily true (false) is an A-statement if, and only if, it is made through the use of a sentence for which it is possible that it is now used to make a true (false) statement and some past or future use of it makes a false (true) statement, even if both statements refer to the same things and the same places.[23]

Thus Danto's six sentences above are A-statements. Let S be any A-statement. The metalinguistic statement "it is true that S" may then be called an *endorsing statement* S*. Such an endorsing statement can be given two rather different interpretations: it can be analyzed pragmatically or semantically. In the former case, Gale argues, although the endorsing statement S* implies nothing about the evidence for S, the making of S* in certain contexts does imply something about the evidence for S. Specifically, the use of S* in a fact-stating context C pragmatically implies that the speaker has what he considers to be adequate evidence for S. Since sentences uttered in the context C are usually believed warranted by the utterer, there is a convention that S* should not be uttered in such a context unless the utterer believes S*, and to disavow this convention would nullify the perlocutionary acts for which S* is usually used in C. Clearly, this is a metametalinguistic criterion, for it is a statement about the use of a statement about S. Gale argues that the apparent indeterminacy of the future contingent arises from this pragmatic dimension, for S* cannot be asserted in context C in the absence of evidence and such evidence may not exist. Thus with respect to tomorrow's sea battle, if the admiral in whose power it is to determine whether or not the battle will take place is still debating whether or not to give the order upon which the occurrence of the battle depends, then he would have to say that the statement "There will be a sea battle tomorrow" is neither true nor false (or not yet true or not yet false), since the evidence for this statement is not yet in. But this does not imply that the statement, considered semantically, has no truth value. Indeed, semantically considered, we may develop a set of rules for the truth of A-statements as follows. Let S be Danto's (1). Then to say (1) is true entails that (5) was true earlier than now and that (3) will be true at any time later than now. And similar rules can be generated for dealing with (3) and (5), and for all the negations. Danto would reply to this that it is a move without effect, since the rule itself involves a statement of what will be the case and this statement is itself indeterminate. But this depends upon taking for granted the point at issue—namely, that future contingents are neither true nor false. Gale, following Rescher, holds that we can regard them as having truth values of the ordinary kind which depend upon how the contingencies come out, and that to assert (5) is simply to say that before s is F (5) is true, when s is F (1) is true, and after s is F (3) is true. That we have not the evidence to decide now whether (5) is true explains why in a certain context we cannot assert (5), but this is a pragmatic rather than a semantic consideration. Accordingly, it appears that the escape from fatalism does not involve any such heroic move as Danto appears to believe. We need not deny ordinary truth values to future contingent propositions.[24]

What now becomes of the claim that there exist past contingencies? If future contingent propositions have truth values, then narrative sentences which contain singular future-referring propositions are also either true or false, and past contingencies in any ontological sense appear to vanish. It will, of course, remain true that we do not know now whether these narrative sentences are true or false, but this is also the case with many sentences whose possession of truth values no one seriously questions. We may, it is true, come to describe some past events in terms other than those which we have used before, but it does not follow from this that the past event is really somehow different, unless one also subscribes to the doctrine of internal relations. Indeed, even if Danto's claim that future contingents are indeterminate were correct, it would not follow that there are real past contingencies unless one also subscribes to some form of the doctrine of internal relations. For to say that, because an event may have a relative property in the future which it does not have now, the event itself has changed is surely to say that the relative property is in some sense constitutive of the event. Moreover, the relative properties here involved could hardly be taken to be essential properties on any view which holds that less than all the properties of the event in question are essential. It thus appears that Danto's argument for real past contingencies is linked to two extremely dubious positions.

Whether or not there are real past contingencies, we have still to meet Danto's argument that, since we cannot predict the behavior of future historians, we cannot determine the significance of past events. For if, as Danto claims, the significance of historical events is ascribed through narrative sentences which relate them to later events, and the choice of which later events are to be included in narrative sentences depends upon the interests of future historians, we must either be able to predict what the choices of future historians will be or we cannot now determine the significance of historical events. But it is certainly difficult to hold that we can predict what choices future historians will make; for, as Danto points out, if we could do that we could also predict what narrative sentences future historians would write and we could then act in such a way as to make those sentences false. Clearly, this would lead to absurd consequences, and so Danto concludes that the attempt to predict what future historians will write is hopeless.

The trouble with this argument is that it proves too much. On Danto's analysis, causal statements are narrative sentences—so, obviously, are predictions which relate a set of antecedent conditions to consequent events. Hence among the statements of the sciences are many which Danto would classify as narrative. But it is clear that scientists can no more predict what future scientists will say or believe than historians can predict what future historians will say or believe. For we know that the sciences have undergone periodic "revolutions" in which new conceptual schemes have replaced old ones, and that such changes in conceptual schemes often transform radically the kinds of questions asked and the kinds of answers accepted in the sciences. Hence, no matter how well confirmed our present statements of physics may appear to be, no one can know now whether or not these statements will be incorporated into a new conceptual scheme "after the revolution," or even if the problems which are now considered crucial in physics will be regarded as scientific problems at all. Danto's argument, therefore, does not serve to distinguish science from history—in neither case can we predict now what future practitioners will be interested in or will believe. But we can, of course, predict, as the sciences do every day, what will occur. Our predictions are, to be sure, couched in the language of our own conceptual scheme, but they are nonetheless predictions and they may well be true—at least their truth can be tested in due course. In other words, our inability to know how future scientists or historians will describe events in no way implies that we cannot describe future events in terms of our own conceptual schemes. Hence whether or not narrative sentences containing future-referring terms are true is not just a matter of what future historians or scientists will believe. To this Danto would agree, but he would also insist that our predictions must be general—that we can only predict that certain types of events will occur, not that certain future individual events will occur or that certain individuals will exist and stand in particular relations to past events. Hence he would still maintain that our predictions about the future must be of a very different sort from our narrative statements about the past. That we cannot make predictions regarding future individuals not now in existence I must agree, although I think Danto is led to overstate the degree of generality necessary for predictions, owing to his belief that a law-like statement can contain no uneliminable reference to an individual. So, if it is granted that it is through narrative sentences that significance is ascribed to historical events, it will still follow from Danto's argument that the significance of past events must be continually revised in terms of the unfolding future. But this returns us at long last to the question of whether or not the significance of past events is ascribed on the basis of their relations to later events or to terminal consequences. And this is a question which requires some analysis.

It should be remarked at the outset that many historians themselves do not accept Danto's view. This issue has come to the fore particularly in the historiography of science, because it is in that field especially that the tendency to ascribe significance to past events in terms of later ones has been pronounced. Because scientists, and many historians of science, have regarded science as a progressive and cumulative discipline—that is, one in which the successive changes in theories represent an asymptotic approach to truth and in which each change preserves what was true in the older theories while adding some new truths to them—the significance of past events in science has often been conceived in terms of their relations to present (and presumably truer) scientific beliefs. Thus special emphasis has been given to anticipations of present views, and discussions of past scientific theories have been in terms of what in those theories was true (judged by modern standards) and what was not. But it is now generally recognized that this approach to the history of science has seriously distorted the nature and the significance of past scientific work. The significance of the work of Aristarchus did not lie in its anticipation of Copernican astronomy; nor do we learn anything of significance about Franklin's electrical theory by being told that his corpuscularian doctrine is an anticipation of the theory of the electron.[25] Historians of science are now calling for a historicist approach which will seek to understand the past in its own terms, not in terms of its relation to later events which happen to interest certain investigators.[26] There is, then, good reason to challenge the claim that all historians ascribe "significance" to events in terms of consequences, at least in the form that Danto and Frankel assert this thesis.

But what does it mean to understand the past in its own terms? It means, I think, to seek for an understanding of past phenomena in terms of the system of thought and action of which they were a part. Of course, this system is in part our construction, as is any theory, and it must usually contain recently discovered principles of which the members of past societies were unaware, but it must also contain the customs and beliefs of those past societies which function both as factual conditions and explanatory generalizations. Consider the following events, each of which is generally regarded as historically significant: a man rides into a city on an ass; a man walks two hundred miles overland to the sea, and when he reaches it collects some salt; a man flies a kite in a storm. What is the significance of these events? For an understanding of the significance of the first, we must refer to the role of the messiah as defined in the prophetic literature of the Old Testament and to the attempt of Jesus to claim that role for his own. For an understanding of the second, we must refer to the structure of British law in India in 1930, to the movement for Indian independence, and to the role of Gandhi. For an understanding of the third, we must refer to the system of beliefs concerning electricity prevailing in 1752, to Franklin's theoretical and experimental work in this field, and to his proposal for demonstrating the electrical character of lightning. In every case, then, it seems that the significance of the event lies in its relation to the system of thought and action of which it is a part. Historians are fond of saying that one must view an event in its context. That context is the system of thought and action of which the event is a component. More precisely, the significance of an event x lies in its relation to the set of law-like statements into the extension of whose terms x falls or which imply statements into the extension of whose terms x falls. Thus it is the role of x, as a cause or effect, or as a confirming or disconfirming instance, which makes x significant at all. Apart from some set of law-like statements which define the system of thought and action in which x is imbedded, x could have no significance. It would be, indeed, that monstrosity of the historical imagination: the wholly unique event.

It is always the problem of the historian to discover that system of thought and action which gives significance to the events he is studying, and the great historian is one who is particularly successful in doing this. Thus the accolades which were for so long bestowed upon Beard's interpretation of the Constitution[27] were not simply in praise of his specific conclusions, but also of the fact that, by employing economic determinism with apparent success, he seemed to have provided a mode of interpretation—a theoretical perspective—which promised to make sense of many events. Similarly, the incredible hold of Turner's frontier thesis has been due to the fact that it provided a set of generalizations which appeared to explain a great many otherwise unexplained phenomena.[28] To cite a more recent example, the achievement for which Miller is acclaimed was no particular historical discovery, but the delineation of the system of thought and action characterizing Puritan New England, which converted what to his predecessors had seemed an arid and unintelligible historical domain into one of the most popular and productive fields of contemporary historical research.[29] And if we look at Bailyn's interpretation of Bacon's Rebellion sketched above, it must be apparent that, there too, what Bailyn is seeking to do is to place these events in Virginia in a context provided by generalizations about the nature of the political system in England and her colonies, and the reactions of various groups of settlers to the functioning of this political system. These interpretations are explanatory in the sense that they provide generalizations which explain particular events, and they give significance to these events by showing how they relate to the general patterns which the interpretation affords.

It is not, therefore, the "terminal consequences" or the long-run consequences of an event which provide its significance. Such effects may, indeed, be involved in the significance if the interpretation contains generalizations which relate events to effects over a considerable time period—something which few interpretations do. But it is normally the near causes and effects of a given event which are relevant for its understanding, since most of our generalizations in relation to which the significance of the event really consists are of a short-term character only. Nor are Danto's narrative sentences invariably the vehicles of significance. The significance of the work of Aristarchus does not lie in his anticipation of Copernicus but in its relation to the context in which it was produced. Sentences causally relating events which occur at different times may, of course, be vehicles for the ascription of significance, but so may sentences relating simultaneous events, as, e.g., functionally related events. It is the fact that causal relations are involved which is crucial for the ascription of significance—not the temporal distance between the events.

A fourth characteristic of historical interpretations is that they are usually presented in narrative form, and this is particularly true when they deal with change. The connection of the narrative form with the subject of change is important and clear-cut—most of the notable historical works which are not narrative, such as Miller's *New England Mind: The Seventeenth Century*,[30] are works which attempt to delineate their subjects at a single time. As Danto has remarked, the explanation of change in history is in narrative form. If we seek to explain this fact, it is useful to consider what the alternative might be. Perhaps the obvious answer is that change might be accounted for by laws of change—i.e., by so-called historical laws which determine the sequence of events which follow upon some set of initial conditions. But as we saw in an earlier chapter, few such laws are known and their discovery has proven extremely difficult. Some of the reasons for this difficulty are evident from the way historical study is structured. For, as we have seen, it is oriented toward the individual culture area or culture component. The sort of generalizations which such an orientation can most easily yield are generalizations about the behavior of individuals in that culture. Where such generalizations relate to change, it is change at an individual level and of the sort that occurs repeatedly within the society, as, e.g., the process of socialization by which the culture is transmitted from generation to generation. But generalizations about processes of change which occur only once or very seldom in a given society—i.e., industrialization, civil wars, or revitalization—are extremely difficult to discover from the examination of that society alone. What can be observed in the single case is that a change is taking place, but before the process of change can be conceptualized and its determinants defined, it is usually necessary to examine a number of instances of the process, and this requires the comparative study of many societies. History as a discipline is not well organized for this undertaking, and as a result few such comparative studies have been done. The usual approach has been to concentrate upon a description of the observed changes taking place in one particular society, and, lacking any broader conceptualization, this has usually taken the form of a chronological narrative of events.

There is an old saying that truth is stranger than fiction. If a novelist were to include in his tale events as bizarre as many that are recounted in the daily newspapers, his readers would find his narrative contrived and unconvincing. This fact points up an interesting difference between scientific explanations and narratives. In scientific explanations, the laws and antecedent conditions are made explicit; hence no matter how bizarre the events to be explained may be, the explanation (if successful) renders that event intelligible by showing exactly what caused it. In narrative writing, on the other hand, the laws are usually not made explicit. The convincingness of the narrative, therefore, depends upon the presentation of the events of the story in such a way that their sequential occurrence seems to follow causally in terms of laws which are part of the common-sense knowledge of the reader. These laws, like most common-sense knowledge, tend to be vague, but they are sufficiently clear to permit the reader to recognize at least gross violations of them. The writer is, therefore, bound by the laws familiar to his readers, and cannot deviate radically from that stock of interpretative knowledge without violating the readers' sense of reality.

What is true of the novel is even more true of the historical narrative, where the liberties of fiction are forsworn. The historian avows that his narrative is true, and this requires that the causal connections alleged to hold between the events of the narrative must hold in fact. To the extent that they do hold and that the reader can supply the necessary law-like principles to support them, the narrative affords a perfectly adequate causal account of the events with which it deals. Nevertheless, the fact that the narrative form permits the writer to shift to the reader the responsibility for providing the necessary laws relieves the historian of the necessity of stating these principles explicitly. The possibility thus exists that the narrative may be used in cases where no explicit laws are known which would support the causal connections claimed to obtain, and that this fact may not be apparent to the reader. This possibility has sometimes proven irresistible to historians hard pressed to make sense of their data. Since causality has the same direction as time, it is easy to perceive x's following temporally upon y as a case of x's following causally upon y, even though no law-like principle is known which will support the latter connection. There is nothing inherent in the nature of the narrative form which compels such dubious expedients, and the better the historian, the less the resort to such devices. Yet it is also true that the more explicit the laws underlying the explanation are made, and the more rigorously the model is spelled out and the explanatory task is conceived, the more the account is likely to deviate from the classical narrative form. As historians have become increasingly concerned in recent years with the explicit formulation of the causal models they employ, there has been a marked increase in the number of nonnarrative historical studies. One may, I think, confidently predict that this trend will continue in the future.

These points can be illustrated by reference to the interpretations of Bacon's Rebellion which we have discussed above. Of the three, Wertenbaker's most nearly resembles an adventure tale. The account is dramatic, with a well-defined hero and villain; it is replete with rousing rhetoric and imaginative recreations which far transcend in richness and detail what the actual data warrant. Washburn's account is also a narrative, but, since it is in part a critical attack on Wertenbaker, it stays much closer to the actual data and is less dramatic. But Bailyn's account is not a narrative, although the discussion does follow a chronological pattern. For Bailyn is viewing the rebellion in a comparative framework, i.e., as one of a number of related revolts, and he is seeking an explanation in terms of social processes which can be applied to the revolts in Maryland, New York, and elsewhere, as well as to the one in Virginia. Like Wertenbaker and Washburn, he leaves implicit most of the generalizations upon which his explanation depends, but the conceptual model employed is much more explicit and much closer to those of the social sciences than the models used by his predecessors.

The fifth characteristic of interpretations upon which there is general agreement is that, although they are regarded as true by their authors, they are not regarded as exclusively true, and the possibility—indeed, the probability—of conflicting interpretations of equal legitimacy is recognized, at least in principle. This point has been particularly urged by revisionist historians, and results from what they regard as the inescapable relativism which afflicts historical knowledge. For according to the revisionists, the historian never deals with all the facts; he selects a particular subset of the facts and develops his interpretation on the basis of this subset. Had a different subset of facts been chosen, a different interpretation would have resulted. Differences among interpretations are thus reduced to differences in criteria for the selection of facts, and such criteria, the revisionists have claimed, are subjective. There are many versions of this argument in the literature, but perhaps the most considered statement of it is due to Morton White.[31] He employs the term "chronicle" to mean the set of all the singular noncausal factual statements involved in a history, and the term "narrative" or "interpretation" to mean the chronicle together with the addition of a set of singular causal statements relating the noncausal factual statements to each other. Where histories differ in their chronicles, they will also differ in their narratives, and they may differ in their chronicles even when they are histories of the same entity. Thus a history of Puritan theology and a history of Puritan polity are both histories of the Puritan churches, but they concern different aspects of those churches, and it would make no sense to say that one was a "better" interpretation than the other. But we do often have histories which present different interpretations of a given entity or event where it does make sense to say that one is superior: e.g., the interpretations of Bacon's Rebellion discussed above. White suggests that the basis for this distinction lies in the choice of factual statements to be included in the chronicle. Every chronicle, White avers, contains three kinds of statements. Some, which he calls charter members of the chronicle, are statements about objects or events which are regarded as the basic facts about the entity whose history is being written. A second class involves statements about those objects or events which are interpreted as the causes of the basic facts, and, in accordance with his doctrine of abnormalism which we will discuss below, White thinks that there is a certain element of relativity involved in the choice of decisive causes for these facts. The third class consists of statements about those objects or events which are interpreted as the effects of the basic facts, and here

White thinks that the choice of effects is arbitrary and a function of the historian's point of view. For there will normally be so many effects of a given event—say, the Civil War—that all of them cannot be recorded, and he believes that there is no way in which one can decide objectively which effects are most important. But the chief element of relativity for him lies in the choice of the basic or charter facts themselves. These, he believes, are chosen on the basis of the historian's interest and his sense of what is memorable or worthy of being recorded. Such a choice is clearly based upon subjective factors,[32] and is not subject to any objective mode of criticism. Accordingly, White holds that, in the last analysis, the choice among historical interpretations is subjective, representing the point of view of the historian, his values, interests, preferences, and desires.

White is careful to point out that he is discussing histories which deal with a single entity, such as a nation, institution, organization, or culture.[33] He furthermore asserts that the "task of the typical narrator is to give a connected account of the development of that central subject."[34] Now the question must be raised as to what it can mean to give an "account" of the "development" of such a subject. In view of what we have already said about the causal nature of interpretation, I think it is obvious that this "account" is supposed to be a causal model, and it is to be a model of the "development," or, to avoid unnecessary implications, of the course of change which has characterized that entity. Such a model must involve at least two characteristics if it is to be adequate. First, it must involve a conceptual scheme which indicates which characteristics of the social entity in question are significant for change. This conceptual scheme will specify the variables upon which the dynamic behavior of the entity depends. Second, it must involve a set of general laws relating these variables in such a way that from a given state description of the entity at one time, together with these laws, it is possible to explain its state at another time. It is only such a model which can provide an explanation of the course of change which that entity has undergone during the time period studied. And, clearly, the decision concerning which variables are relevant to the dynamic behavior of the system is not one which can be settled on the basis of a criterion of memorability. It is not memorability or interest, but the ability of the variables chosen to account for the phenomena involved which must decide what the charter members of the chronicle are to be. The question here concerns the adequacy of the model as an explanatory device, and that adequacy has to be assessed in just the same way that the adequacy of any explanatory device is assessed. That is to say, we are dealing here with a theory about the dynamic behavior of a social entity, and that theory must be confirmed or disconfirmed just like any other theory of social science.

The point may be illustrated by reference to the interpretations of Bacon's Rebellion discussed above. We have already remarked that the events discussed—i.e., the chronicle—in Wertenbaker's account are quite different than those discussed by Bailyn. This difference is not due simply to an argument over memorability. Bailyn is seeking an account of the rebellion in terms of the changing distribution of power in the social structure of Virginia; Wertenbaker is seeking an account in terms of a conflict between democracy and tyranny. These alternative conceptual schemes make different sets of facts significant, and so lead to the inclusion of different factual statements in their respective chronicles.

Why does White believe that this choice of charter facts is subjective? The answer is that he subscribes to the revisionist historiography: he believes that the facts are selected prior to the formulation of an interpretation—so that interpretation can play no role in determining what facts are to be chosen—and that the interpretation is then elaborated to explain just these selected facts. Accordingly, White can find no justification for choosing these particular facts; thus he concludes that the choice is subjective. But this view, as I have argued throughout this book, is false. Historical interpretations explain evidence; the facts are part of the interpretation and they, like the generalizations, are postulated to give order and reason to the observations. That these postulates are arbitrary, in the sense that the interpretation is underdetermined by the empirical data, is as true of history as it is of physics, but this does not entail the existence of caprice in either domain. Theory gives observations their meaning, and observations give theory its warrant, in history as well as in every other domain of empirical knowledge.

But could not White rephrase his argument by claiming that the choice of evidence to be explained is arbitrary and subjective? The answer is clearly no, for what such a claim ignores is the searching function of theory. Theories and interpretations are guides to further research. The domain of evidence relevant to a theory is not closed once the theory has been elaborated; perhaps the most important functions of theory are to help us to discover new observations, as well as the relevance of observations we had previously considered irrelevant. There is, as every work on the philosophy of science points out, a continual interplay between observation and theory. And this is as true of historical interpretations as it is of the quantum theory. However arbitrary the choice of the starting point for an investigation may be, once theory begins to be generated to account for data, the fertility of the theory and the demands of consistency and empirical warrant rapidly reduce the elements of subjectivity to that inescapable modicum which graces all science.

The distinction which White drew among charter facts, their causes, and their effects is based upon his view that the choice of charter facts is subjective. Since that view can be rejected, so can the distinction between the three kinds of facts: the same factors govern the choice of all facts. But it is worth pursuing White's view of the subjective character of the choice among causes because on this issue he has advanced a doctrine which he calls "abnormalism."[35] Historians, he argues, very rarely cite the whole cause of an event, meaning by that all the conditions which together are sufficient for the production of the event. Rather, it is common for them to cite one cause, or a small number of causes, as "decisive" or "primary" or "real," and to ignore the remainder. To explain why historians choose a particular cause as decisive, White asserts that the events we usually seek to explain are those which are regarded as being abnormal or unusual.[36] To explain such an event, he holds, we seek among the causes of the event for that one which is itself abnormal. Thus, to use White's example, a woman married to a man with an ulcerous stomach might identify the cause of his stomach upset as his eating of parsnips. She would not identify the ulcerous condition as a cause since he always has the ulcerous condition but his stomach is usually not upset; since he rarely eats parsnips, they are the abnormal feature of the situation which is cited to explain the abnormal event. Furthermore, White notes, when we speak of the decisive cause, and so of what is abnormal, we do so from a particular point of view. Thus the doctor might say that the cause of the man's upset stomach was his ulcerous condition, thinking of non-ulcerous stomachs as the norm for human beings and of this man's condition as abnormal. Specifically, White argues, suppose the following explanatory deductive argument to hold:

> Whatever is P and R is Q
> a is P
> a is R
> Therefore
> a is Q.[37]

Now if most P's are not Q's, and if most R's are not Q's, then which condition, P or R, is to be selected as *the* cause of a being Q is relative to the point of view of the investigator. He can argue that P is the cause because it is P that makes the difference, since most R's are not Q's; or he can equally argue that R makes the difference, since most P's are not Q's. Hence White holds that there is an irreducible element of relativity involved in the decision as to which cause is decisive.

Several comments are in order on this doctrine. First, White is not consistent. In presenting abnormalism, he states explicitly that the doctrine applies to the explanation of those events which are themselves regarded as abnormal. Later in the book, however, he rejects the thesis that historians choose to include only those facts which are regarded as abnormal,[38] so that the doctrine of abnormalism can apply at most to a subset of the facts with which historians deal. How large or how significant a subset this is depends upon the emphasis which historians place upon abnormal events as opposed to common ones, and this is a question of what interpretation is being used. But as we have just seen, the choice of interpretation is not as subjective as White believes. Second, abnormalism is not easily generalized from the domain of the abnormal event to that of all events with which historians deal. For, while White is certainly right that historians often distinguish the decisive or most important causes from others, there are a variety of senses in which historians hold that one cause may be said to be more important than another. Thus, for example, A may be said to be a more important cause of C than B is if (1) A and B are necessary conditions for C, but A varies frequently while B varies seldom; (2) A and B are both necessary conditions for C, but a greater change in C is associated with a proportional change in A than with an equal proportional change in B; (3) A and B are not necessary conditions for C, so C can occur if A does and also if B does, and A occurs more frequently than B; (4) joint occurrence of A and B is not a necessary condition for C, and C occurs relatively more frequently when A occurs and B does not than when B occurs and A does not; and (5) A is a fundamental theoretical term of a theory T which explains C when reference to B is also included, but reference to B is not generally necessary in explanations involving T while reference to A is.[39] With respect to common, or normal, events, these senses of "more important" are certainly closer to usage and appear to be more adequate than the one chosen by White, so the utility, if any, of abnormalism appears limited to the domain of abnormal events. And even here, one must beware of the dictum that abnormal events have abnormal causes. Since if a concatenation of factors C_1 & . . . & C_n causes E at one time, it causes E at any time, it follows, if E is rare, that the concatenation C_1 & . . . & C_n rarely occurs. This does not mean, however, that C_1 . . . C_n are each rare events, or that any one of them is a rare event—it only means that their concatenation is a rare event. Abnormalism, as a methodological precept, therefore needs to be handled with some care. Third, White's claim that in certain circumstances the choice of the decisive cause is relative to the historian's point of view may be granted, but what the claim implies is that in such circumstances no such choice should be made. Thus in the explanatory deductive argument given above, if the probability that P is Q equals the probability that R is Q, there is simply no basis for calling one decisive and the other not, and any such choice is not merely subjective, it is absurd. What the argument shows, then, is that decisive causes ought not to be chosen under such conditions. To this White might well reply by urging upon us the case of the celebrated woman who must cook for a man with an ulcerous stomach, and ask if her behavior, and the doctor's, do not show that decisive causes may be reasonably chosen in such circumstances. But the reply is that White has misconceived his own example. For, as his argument makes clear, the woman's reasoning is based upon the premise that her husband rarely has an upset stomach, while the doctor's reasoning is based upon the premise that people with ulcerous stomachs frequently have upset stomachs—hence, since her husband has an ulcerous stomach, he frequently has an upset stomach.[40] That is, not only are the two explanatory arguments not the same, but they also contain contradictory premises. And since the two arguments are not the same, it is hardly surprising that they lead to different conclusions. Thus, White's example does not show that it is reasonable to choose one of several causes as "decisive" in the circumstances proposed. If the woman and the doctor really argued, as White says they did, i.e.,

Whoever has an ulcerous stomach and eats parsnips has an upset stomach.
The husband has an ulcerous stomach.
The husband ate parsnips.
Therefore, the husband has an upset stomach.

and if the probability that a man with an ulcerous stomach has an upset stomach equals the probability that a man who eats parsnips has an upset stomach, then there would be no warrant for choosing either cause as decisive.

On the basis of the considerations advanced above, it would appear that historical interpretations are not different in kind from scientific theories. It is certainly true that they are not formulated in the same manner as theories of physics or chemistry—that is, they are not axiomatized, and some of their component statements, especially general statements, are only implicitly asserted. But axiomatic formulation is a matter of style, not content. As Quine has remarked, for certain purposes "a man's theory on a given subject may be conceived, nearly enough, as the class of all those sentences, within some limited vocabulary appropriate to the desired subject matter, that he believes to be true."[41] In this sense, historical interpretations qualify as theories and, moreover, as explanatory theories. Like all such theories, they purport to provide a causal explanation, in the broad sense of the term "causal" that includes those conditions upon the fulfillment of which a given sort of event ensues. They are based upon, and serve to account for, empirical evidence, and they are judged by the same criteria of empirical adequacy, simplicity, and consistency with our other knowledge which apply to all theories of science. Nevertheless, it is notorious that historians usually suppress the generalizations upon which their explanations are based, present their interpretations in narrative form, resort to literary devices to make their accounts convincing, and are openly skeptical about the scientific character of their own discipline. I have tried above to indicate some of the reasons for this situation, but the principal ones remain to be discussed. The skepticism which historians generally feel toward claims that history is a science is based upon a very clear-eyed recognition of the enormous difficulties which surround the question of confirmation in history. It is to this question that we now must turn.

NOTES

1. Thomas Jefferson Wertenbaker, *Virginia Under the Stuarts, 1607–1688* (Princeton: Princeton University Press, 1914) ; *Torchbearer of the Revolution* (Princeton: Princeton University Press, 1940) ; *Bacon's Rebellion, 1676* (Williamsburg: Virginia 350th Anniversary Celebration Corp., 1957).

2. Wertenbaker, *Bacon's Rebellion*, p. 8.

3. Wertenbaker, *Bacon's Rebellion*, p. 55.

4. Wertenbaker, *Touchbearer*, p. 209.

5. Wertenbaker, *Torchbearer*, p. 98 ff.

6. Wertenbaker, *Bacon's Rebellion*, p. 58.

7. Wilcomb Washburn, *The Governor and the Rebel* (Chapel Hill: University of North Carolina Press, 1957).

8. Washburn, *Governor*, p. 162.

9. Washburn, *Governor*, p. 154.

10. Washburn, *Governor*, p. 60 ff.

11. Bernard Bailyn, "Politics and Social Structure in Virginia" in *Seventeenth-Century America*, ed. J. M. Smith (Chapel Hill: University of North Carolina Press, 1959), pp. 90–118.

12. Morton White, *Foundations of Historical Knowledge* (New York: Harper and Row, 1965), p. 221 ff.

13. William Waller Hening, *The Statutes at Large: Being a Collection of All the Laws of Virginia* (Richmond: Samuel Pleasants, 1810), vol. II, pp. 341–65.

14. Washburn, *Governor*, 60 ff.

15. Charles Frankel, "Explanation and Interpretation in History" in *Theories of History*, ed. Patrick Gardiner (Glencoe, Ill.: Free Press, 1959), p. 421.

16. Arthur C. Danto, *Analytical Philosophy of History* (Cambridge: Cambridge University Press, 1968), p. 11.

17. Danto, *History*, ch. 8.

18. Frankel, "Explanation."

19. Danto, *History*, ch. 9.

20. Danto, *History*, p. 188.

21. Danto, *History*, p. 197.

22. Nicholas Rescher, "Truth and Necessity in Temporal Perspective" in *The Philosophy of Time*, ed. Richard Gale (New York: Doubleday, 1967), pp. 183–220.

23. Richard M. Gale, *The Language of Time* (London: Routledge and Kegan Paul, 1968), p. 49.

24. Gale, *Language*, ch. 8.

25. Robert A. Millikan, "Benjamin Franklin as a Scientist," *Journal of the Franklin Institute* 232 (1941): 417 ff.

26. George W. Stocking, Jr., "On the Limits of 'Presentism' and 'Historicism' in the Historiography of the Behavioral Sciences" in George W. Stocking Jr., *Race, Culture, and Evolution* (New York: Free Press, 1968), p. 12.

27. Charles A. Beard, *An Economic Interpretation of the Constitution of the United States* (New York: Macmillan Co., 1913).

28. Frederick Jackson Turner, "The Significance of the Frontier in American History" in Frederick Jackson Turner, *The Frontier in American History* (New York: Henry Holt, 1920), pp. 1–38.

29. Perry Miller, *The New England Mind: The Seventeenth Century* (New York: Macmillan Co., 1939).

30. Miller, *New England Mind*.

31. White, *Foundations*, ch. 6.

32. White, *Foundations*, p. 259.

33. White, *Foundations*, p. 221.

34. White, *Foundations*, p. 221.

35. White, *Foundations*, ch. 4.

36. White, *Foundations*, p. 115 ff.

37. White, *Foundations*, p. 120.

38. White, *Foundations*, p. 247 ff.

39. Ernest Nagel, "Some Issues in the Logic of Historical Analysis" in *Theories of History*, ed. Gardiner, p. 383 ff.

40. White, *Foundations*, p. 118.

41. Willard V. Quine, *Ontological Relativity and Other Essays* (New York: Columbia University Press, 1969), p. 309.

V

Historical Confirmation I

In the preceding chapters, I have presented a description of historical knowledge which may suggest that history is very like the sciences. Thus I have claimed that historical explanations involve covering laws, that historical interpretations are really causal models, and that historical entities and events are theoretical constructs. If these claims are true, one might expect historians to be engaged in deriving predictions from their "theories" and in testing these predictions against systematically collected data. Yet it is notorious that this is not what historians do, or at least it is not what they say they do. Certainly in facing the relation of theory to data, the historian is an unflinching empiricist—so much so, in fact, that he often refuses to admit that he theorizes at all—yet his stance is very different from that of the physicist or chemist, or even the sociologist. And this difference does not stem from any "confusion" on the historian's part. It stems, rather, from a very clear-eyed recognition of the difficulties which the character of historical data places in the way of confirmation.

Let us begin by assuming for the sake of argument all that the Hempelian could ask—that the covering laws are made explicit and that the interpretation is formulated explicitly as a causal model. Such a theory would then assert that, at a particular past time and place, certain sorts of events occurred and certain objects existed, and that these objects and events are related to each other and to observables by explicitly formulated laws. Predictions derived from this theory must, if they are to be testable, relate to observations which can be made now. Let us, therefore, explore the question of whether or not such predictions can be confirmed. There are at least three separate factors which affect the probability that such confirmations can be made.

From a theory concerning the structure and functioning of the English political system in the fifteenth century, one may well be able to deduce the occurrence and characteristics of many events of that time and place. But these consequences of the theory cannot be directly tested, because they refer to events no longer observable by us. The only consequences which are directly testable are those which concern something we can observe now. Some of these consequences may concern physical objects which do not involve inscriptions, but the consequences which have most concerned historians have been those which involve inscriptions occurring upon objects now observable by us. We have already discussed the difficulties involved in attributing reference and meaning to such inscriptions, and that discussion need not be reviewed here. But even assuming that reference and meaning can be correctly attributed to such inscriptions, how are the inscriptions related to the events or objects which are postulated to exist in the theory? That relation is highly complex, but it is obvious that, to be related to the postulated object and events at all, the inscription must either be a response, or must encode responses of its author, or of others, to those objects or events. Whether the inscription is itself such a response or only encodes such responses, we are in any case dealing with responses to objects and events which are treated as stimuli and which are not now observable by us, but only postulated in the model. Accordingly, our testable consequences must involve statements to the effect that a subject, so related to the stimuli in question as we suppose the author of the inscription, or those whose responses the inscription encodes, to have been, would have responded in such and such a way. The first question we have to face, therefore, is whether or not we can make statements of this sort, and if so, what warrants we have for them.

Statements as to how a person is likely to respond to a given stimulus under standard conditions are used in many fields. Perhaps the most obvious example is in law, where the credibility of testimony is frequently assessed on this basis. Scarcely less obvious is psychiatry, where many diagnostic procedures rely upon such statements to discriminate normal from abnormal responses—e.g., projective tests such as the Rorschach or the TAT have diagnostic value just because we have empirically warranted generalizations respecting how normal and abnormal subjects respond to the stimuli of the plates. Clearly, it would be easy to find other examples. But in all such cases, what constitutes a "normal" response is a function not only of the mental health, but also of the perceptual and conceptual system of the person in question. Anthropologists have established beyond question the fact that responses on projective tests vary from culture to culture in such a way that a response pattern which is the norm for one culture is not the norm for another.[1] One cannot, therefore, determine how a person is likely to respond to a given stimulus, even under so-called standard conditions, without specifying the perceptual-conceptual system of his culture.

What is true in general is, of course, true in particular of historical subjects. Events which might appear to us utterly mundane have been viewed in other times and places as miraculous and as clear evidence of divine intervention. One cannot, therefore, formulate principles concerning the response to be expected to particular stimuli in historical cultures without taking into account how people in those cultures perceived and conceived events and objects. Accordingly, whatever theory we are to use to relate stimulus and response, we shall be forced to include a characterization of the stimulus in terms of the categories of perception and conception of the historical culture. We thus have two options: we can formulate our theory to begin with in these terms, so that the only characterization of the stimulus employed is one which utilizes the categories of the culture in question, or we can include in our theory a characterization of the stimulus and response which does not involve the categories of the culture, in which case we have to explain how this characterization of the stimulus and the response is related to those which involve only the categories of the culture. Let us explore these alternatives.

If we choose the first, whatever we say about the stimulus must be said in the terms of the culture. There are two cases which arise here. First, among the responses made to the stimulus there may be enough which can be taken as descriptions of the stimulus object to permit us to develop a characterization of it from these responses. Our problem then will become that of relating the stimulus so described to other responses, which may be encoded in the inscription or may be the inscription itself. If they are encoded in the inscription, the responses also come to us through a description in terms of the categories of the culture; if the response is the inscription (and the inscription is always a response to some stimulus), the categories used in describing the response may be either those of the historical culture or of our own. In either event, the determination of the stimulus-response relations in this situation is a straightforward inductive problem. Second, we may not have responses which can be interpreted as describing the object, but only behaviors, or descriptions of behaviors, which we believe to be responses to this otherwise-unknown object or event. Inscriptions, after all, are often performatives, which do not describe their stimuli but react to them. In this case, the stimulus object is clearly a postulate, and our warrant for postulating it lies in the fact that this postulate gives coherence to the data. Such a warrant exists only where the postulate can be shown to integrate a variety of responses into a pattern, and the more relations among the data it can account for, the stronger it is. It is, therefore, particularly important in such cases that these relations be fully developed. But we shall also have to account for the fact that the stimulus is not described. The fact that a stimulus is responded to, and yet is never overtly characterized, requires explanation, whether in terms of psychological repression or cultural taboo, and this in turn involves the use of the perceptual-conceptual system of the culture. Whichever case obtains, we can develop statements of relationship between stimuli and responses, subject to the normal difficulties of inductive inquiry. But the relations discovered will be specific to the particular historical culture in question. Since the stimuli are characterized in terms of the categories of that culture, the relations found cannot be generalized to other cultures in which different perceptual-conceptual categories are operative. We are thus limited to the patterns of one culture, and our results may not apply to other cultures at all.

If we seek to develop theories of greater generality which can apply to many cultures, we shall be forced to adopt the second option. That is to say, we shall have a general theory concerning, say, the food quest, in which events and objects are characterized by the terms of the theory. We shall then require rules which carry the stimulus as characterized by our theory into that stimulus as perceived within a particular culture, since it is only as perceived within a particular culture that members of that society respond to it, and rules which carry the responses actually made in that culture into those described by our theory, since otherwise we would not know whether the predicted response occurred. Our problem, therefore, is to generate statements of this sort. So far as the stimulus object is concerned, perhaps the most obvious and certainly the most satisfactory way of doing this is to make a direct comparison between the stimulus as described in our theoretical terms and as described through the categories of the culture. This is, of course, what we do in the cross-cultural use of projective tests. But for historical cultures, this requires that we be able to observe the actual stimulus described—a condition which can be met only where the object has endured or can be reconstructed from archaeological evidence. Cases of this sort, of course, exist; nevertheless, it is still true that most of the stimuli with which we are likely to be concerned are not recoverable in this fashion and, therefore, other methods must be used. Ideally, one would like to invoke a well-confirmed, cross-cultural theory of cognition which would relate perceptual-conceptual systems to other cultural variables, but no such theory is now in existence and there is no reason to expect that one will be forthcoming in the immediate future. We must, therefore, treat our identifications as hypotheses to be confirmed by indirect evidence. Thus, in medical history, we are often confronted with characterizations of a disease such as "the putrid sore throat." Historical descriptions of disease do not usually include the data which would be used today in making a diagnosis (i.e., blood analysis, temperature records, etc.), so we must look for a disease the presence of which would account for the data. In making this hypothesis, we are correlating symptoms of the disease as we know it to characteristics of the disease as perceived by members of the culture, and the justification for adopting the hypothesis is that these two characterizations can be adequately matched and the discrepancies attributed to differences in perception and conception. Thus, if we find with respect to diphtheria that only certain categories are used in this culture in describing and treating it, we should expect that the same or analogous categories will be used for similar diseases. We should then be very surprised, indeed, to find diphtheria discussed in terms of an imbalance of the humors while scarlet fever is described in terms of bacteriological infection. It is upon this sort of indirect proof that we shall usually have to rely in confirming statements which relate stimuli as characterized in our theory to those stimuli as characterized in the culture in question.

When we come to responses, the case is somewhat altered, since the fact that the response is encoded in the inscription means that we do in some sense observe it. But to relate the response observed to the general theory in question requires a classificatory hypothesis asserting that the response observed falls into one of the response categories of the theory. Thus, the responses observed may be those which Cotton Mather recorded in his diary and which relate to his efforts to find divine favor.[2] The theory may be McClelland's theory of achievement motivation, and the response categories in question those used in that theory for scoring written material for achievement motivation.[3] It may be granted that many of the statements made by Mather would be scored as high in achievement imagery if they were written by a contemporary student in Psychology I—the question is, how should they be scored, given that they were written in the late seventeenth century by a New England divine? In general, any classification involves the hypothesis that the x being classified falls under some class A. But where the theory is a cross-cultural theory, and the x being classified is a symbolically mediated response, the response which is classed as A will be one thing in one culture and something quite different in another culture. To make the classification we shall, therefore, require a translation of the criterion for x being an A into the relevant terms of each culture. What behavior is achievement oriented will be one thing among the Cheyenne Indians and quite another on Madison Avenue. Here again our statements must utilize the perceptual-conceptual system of the culture in question.

The above discussion has been elaborated at the risk of some tedium to bring out an essential point. Whether we limit ourselves to theories specific to one culture or seek to construct theories having cross-cultural scope, we must seek for theories which involve the perceptual-conceptual system of the historical culture. Except in cases where the data do not involve symbolically mediated responses, a purely structural theory—one which involves no reference to the perceptual-conceptual system—cannot be constructed for historical subjects. The reason for this is that the characterization of the stimulus must be derived from the symbolically mediated responses. Thus, even with kin terms, one cannot begin a componential analysis of the historical lexicon by first noting what persons are called by what terms, since to establish that fact, one must use a characterization of the persons involved which is given in terms of the perceptual-conceptual system of the culture, and infer from that characterization what the relationship among these persons is. But, as this example should make clear, questions of psychological reality blend into those of translation. To know that the term "pater" is used in an antique tongue to refer to a father, one must be able to translate enough of what is said about a pater to be certain of the term's reference. One cannot, in this case, simply observe that the use of "pater" is correlated with appearances of certain objects, since it is not the objects which appear in our inscriptional data, but the symbolically mediated responses to them. At some point, we are compelled to accept a translation of at least some of these symbols, and to assume that that translation gives us an accurate rendering of what the author perceived and thought. This assumption may later be questioned, and revised, when further analysis leads to difficulties; nevertheless, we must set out from an initial translation and correct it as we go. Since our only access to a historical culture is through responses mediated by the perceptual-conceptual system of that culture, we must always seek the reconstruction of that system if we are to understand that culture at all.

Let us assume that the historian has been able to develop a reasonable basis for connecting responses to stimuli through the mediation of a perceptual-conceptual system: has he thereby taken account of all the factors which affect the probability that he can test his hypothesis? The answer is clearly no, for there is a second set of factors which enter as determinants of the observations he can make now—namely, those which affect the chances that the responses in question were recorded. For a subject's response to become a possible object of observation for a historian, that response, or a response to that response, must be somewhere recorded in a form which can endure. Let us, therefore, ask what factors govern the process of recording.

It is essential to distinguish here the cases in which there exists an institutionalized recording procedure from those in which no such procedure is present. Many institutions have as a part of their structure processes for the recording, transmission, and storage of data concerning either the institution itself or certain other social groups or processes. For example, the journals of a legislature, such as the *Congressional Record,* the register of a parish, the tax lists of a city, the United States Census, and the minutes of a university committee are all records generated by an institutionalized procedure. Where such a procedure exists, there is a high probability that responses of certain types will be recorded. But what these types of responses will be depends upon the rules which govern the generation of the record. An example may serve to make this clear. Not long ago, I attended a meeting of a university committee of which I was a member, and the minutes of the preceding meeting were introduced for approval. The members of the committee were shocked to discover that the minutes recorded some highly derogatory remarks, made by a committee member about another committee. By unanimous vote, this section was stricken from the minutes before they were approved. Yet the section stricken was, in fact, a quite accurate record of what had occurred in the preceding meeting. Accuracy, however, was not the point at issue: the institutionalized rules which govern the generation of committee minutes in a university require that evidence of conflict be muted and, particularly, that overt expressions of hostility or contempt be suppressed. The members of this committee did not perceive the question as one of accuracy: they all saw it as a question of what was "appropriate" to include in the minutes.

This example is typical of the operation of institutionalized recording procedures. The relation between the record generated and that of which it is a record cannot be assumed to be one of accurate description. Rather, the process by which the record was generated must be analyzed to discover empirically how the two are related. No one who wishes to study conflict in universities can rest with the formal minutes of committees as data. And the same point holds for all records generated in this way. Unless we know the procedure for generating the record and the rules which govern its generation, we cannot assess its relation to that of which it is a record. Very often these rules are quite explicit, and they may even be among the formally stated rules governing institutional operation. Thus, for example, the methods used in generating records of votes in presidential elections are highly explicit and yield quite accurate records of certain characteristics of voting (e.g., the total vote per political unit for a candidate), while rigorously excluding the recording of other characteristtics (e.g., how each individual voted). In other cases—as, e.g., that of university committee minutes—the rules are informal, implicit, and vague, resting upon a shared sense of appropriateness of behavior rather than upon any specific formulation of rules.

The same remarks, of course, apply to the question of the completeness of such records—i.e., to the probability that a response made was recorded at all. Thus one of the first questions a historian asks of any record is, how complete is it? If, for example, one is working with a colonial Pennsylvania shipping register, it is critical to know whether all ships are registered or only some ships, and if the latter, which ones are left out. Analysis in this case reveals that ships in the coastal trade were not registered, so the record can be used only in cases where the coastal trade can be ignored. Such problems are, of course, well known to every historian. It is, in fact, rare that any record can be found which is complete—i.e., where the probability is one that the entire set of responses of a given sort were recorded. The labor, time, and ingenuity which are poured into the investigation of the completeness of records are incomprehensible to those contemporary social scientists who are able to generate their own data.

It must not be supposed that all documents produced through institutionalized procedures and used by the historian are designed to be records. Most of these documents are used by the institution in some instrumental capacity, and even records are usually generated because they fulfill practical purposes. Thus diplomatic notes are invaluable sources for the study of diplomatic history, but they are, of course, not designed (at least primarily) for purposes of record: they are, rather, means by which one government tries to influence another. Laws, directives, treaties, military orders, financial accounts, catalogues, deeds, wills, etc., are all documents generated for some institutional purpose. It is this very fact which often makes them such excellent sources for the historian, for one is here observing the act itself rather than a record of it. And even when they are used as records, it is often possible to show that, in order to serve their institutional purposes, the documents must be either highly accurate or biased in a special way, and that the rules governing their generation are accordingly so drawn as to guarantee that they have the desired characteristics.

I have stressed the importance of institutionalized recording procedures because, where such procedures exist, they greatly facilitate the search for data to confirm hypotheses. If one knows that a particular institution has an institutionalized record-creation procedure, one knows at once where to look for certain types of data. Conversely, an institution like the family, which has no institutionalized procedure for the generation of records, poses severe data problems. Systematic historical study of the family is very largely limited to questions regarding births, marriages, divorces, deaths, property transfer, and, for nonmigrants, vertical mobility, because this is the sort of data recoverable from the census, wills, city directories, parish records, etc.—i.e., from the references to the family which appear in the formal records of other institutions.[4] The fact that the family has no institutionalized recording procedures of its own severely limits the character of the investigations which can be undertaken and throws a heavy burden on records produced by noninstitutionalized methods.

The class of documents which are not institutional products, but which may afford data for the historian, is extremely heterogeneous. It includes most letters, diaries, autobiographies, essays, articles, etc.—all documents produced by individuals as a result of other than institutionalized procedures. So far as the relation of such documents to the stimuli which produced them is concerned, many of the remarks above apply. It is a methodological truism of social science that a subject should not be asked to make responses which he cannot or will not make. The same principle obviously applies to documentary analysis. Data respecting a man's weaning or toilet training cannot be obtained from his recollections since he himself cannot recall these experiences. Furthermore, only certain sorts of questions will be regarded as appropriate for discussion in letters or autobiographies, or even diaries, and the conventions governing appropriateness vary over time. Lincoln Steffens tells the following charming anecdote:

> It is related of Frederick C. Howe that when he had laid the finished manuscript of his autobiography proudly before his wife and she had read it, she looked up at him with the humor that is all hers and said, "But, Fred, weren't you ever married?"
> "Oh, yes," he answered. "I forgot that. I'll put it in."[5]

Anyone who has studied nineteenth-century American autobiographers knows that Howe's omission was a direct reflection of his nineteenth-century upbringing: males of that period who wrote autobiographies rarely devoted more than a paragraph to their entire married lives, and it is not rare for the wife and family to go wholly unmentioned. Compare this with the conventions in operation today, which make discussion of one's family life quite appropriate. Hence, the interpretation of documentary evidence of this sort requires the use of a theory which relates the content of the document to the stimuli which evoked the document and to the postulated events and objects.

For this class of documents, too, it is highly important to avoid what Austin has called the descriptive fallacy. Most letters are not written to record events for posterity; even if they are written to convey news, the news conveyed and the manner in which it is conveyed will be functions of the recipient as well as of the events themselves. Letters are often instruments and are replete with exercitives, commissives, behabitives, expositives, and even verdictives. The same is true of diaries, and even of autobiographies, which can never be assumed to be accurate historical records. Yet it is often possible to use such documents to study relations between people, or between people and events, even though every constative sentence in the document may be false.

From the standpoint of the historian seeking evidence of the past, documents of this class are the most difficult to use in confirmation because the probability is so low that a document containing the needed observations was ever produced. Thus, for example, when Morgan was trying to determine what took place in Virginia's House of Burgesses on May 30 and 31, 1765, there were certain obvious places to look, because this body, like most legislatures, had an institutionalized procedure for record creation. But who could have predicted that an unknown French traveler, who happened to visit the Burgesses on those days, would leave an account in his journal? As Morgan has remarked, "Of all the spectators and of all the thirty-nine Burgesses, this anonymous stranger was the only one who left a message for future historians, and though his account contains at least one recognizable error of fact, it is the only direct road that we can follow back to those critical days when Virginia pointed the way to freedom."[6] That such an account should have been created at all is so much a matter of chance that it is quite hopeless to talk of "predicting" or "deducing" its existence from any general theory of record creation. Yet the importance of such evidence cannot be overstated, for it offers one of the few ways to check the accuracy of official records, and it is the chief reliance in cases where no institutionalized record-producing system exists.

After what has been said about the nature of record creation, the problem of confirming historical predictions certainly appears difficult enough, but we have yet to mention what is commonly cited as the greatest difficulty—the problem of preservation. Once a document has been created, what is the probability that it will survive for n years? There is, so far as I know, not a single study which affords an empirical basis for answering this question. Nevertheless, there are some factors which are obviously influential in determining this probability. The chance that a document will survive for any extended period is related to the number of copies that exist in geographically separated locations, since it may be assumed that the probabilities of survival of the copies so circumstanced are independent of each other. From this standpoint, printing is probably the greatest single safeguard of survival. Nevertheless, the production of multiple copies is by no means sufficient to guarantee survival; of all the hundreds of copies of the *New England Primer* printed in the colonies before 1727, not one has survived.[7] In this case, social values clearly played a decisive role. Although, in New England, school books were considered of great importance as instruments of education, their very abundance and the utilitarian nature of the value accorded them produced almost complete unconcern with their preservation, while books such as family Bibles were cherished as heirlooms. Printing alone, then, is not enough; it must be supplemented by social evaluations which make the preservation of the item desirable. Such social values are often implemented through institutionalized procedures for assuring preservation, which find expression in the acquisitions policies of libraries and repositories.

Many documents which are generated by an institutionalized procedure also have associated with them institutionalized procedures for insuring preservation, and this is particularly true if the document has a recognized recording function. Thus the United States Census, the journals of a legislature, the register of a parish, the records of a probate court, and the records of a customshouse usually are subject to rules which are intended to insure preservation indefinitely. In other cases, e.g., accounts of a business, case records of a hospital, etc., the preservation procedure may specify holding the records for a fixed period and then destroying them. And in still other cases, documents produced by an institution may be regarded as purely instrumental, so that no effort at preservation is made. But if there is an institutionalized procedure for preserving documents, then there is at least a *prima facie* reason for expecting them to survive.

Where no institutionalized procedure exists, the probability of preservation is obviously much lower. Consider the number of private letters that pass through the mails each day, and ask yourself what proportion of these are still in existence after one year. Obviously, an enormous number of factors influence the preservation of such documents—the saving propensities of individuals, the concern of loving daughters for their fathers' reputations, the question of whether or not individuals are migratory, the size of dwellings, etc. So various, so random, and so unpredictable are these factors that it is quite impossible to predict the fate of a given document for any appreciable length of time.

When to the factors already discussed are added flood, fire, war and riot, earthquake and storm, something of the true situation becomes apparent. The many cities of Europe which, despite their having taken all reasonable precautions to conserve their records, had them utterly destroyed during World War II, are a testimony to the impossibility of guaranteeing the preservation of documents. Factors of this sort affect all documents, whether they are subject to institutionalized procedures or not, and over any appreciable length of time they are simply beyond our present powers of prediction.

Finally, the fact that a document has been preserved does not automatically bring it within the purview of the historian. The Dead Sea Scrolls had been preserved for hundreds of years before a Bedouin lad accidentally discovered where they were. Here again, the existence of institutionalized preservation procedures is of immense help, since the knowledge of such procedures usually gives good indication of where to look for documents. While the search for lost inscriptions is pursued with unabated vigor in the caves along the Dead Sea and the attics of New England, much of the contemporary historian's problem is to locate relevant documents already in institutions. The forest of guides, bibliographies, indices, and catalogues which have been developed as aids in this quest are still quite inadequate as means of fulfilling the imperative of the profession to find all the relevant data which remain.

If, then, we return to the issue from which we set out, and we suppose a historian who has generated an interpretation concerning a given past society, and we further suppose that from his model he has derived a number of predictions which he wishes to test, the question must be faced as to whether or not he can reasonably expect to find the data necessary to confirm or disconfirm these predictions. Let us leave aside the questions of sampling and measurement, to which we shall return below, and simply ask what the chances are that he can make any of the necessary observations. Even if he can specify, in terms of a theory concerning the perceptual-conceptual system pervading the society he is studying, and in terms of the rules governing the recording of responses, what observations would confirm or disconfirm his hypotheses, the chances that a document affording these observations was ever created, times the conditional probability that the document was preserved, given that it was created, will almost certainly be very slight. Accordingly, no historian formulates his endeavor in terms of testing hypotheses by deriving from those hypotheses consequences concerning what should be observed in the data. The chances are that the predicted observations cannot be made.

This situation may be illustrated by a simple example. When Lynde Wheeler wrote his biography of Josiah Willard Gibbs, he found among Gibbs's belongings a model of a thermodynamic surface made by Clerk Maxwell. It seemed clear to Wheeler that Maxwell must have sent the model to Gibbs, but he was bothered by the fact that he could find no letter of transmittal from Maxwell. Wheeler had to decide whether or not there had been such a letter: if there had, Maxwell had sent the model to Gibbs and the letter of transmittal was lost; if there had not, then Maxwell had not sent the model and so the question of how Gibbs got it remained open. Wheeler's problem therefore was to decide which of two alternative hypotheses to adopt—the document was created but not preserved, or it was never created. To estimate the probability of the former hypothesis, he examined Gibbs's practice with respect to his scientific correspondence and found ample evidence that Gibbs was meticulous in preserving such documents. On the basis of this evidence, Wheeler should have chosen the latter alternative; nevertheless, he was so impressed with the difficulty of explaining how Gibbs got the model if Maxwell had not sent it that he elected the option that the letter was lost. Subsequently, there turned up a letter from J. J. Sylvester to Daniel Coit Gilman which indicated that Maxwell had had the model in his possession only a fortnight before he died. This fact led Wheeler to reverse his interpretation and to argue that the model was probably sent after Maxwell's death—hence no letter from Maxwell was ever written.[8]

This rather minor incident serves to illustrate the sort of difficulty a historian confronts when a document, which should exist if his theory is correct, cannot be found. Because of the multiple sources of error which exist in this situation, failure to make the required observation does not disconfirm the hypothesis. Note too that the collaterial evidence which enabled Wheeler to make his final decision was found in a place where it could not reasonably have been predicted to occur. The probability that this evidence would have turned up in a letter of Sylvester's seems to me to be vanishingly small, and indeed the discovery of this letter was, so far as Wheeler's research was concerned, purely accidental. But this is so often the case in historical research that it can be called the normal situation.

This discussion should suffice to show at least some of the reasons why historians have avoided the methodological models which scientifically minded philosophers have prescribed for them. Given the enormous problems involved in historical data, no historian begins by elaborating a theory about a past situation, deriving consequences, and *then* seeking data to confirm these consequences. To do so would be, at best, an extremely inefficient procedure, since the probability that the required observations can be made is very slight. It is for this reason that historians have been overwhelmingly data-based. It is standard procedure for a historian to begin with a body of data—a set of manuscripts, a cache of records, a trunkful of letters—and to develop his study on the basis of what this set of documents will provide evidence for. This preoccupation with data rather than theory has produced among historians a concomitant unwillingness to pursue theoretical questions or implications which are not directly relevant to a given data-base. Frustrated by the incompleteness of the historical record, and harassed by the knowledge that a malevolent fate will inevitably deny them some portion of the data needed to confirm even the simplest theory, many historians have even renounced theorizing altogether and claimed that they simply "tell it like it was," or as their limited data suggest that it was. This stance has led many to assume that history is antiscientific and atheoretical. But such a conclusion is naive. The historian has every reason to be concerned with his data-base, and to be skeptical of theory which cannot be brought to bed with whatever data flood, fire, and loving daughters have left him. Even those modern historians who have succumbed to the lure of the social sciences, and have begun to think and write in terms of "theories" or "models" tested against "systematically collected data," have in all cases with which I am familiar drawn up their theories only after having chosen a data-base and determined just what observations could be systematically garnered from those data. In such cases, what is happening is very clearly a modification of the classical methods which is designed to accommodate these methods to the wayward character of historical data. Let us look now briefly at what this modification involves.

Availability of an adequate data-base is a prime determinant of problem choice. It may be the case that, in many fields of science, problems are chosen primarily in terms of their theoretical interest; in history, data availability is at least as important a determinant. Thus, for many reasons, we would like very much to know the details of Puritan child rearing; this is a question of major consequence in evaluating different theories about Puritan culture. Unfortunately, there are virtually no data on the subject, and hence there are virtually no studies of it. Theoretical importance alone is not enough; without the data-base the study is impossible. Indeed, in historical research the problem for investigation is frequently chosen solely on the ground of data availability. Many a book has been written just because the author had access to a hitherto unexplored set of data and decided to make the most of it. If one asks a historian why he chose to write on a particular topic, all too often one gets the answer that Leigh Mallory gave when asked why he wanted to climb Everest—"because it's there." What this really means is "because the data are there."

Nevertheless, historians can rarely stop with a particular cache of data. The research begins with this cache but, as soon as an interpretation begins to be formulated, questions arise which it alone will not suffice to answer. The historian is driven to search for other data which will enable him to "fill out the picture"—i.e., to test some of the implications of the interpretation he is forming. This search is guided by the kinds of considerations about response encoding and record creation, preservation, and location which we have discussed above. Because the outcome of the search is so doubtful, and because failure to find data of a given category can be due to so many factors, the process of searching for new data to test an interpretation is rarely formulated in terms of explicit hypothesis testing. Nevertheless, that is what is really going on. Over and over again, the historian puts to himself the question: "If the situation was as I think it was, what ought I to be able to find?" The answer to that question, of course, depends upon a detailed knowledge of all the considerations involved in translating past responses to stimuli into presently observable inscriptions which we have discussed.

It is very frequently the case that the data necessary to answer a given question about a historical subject cannot be found. In this case, the inquiry may have to be abandoned. But there is an alternative—namely, to make some available data-set do the job. Thus, in a recent book, John Demos wanted to determine how the Puritans of Plymouth viewed the adult years of life—i.e., whether adulthood, like childhood, was viewed as a progression through a sequence of phases or as a single, undifferentiated whole. For this question, there was simply no direct evidence. So Demos adopted the strategy of using the age at which men assumed positions of leadership in the colony as an index of the attitudes toward age.[9] Behind this strategy lies, of course, a theory—one which holds that in Plymouth leadership was associated with certain attributes, such as competence, respect, and authority, and which further holds that if leaders are drawn from a particular age-class, these attributes must have been viewed as more characteristic of members of that age-class than of other age-classes. Thus, as this example illustrates, the problem of historical data can also be met by an increased elaboration of theory. In a very real sense, it can be said that, in eschewing theory on the ground that their data would not bear it, historians have chosen the wrong alternative. Theory may well offer the best, and perhaps the only, answer to their difficulties.

What would such a theory look like? In the case noted above, data bearing directly upon the variable of interest could not be found; hence, another variable, concerning which data was available, was chosen to serve as an index of the variable of interest. In such cases we are inferring something about an unobservable variable from the characteristics of an observable one. The connections between the two variables must be provided by a theory which asserts that the two are so related that values of one can be inferred from values of the other. It is not difficult to see how such a theory can be generated; indeed, it seems altogether too easy to generate such a theory, since the data appear to put no limit on the theoretical connections which a whimsical mind might invent. Thus given an observable variable x and any unobservable variable y, one can always invent some theory which connects them, and as long as we have no data on y directly there would appear to be no way to prove the theory false. But this is not quite the case; there are constraints on our theorizing, and these constraints may in some cases be quite formidable.

One type of constraint is generated by independent evidence concerning the postulated relation derived from other societies. Thus where we know that in societies of a given type, A, x and y are strongly correlated, we have some warrant for projecting this relation onto our data if we are studying an A-type society. And where our theorizing is based upon laws of universal scope, such as the laws of learning, we have even stronger warrants. Nevertheless, this procedure is subject to difficulties which we have discussed before—namely, that we are projecting relations onto a society which has not been previously examined and in which factors may be present which make the projected laws inapplicable. If this were our only warrant, we should be on weak ground indeed.

But this is not our only warrant. So long as we deal with x and y only, and y is unobservable, it is indeed true that everything is in the wind. But if we elaborate the theory, drawing further relations between y and z, y and w, and y and v, all of which are observable and, according to our theory, correlated with y, we can then put this set of claims to a test by intercorrelating x, z, w, and v, and examining the intercorrelation matrix. The well-known methods of factor analysis permit us to determine whether the intercorrelations are sufficiently strong to justify the hypothesis that these variables are all indices of a single unobserved factor. If they are, our theory gains considerable confirmation, even though y remains unobservable throughout, and the identification of y with the factor underlying x, z, w, and v remains hypothetical. Thus, by elaborating the theory so as to tie the variables which we cannot observe as tightly as possible to those which we can observe, we can often generate statements about the relations of these observables which are testable and which, if true, confer confirmation upon the theory as a whole.

As this procedure should indicate, the line between what is observable and what is not is much less clear in history than in other disciplines. Indeed, in physics it is usually assumed that the difference between what is observable and what is not reflects a difference in kind which can be defined by general criteria. But in history, which variables are empirically determinable and which are not is very largely a matter of chance; until we have examined the data-base, there is no way to tell which variables are determinable from it. Hence, the interrelations between theory and data in history are peculiarly complex, and theory must be continually readjusted to compensate for the vagaries of the data. Where data-gaps exist which make observation impossible, there theory must be elaborated so as to articulate with the observations which can be made. And even where data are abundant and rich, it is worth while consciously to seek the theoretical questions which that luxurious data-base will answer. But in both cases, deliberate theorizing is essential. The only surrogate for missing data is present data from which the missing data can be inferred, and such inferences are possible only where theoretical connections are drawn between what we can see and what we cannot. Such theoretical hypotheses of connection need not themselves be untestable, as the above-cited application of factor analysis should make clear.

Finally, it is in terms of the considerations presented above that one must evaluate the oft-repeated claim that historical theories and explanations are usually of an *ex post facto* character. There is some truth to this claim, for the simple reason that in many cases the theory is elaborated to explain a given data-base. But this is not a fact which should concern us. The ability of a theory to explain data already before us does as much to confirm the theory as does its ability to predict; logically, any complete explanation is equivalent to a prediction. Moreover, new data are continually turning up against which the theory can be tested. Sometimes these new data can be predicted from the theory, but, for reasons already discussed, this is not the general case; usually we discover the relation of the data to the theory only after the data are in hand. Nevertheless, the fact that a theory turns out to explain data which it was not known to explain at the time the theory was developed is surely as strong evidence for the theory as its ability to predict the character of the actual data found. The so-called *ex post facto* character of historical explanations does not, therefore, tell against their truth.

The considerations advanced above should suffice to show both that historical theories are somewhat different from those in other fields and that their confirmation is confronted with harsh difficulties. Any historical theory must contain within itself the principles necessary to relate the events and objects postulated in the theory to the observations which serve as the evidence for the theory, and this involves an immensely complex structure of rules. The journey from the Battle of Bosworth, as we postulate it to have been, to the observations made now upon which that postulate ultimately rests is so long and tortuous that one may well wonder whether, in fact, it can be traversed. Yet the problems facing historical confirmation which have been discussed so far are by no means the most serious ones. Even when the difficulties which we have described are overcome, there remain serious problems to be dealt with—problems so serious that it cannot be said with certainty at present that they are solvable. To these problems we shall turn in the next chapter.

NOTES

1. A. I. Hallowell, *Culture and Experience* (Philadelphia: University of Pennsylvania Press, 1955); George Spindler, *Sociocultural and Psychological Processes in Menomini Acculturation* (Berkeley and Los Angeles: University of California Press, 1955); Anthony F. C. Wallace, *Culture and Personality* (New York: Random House, 1969).

2. Cotton Mather, *Diary* (New York: Frederick Ungar, n.d.) vol. I.

3. David C. McClelland, *The Achievement Motive* (New York: Appleton-Century-Crofts, 1953).

4. Philip J. Greven, Jr., *Four Generations* (Ithaca: Cornell University Press, 1970); John Demos, *A Little Commonwealth* (New York: Oxford University Press, 1970).

5. Lincoln Steffens, *The Autobiography of Lincoln Steffens* (New York: Harcourt, Brace, and Co., 1931), p. 153.

6. Edmund S. and Helen Morgan, *The Stamp Act Crisis* (New York: Macmillan Co., 1963), p. 122.

7. Paul Leicester Ford, ed., *The New-England Primer* (New York: Columbia University Press, 1962), introduction.

8. Lynde P. Wheeler, *Josiah Willard Gibbs* (New Haven: Yale Press, 1951), 2nd ed. rev. 1952.

9. Demos, *Commonwealth*, p. 171 ff.

VI

Historical Confirmation II

I have argued above that, if the historian is to provide explanations either for his data or for his "facts," he must not only use laws but must seek for and discover laws. Some of these, such as the laws of learning, will hold good for all men at all times; some, such as those of Keynesian economics, for all societies of a given type; and others, like those applying to the customs of Puritan New England, for only a special time and place; but in the present state of our knowledge all three types are necessary to provide an adequate account. The laws of cross-cultural scope have generally been discovered by the social scientists, but those which relate to specific past societies must be discovered by historians if they are to be discovered at all. The social sciences deal primarily with the contemporary world, and their findings, however correct for our time, may not apply to societies in the past. Even if the historian wishes to apply some theory of contemporary social science to his data, he cannot simply assume that the application can be made—he must rather show that the theory is applicable to the specific society which he is studying. This means that he must entertain the theory as a hypothesis to be tested against his data—not force his data to fit the theory. Thus the historian finds himself facing the problem of how law-like statements can be confirmed using the data from a society in the past.

It thus appears that historians must seek to establish the truth of law-like statements about the past. By what method is this done? If we look to prevailing historical practice, the answer is fairly clear. If the generalization is made explicit, it is supported by the citation of "representative" examples which illustrate the pattern. These examples are usually few in number, though it is understood, and often said, that their number could easily be multiplied. The examples presented are alleged to be "representative" in the sense that they are typical of, or very like, the multitude of other examples which could have been cited, though in many cases what is called a "representative" example is really a particularly "good" or striking example. In many if not most cases, however, the generalization is not explicitly stated, but is used implicitly to justify the attribution of a particular causal connection. If the particular connection is challenged, the historian will defend himself by saying that that is how people behaved in that society, and, if further pressed to justify this claim, will cite "representative" examples to support his thesis. Thus whether the generalization is explicit or implicit, the support for it comes from a relatively small number of illustrative examples which are believed to be typical or "representative." Most historians believe that the generalizations they affirm are true—that the scholar who has "immersed himself" in the "period" really knows how people behaved in that time and place—yet few regard their generalizations as proven by this procedure. Hence historians refer to their generalizations as "interpretations" of the data, meaning that, although they believe them to be true, they cannot prove them to be so.

Before the philosopher-critic attacks this procedure, it might be well to ask what other procedures are open to the historian. Granting, as virtually every historian will, that this method of supporting generalizations is inadequate to confirm them in any scientific sense, what else could be done? Specifically, philosophers have often demanded that historians be "scientific." Since a science is sometimes defined as a discipline which seeks to discover and establish law-like generalizations, and since on the analysis given here history is certainly such a discipline, it may seem obvious that historians ought to follow the "scientific method," whatever that may be. If history is a science, it is a social science. The question which must be asked, then, is whether or not it is possible for the historian to employ the methods of confirmation currently used in the social sciences.

We may distinguish five methodological problems which beset the historian in his efforts to confirm law-like statements—the problems of quantity, aggregation, sampling, informant bias, and measurement. Of these, the first two are the only ones for which there is at present much hope of a solution. Until recently, historians have chosen their subjects in terms of the amount of data available, and have avoided not only those subjects with very few data, but those with too many as well. Thus a subject which would involve analyzing the county election returns for the United States over a ten-year period has been, until recently, beyond the ability of any person in the profession. This limitation on problem choice reflects, of course, the tradition of humane scholarship which has dominated the profession and which has defined the appropriate working unit as the single scholar rather than a team of scholars. But it also reflects the hard economic fact that funding for large-scale multi-person projects in history has been, and is now, largely nonexistent. Accordingly, a feasible research project in history generally means something which a single scholar can complete within a few years time. But two new developments have tended to alter this situation. The first is the computer, which now makes possible the almost instantaneous manipulation of quantities of data which would require years of hand labor. The second is the development of institutional arrangements, such as the InterUniversity Consortium for Political Research, through which quantities of data can be processed and made available for the use of scholars. The effects of this combination of factors are already evident, particularly in political history, and will become increasingly so as time goes on. But it is important to note that these new developments are useful only under certain special conditions. All that the computer does, in this type of application, is to enable masses of processed data to be manipulated quickly. But not all data are equally amenable to computer application. In those cases where complete data exist in a standard format, and the problem is to obtain certain summary statistics and their interrelations—e.g., county election returns, or congressional roll calls—the computer is working wonders. But there are very few such areas. The solution of the problem of dealing with large quantities of standardized data leaves unsolved other fundamental difficulties.

A second major problem confronting the historian is that of inferring individual behavior from aggregate data—what is often called the "ecological" problem. It is desirable in any sort of research that one be able to observe directly the unit of interest—the thing one is studying.

There are, however, cases in which the unit of interest cannot be observed, and information about it must be inferred from some other unit of observation. The family of these cases which is usually called "ecological" is one in which the unit of observation is a set of which the unit of interest is a member. Examples of this sort are legion. The unit of interest may be the individual voter, while the unit of observation is the county; the unit of interest may be the individual soldier, while the unit of observation is the platoon, etc. The problem of ecological inference is, given measurements on the unit of observation, what can be inferred about the characteristics of the unit of interest. We may, for example, know the mean income for a county, or the percent of its vote Democratic, or any of a number of similar statistics. But what, if anything, can we infer from them about the characteristics of individuals in that county? This is particularly critical in history because, in those cases where statistical evidence has been collected and reported in the past, it has very often been reported for aggregates only. Thus election statistics are always reported by precinct, ward, or county, but not by individual. Census data, though available at the individual level in the manuscript returns, are reported publicly as measurements on the county and state. It is therefore relatively easy to determine for a particular county at a given time in the past the percent of the vote Democratic, the percent of the population Catholic, the mean value of agricultural products, etc., although it is enormously difficult, if not impossible, to determine how any individual in that county voted, what his religion was, or the value of the produce he raised. It is therefore very tempting to try to infer the characteristics of the individuals belonging to the aggregate from the information about the aggregate itself. Indeed, many studies have been done which used correlations on the population of "ecological" units or aggregates to estimate correlations at the individual level.[1] Thus, e.g., the percent of the vote Democratic and the percent of the population Catholic might be correlated over a population of counties, on the assumption that the resulting correlation is essentially similar to the correlation of the attributes Catholic and Democratic voter at the individual level.

As W. S. Robinson[2] showed in a classic paper, this inference is invalid. If r_e denotes the ecological correlation, r_t the correlation at the individual level, and r_w the within-areas correlation, x and y are the two variables of interest, and η_{xA} and η_{yA} are the correlation ratios of x and y on area, then Robinson showed that

$$(1) \qquad r_e = \frac{r_t}{\eta_{xA}\,\eta_{yA}} - \frac{r_w\sqrt{1-\eta_{xA}^2}\,\sqrt{1-\eta_{yA}^2}}{\eta_{xA}\,\eta_{yA}}$$

In other words, he showed that what had been regarded as a bivariate problem involving only x and y was, in fact, a trivariate problem, where the third variable was the nominal one which determined the aggregation of individuals into ecological units. From Robinson's formula, it follows that $r_e = r_t$ if, and only if,

$$r_w = r_t \left\{ \frac{1 - \eta_{xA}\,\eta_{yA}}{\sqrt{1 - \eta_{xA}^2}\,\sqrt{1 - \eta_{yA}^2}} \right\}$$

Since the minimum value of the coefficient of r_t is 1, r_e can be used to estimate r_t only if r_w is at least as large as r_t. But since small areal units are usually more homogeneous with respect to social variables than are larger units, this will very rarely be the case.

By a procedure exactly analogous to that by which (1) is derived, it may be shown that

$$(2) \qquad \beta_t = \beta_w + \eta_{xA}^2\,(\beta_e - \beta_w)$$

where β_t is the bivariate regression coefficient of y on x at the individual level, β_w is the within-areas regression coefficient, β_e is the ecological regression coefficient, and η_{xA} is the correlation ratio of x on area.[3]

Robinson's paper seemed to raise unanswerable objections to ecological inference, and these objections do, indeed, remain unanswered in many respects. However, some methods have been developed by Leo Goodman which provide solutions to the problem under certain conditions. His paper of 1959[4] attacked the problem at several levels of measurement and dealt with cases involving varying numbers of variables. For the sake of simplicity, the following discussion is limited to the bivariate case, and to two combinations of measures—that in which we have nominal measurement at the individual level but at least interval measurement at the aggregate level, which I shall hereafter call Case I; and that in which we have at least interval measurement at both the individual and the aggregate levels, which I shall hereafter call Case II.

Let us consider first the case in which the variables of interest are nominal, e.g., race and literacy. Nominal variables do not admit of ratio or interval measures, and since the Pearsonian coefficients require at least an interval level of measurement, they are, strictly speaking, inapplicable in this case. Nevertheless, an application of such methods to dichotomous nominal variables can be made by using dummy variables —i.e., we let one value of the dichotomous nominal variable have the measure "1" and the other the measure "0." Strictly, the symbols "1" and "0" are here employed like telephone numbers—they are merely numerical names for the values. Arithmetic operations cannot be applied to mere names, numerical or other, but they can be applied to the frequencies with which such names occur in a given population of items. Thus we may interpret the mean of such a dummy variable as the proportion of items in the population which have the numerical name "1"; similarly, the standard deviation becomes $\sqrt{PxQx}$ —the root of the product of the proportion of items in the population having the numerical name "1" and the proportion having the numerical name "0." Correlation and regression coefficients are also interpretable as relations among proportions. The Pearsonian correlation coefficient applied to dummy variables becomes

$$\frac{Pxy - PxPy}{\sqrt{PxQx}\,\sqrt{PyQy}}$$

where Pxy is the proportion of items in the population which have the numerical name "1" with respect to both the variables x and y, Px and Qx are interpreted as above, and Py and Qy have the corresponding interpretations with respect to y. The resulting interpretations are useful, but the formulae must not be assumed to have the same meaning that they have in cases where the variables of interest admit of interval measure. In particular, a proportion is a characteristic of an aggregate, not of an individual. Hence correlation and regression coefficients applied to dummy variables yield results which are ecological by definition—that is, they characterize aggregates, not individuals. Race and literacy cannot have a correlation of .4 at the individual level, nor can there be a regression of .4 of illiteracy upon race, for what could it mean to say that an increase in nonwhiteness of one unit yields an increase of illiteracy of .4

units? Such symbols become meaningful only if we understand them to mean that an increase in the proportion of nonwhiteness of one percent yields an increase in the proportion of illiterates of .4 percent. Thus in the above formulae (1) and (2), the symbols r_w and β_w are in fact meaningless in this case, for there is no within-areas correlation or regression.

Suppose we are interested in the relation of literacy and race in a Negro-white population, e.g., suppose we have a racially mixed population of n members, $n_{.1}$ of whom are Negro, $n_{.2}$ of whom are white, $n_{1.}$ illiterate, and $n_{2.}$ literate. The population may be described by the following table, where n_{ij} is the frequency in the cell at the intersection of the ith row and the jth column.

	N	W	
I	n_{11}	n_{12}	$n_{1.}$
L	n_{21}	n_{22}	$n_{2.}$
	$n_{.1}$	$n_{.2}$	n

In his 1959 paper, Goodman noted that the proportion of individuals in this population who are illiterates, $\dfrac{n_{1.}}{n}$, may be written as

$$(3) \qquad \frac{n_{1.}}{n} = \frac{n_{12}}{n_{.2}} + \left[\frac{n_{11}}{n_{.1}} - \frac{n_{12}}{n_{.2}} \right] \frac{n_{.1}}{n}$$

The ratios $\dfrac{n_{11}}{n_{.1}}$ and $\dfrac{n_{12}}{n_{.2}}$ may be called the column T-probabilities: they define respectively the probability that a randomly chosen member of the set of individuals in column one will fall into row one, and that a randomly chosen individual from the set of individuals in column two will fall into row one. If we let y_i be the percent of the population illiterate and x_i the percent Negro, we have $y_i = \alpha + \beta x_i$, where $\alpha = \dfrac{n_{12}}{n_{.2}}$ and $\beta = \left[\dfrac{n_{11}}{n_{.1}} - \dfrac{n_{12}}{n_{.2}} \right]$.

Hence if a number of populations or areas are considered for which $\dfrac{n_{11}}{n_{.1}}$ and $\dfrac{n_{12}}{n_{.2}}$ are constants, a perfect linear relation will exist between y_i and

x_i. In this case, α and β could be estimated by the usual least-squares methods of fitting the regression line.

In fact, $\dfrac{n_{11}}{n_{.1}}$ and $\dfrac{n_{12}}{n_{.2}}$ vary from population to population or from area to area. Nevertheless, if the number of cases is large, the observations (i.e., the individuals) are independent of each other, and if the expected values of $\dfrac{n_{12}}{n_{.2}}$ and $\dfrac{n_{11}}{n_{.1}}$ are constant regardless of the variation in x_i— if $E\left[\dfrac{n_{12}}{n_{.2}}\,\Big|\,x_i\right] =$ a constant and if $E\left[\dfrac{n_{11}}{n_{.1}}\,\Big|\,x_i\right] =$ a constant for all i—then standard regression theory can be applied with $\alpha = E\left[\dfrac{n_{12}}{n_{.2}}\,\Big|\,x_i\right]$ and $\beta = \left\{E\left[\dfrac{n_{11}}{n_{.1}}\,\Big|\,x_i\right] - E\left[\dfrac{n_{12}}{n_{.2}}\,\Big|\,x_i\right]\right\}$. The latter assumption, it should be noted, formulates the condition of linearity which underlies all linear regression theory in a form applicable to Case I. From these estimates, we can then readily determine the actual cell proportions and frequencies, and thus reconstruct the entire two-by-two table relating race and literacy. It should be noted that, although this is an "ecological" regression since y_i and x_i are variables characterizing aggregates, yet, under the assumptions given, the estimates obtained are unbiased estimates of the cell entries. From such a table, we may then compute a correlation statistic such as ϕ.

The method just discussed has one weakness which can be troublesome: namely, when the true values of the parameters α and $\beta - \alpha$ are close to 1 and 0, the estimating procedure may yield estimates which lie outside these bounds and so are inadmissible as estimates of probabilities. This does not reflect any bias in the estimating procedure itself: the difficulty arises from the fact that the estimators have a nonzero variance, and that only estimates lying between 1 and 0 can be interpreted as probabilities. Recently, Iversen[5] has provided a partial solution to this difficulty. Equation (3) takes the row proportion as the dependent variable and the column proportion as the independent one. Clearly, an analogous equation can be constructed using the opposite choices; viz.

$$(4) \qquad \frac{n_{.1}}{n} = \frac{n_{21}}{n_{2.}} + \left[\frac{n_{11}}{n_{1.}} - \frac{n_{21}}{n_{2.}}\right]\frac{n_{1.}}{n}$$

Let this equation be written as

$$y'_i = \alpha' + \beta' x'_i$$

Iversen has shown that if α and $\beta - \alpha$ are both admissible estimates, in the sense that $0 < \alpha < 1$ and $0 < \beta - \alpha < 1$, then α' and $\beta' - \alpha'$ are both inadmissible, one being greater than one and the other less than zero. Conversely, if α' and $\beta' - \alpha'$ are admissible, then α and $\beta - \alpha$ are inadmissible. Hence if equation (3) yields estimates which are inadmissible, we can switch to equation (4) to obtain admissible estimates, and vice versa. Unfortunately, this solution to the problem is not complete, since it is also possible that one member of the pair α, $\beta - \alpha$ is admissible although the other is not, and also that one member of the pair α', $\beta' - \alpha'$ is admissible although the other is not. Nevertheless, if one pair of estimates is admissible, Iversen's method permits us to find it.

Iversen has also made a number of significant additions to Goodman's work. For Case I, we can conceive the marginals in four different ways: (a) we can regard both row and column marginals as random variables; (b) we can regard the row marginals as random variables and the column marginals as fixed; (c) we can regard the column marginals as random variables and the row marginals as fixed; or (d) we can regard both row and column marginals as fixed. Iversen has shown with respect to maximum likelihood estimates of the T-probabilities that (a) reduces to either (b) or (c). He has developed maximum likelihood methods for estimating the T-probabilities in cases (b) and (c) for two-by-two tables and has indicated how these methods can be generalized to r by c tables. He has explored the problem of least-squares estimates of T-probabilities for the two-by-two tables and has proposed a nonlinear model for use with variable T-probabilities. He has also made a notable contribution to (d) by devising a number of different statistics which can be used to estimate the cell entries when both marginals are regarded as fixed. Although in (d) one is dealing, not with estimators and parameters, but with ways in which some elements of the data can be expressed in terms of others, Iversen has nevertheless adapted methods of least-squares estimation to this problem and has shown how an upper bound to the bias of these "estimates" can be determined. Although these "estimates" may differ considerably from the true values, his results constitute a significant contribution to our ability to deal with Case I.

In 1961 Blalock published a book[6] in one chapter of which he elaborated some further consequences of Goodman's work. If we turn to the case where the variables of interest admit of at least interval measure at the individual level as well as at the aggregate level—i.e., Case II— Goodman has shown that there are in general two situations in which ecological inference is valid. These situations are defined by the way in which individuals are grouped to form the aggregate units. That this should be so is scarcely surprising. Robinson showed that it is the presence of the nominal variable aggregating individuals into ecological units which complicates the relation between the ecological correlation coefficient and the individual correlation coefficient; accordingly, it is reasonable that the solution to the problem of ecological inference should depend upon controlling the effects of this nominal variable, and hence upon how aggregation is done. If the aggregation is done either (a) by grouping people according to their scores on the independent variable, or (b) grouping them randomly into large aggregates of equal size, then the ecological regression coefficient is a good estimate of the individual regression coefficient, and in the latter event—i.e., (b)—the ecological correlation coefficient is a good estimate of the individual correlation coefficient. That (a) is true is obvious from equation (2), for to say that the individuals are grouped on the basis of their scores on the independent variable is to say that $\eta^2_{xA} = 1$; hence

$$\beta_t = \beta_w + 1 \ (B_e - \beta_w) = \beta_e$$

In this case, (1) becomes

$$r_e = \frac{r_t}{\eta_{yA}} \quad \frac{r_w \sqrt{1 - 1} \ \sqrt{1 - \eta^2_{yA}}}{\eta_{yA}} \quad \frac{r_t}{\eta_{yA}}$$

Should the correlation of x and y be perfect, η_{yA} will also equal 1, but if it is less than perfect the relation of the nominal variable to y remains as a disturbing factor. The more η_{yA} departs from 1, the greater the difference between r_t and r_e will be, and the less accurate r_e will be as an estimator of r_t.

The proof of (b) is somewhat more complex. Let σ_x^2 and σ_y^2 be the population variances of x and y respectively, and $\sigma_{\bar{x}}^2$ and $\sigma_{\bar{y}}^2$ the weighted ecological variances—i.e., the variances of the aggregate means, weighted by the proportion of the population in that aggregate. Since $r_t = \beta_t \dfrac{\sigma_x}{\sigma_y}$ and $r_e = \beta_e \dfrac{\sigma_{\bar{x}}}{\sigma_{\bar{y}}}$, r_t will be equal to r_e whenever $\dfrac{\sigma_x^2}{\sigma_y^2} = \dfrac{\sigma_{\bar{x}}^2}{\sigma_{\bar{y}}^2}$ and $\beta_t = \beta_e$. Let us explore first the conditions under which

$$(5) \qquad\qquad \frac{\sigma_y^2}{\sigma_x^2} = \frac{\sigma_{\bar{y}}^2}{\sigma_{\bar{x}}^2}$$

Assume a population of N items divided into k aggregates of n_i members each $(i = 1 \ldots k)$. Assume also that n_i is large enough so that sampling fluctuations can be ignored and that the assumptions of linear regression analysis hold, so that $E(y_i \mid x_i) = A + Bx_i$ for each aggregate i, and $\sigma^2(y_i \mid x_i)$ is the variance of y_{ij} about the regression line in the ith aggregate. We may obtain the expected values of σ_y^2 and $\sigma_{\bar{y}}^2$ as follows. First,

$$E(y_{ij} - E(y_{ij}))^2 = E(y_{ij} - (A + Bx_i))^2 = \sigma^2(y_i \mid x_i).$$

$$E\left\{ \frac{\sum_i \sum_j (y_{ij} - E(y_{ij}))^2}{N} \right\} = \frac{\sum_i \sum_j E(y_{ij} - E(y_{ij}))^2}{N} = \sum_i \frac{n_i}{N} \sigma^2(y_i \mid x_i) =$$

$$\sum_i w_i \sigma^2(y_i \mid x_i) \text{ letting } w_i = \frac{n_i}{N}.$$

Second, $E(\bar{y}_i - E(\bar{y}_i))^2 = E\left(\bar{y}_i - E\left(\dfrac{\sum_j y_{ij}}{n_i}\right)\right)^2 = E\left(\bar{y}_i - \dfrac{\sum_j E(y_{ij})}{n_i}\right)^2 =$

$$E(\bar{y}_i - (A + Bx_i))^2 = E\left\{ \frac{\sum_j y_{ij}}{n_i} - (A + Bx_i) \right\}^2 =$$

$$E\left\{ \frac{\sum_j (y_{ij} - (A + Bx_i))}{n_i} \right\}^2 = \frac{n_i \sigma^2(y_i \mid x_i)}{n_i^2} = \frac{\sigma^2(y_i \mid x_i)}{n_i}.$$

Hence, $E\left(\sum_i w_i (\bar{y}_i - E(\bar{y}_i))^2\right) = \sum_i w_i \dfrac{\sigma^2(y_i \mid x_i)}{n_i} = \sum_i \dfrac{1}{N} \sigma^2(y_i \mid x_i).$

Then if we substitute for σ_y^2 and $\sigma_{\bar{y}}^2$ in (5) their expected values, (5) holds whenever

$$\frac{\underset{i}{\Sigma}\, w_i \sigma^2(y_i \mid x_i)}{\sigma^2_{\bar{x}}} = \frac{\dfrac{\underset{i}{\Sigma}\, \sigma^2(y_i \mid x_i)}{N}}{\sigma^2_{\bar{x}}}$$

i.e., whenever

$$\frac{N(\underset{i}{\Sigma}\, w_i \sigma^2(y_i \mid x_i))}{\sigma^2_x\, (\underset{i}{\Sigma}\, \sigma^2(y_i \mid x_i))} = \frac{1}{\sigma^2_{\bar{x}}}$$

i.e., whenever

$$\sigma^2_{\bar{x}} = \frac{\sigma^2_x\, (\underset{i}{\Sigma}\, \sigma^2(y_i \mid x_i))}{N(\underset{i}{\Sigma}\, w_i \sigma^2(y_i \mid x_i))}$$

If $w_i = \dfrac{n_i}{N} = \dfrac{1}{k}$, this becomes

$$\sigma^2_{\bar{x}} = \frac{\sigma^2_x\, (\underset{i}{\Sigma}\, \sigma^2(y_1 \mid x_1))}{\dfrac{N}{k}(\underset{i}{\Sigma}\, \sigma^2(y_i \mid x_i))}$$

or

$$\sigma^2_{\bar{x}} = \frac{\sigma^2_x}{\dfrac{N}{k}}$$

However if the aggregates are formed by random choice, each $\bar{x}_i$ is the mean of a random sample. Further, if $w_i = \dfrac{1}{k}$, then $n_i = n$ for all i. Hence

$$E\left\{\underset{i}{\Sigma}\, \frac{n}{N}(\bar{x}_i - \mu)^2\right\} = \underset{i}{\Sigma}\, \frac{n}{N}\, E(\bar{x}_i - \mu)^2 = \underset{i}{\Sigma}\, \frac{n}{N}\, \frac{\sigma^2_x}{n} = \frac{k\sigma^2_x}{N} = \frac{\sigma^2_x}{\dfrac{N}{k}}.$$

Accordingly, if the aggregates are of equal size and their composition is determined by random choice,

$$\frac{\sigma^2_y}{\sigma^2_x} = \frac{\sigma^2_{\bar{y}}}{\sigma^2_{\bar{x}}}$$

To show that under these conditions $E(\beta_e) = \beta_t$ we assume again that n_i is large enough so that sampling fluctuations can be ignored, and $E(\sigma_{\bar{x}}^2) \neq 0$. Then

$$E(\beta_e) \doteq \frac{E(\sum_i n_i \bar{x}_i \bar{y}_i - \mu_x \mu_y)}{E(\sum_i n_i \bar{x}_i^2 - N\mu_x^2)}$$

where, as above, μ represents the population mean. Beginning with the denominator, we have, where the aggregates are randomly chosen,

$$E(\bar{x}_i) = \mu_x$$

$$E(\bar{x}_i^2) = \text{Var}(\bar{x}_i) + \mu_x^2$$
$$= \frac{\sigma_x^2}{n_i} + \mu_x^2$$

$$E(n_i \bar{x}_i^2) = \sigma_x^2 + n_i \mu_x^2$$

$$E(\sum_{i=1}^{k} n_i \bar{x}_i^2) = k\sigma_x^2 + N\mu_x^2$$

$$E(\sum_{i=1}^{k} n_i \bar{x}_i^2 - N\mu_x^2) = k\sigma_x^2$$

Similarly, for the numerator, we have

$$E(\bar{x}_i \bar{y}_i) = \text{Cov}(\bar{x}_i \bar{y}_i) + \mu_x \mu_y$$
$$= \frac{\sigma_{xy}^2}{n_i} + \mu_x \mu_y$$

$$E(n_i \bar{x}_i \bar{y}_i) = \sigma_{xy}^2 + n_i \mu_x \mu_y$$

$$E(\sum_{i=1}^{k} n_i \bar{x}_i \bar{y}_i) = k\sigma_{xy}^2 + N\mu_x \mu_y$$

$$E(\sum_{i=1}^{k} n_i \bar{x}_i \bar{y}_i - N\mu_x \mu_y) = k\sigma_{xy}^2$$

Hence,

$$E(\beta_e) \doteq \frac{k\sigma_{xy}^2}{k\sigma_x^2} = \frac{\sigma_{xy}^2}{\sigma_x^2} = \beta_t$$

These results are approximate and hold only under the conditions stated.*

---

* Recently, W. P. Shively[7] has written a paper in which he has considerably confused the issue. As we have noted above, one of the assumptions which underlies Goodman's method for Case I is the assumption that

$$E\left(\frac{n_{11}}{n_{.1}}\,\middle|\, x_i\right) \text{ is constant and } E\left(\frac{n_{12}}{n_{.2}}\,\middle|\, x_i\right) \text{ is constant—i.e.,}$$

that the linearity condition is met. Given this assumption, Goodman's method yields an unbiased result. But we have also seen that in Case II the ecological regression coefficient is an unbiased estimate of the individual regression coefficient only if grouping is done on the basis of the scores on the independent variable or at random. From these observations, Shively has concluded that the linearity condition must be *equivalent* to the grouping assumption. He has, in other words, confounded Case I with Case II; he has concluded that, if unbiased estimates are possible in the latter case only where the grouping assumptions are satisfied, then this must be true also in the former case, and since, in the former case unbiased estimates are possible if the linearity assumption is met, he has therefore concluded that the linearity assumption is equivalent to the grouping assumption. Thus he holds that Goodman's method for dealing with Case I is biased unless the grouping assumption is met, and cites as evidence for such bias the fact that the method sometimes yields proportions less than zero or greater than one.

These conclusions of Shively's are in error. In the first place, the linearity condition is a condition of any application of linear regression analysis—it is as much a condition of Case II as of Case I. This is clear in Blalock's treatment, which is explicitly based on Goodman's paper. Where we have interval variables at both the individual and aggregate levels, ecological inference requires *both* the linearity assumption and the grouping assumptions; where we have nominal variables at the individual level, the grouping assumptions are irrelevant. That the two sets of assumptions are not equivalent is easily shown by considering Shively's claim that where the aggregation is done on the basis of the x scores, $n_{11}/n_{.1}$ must be constant. Consider the following population:

	x_1	x_2	
y_1	31000	75000	106000
y_2	53000	41000	94000
	84000	116000	200000

Suppose that this population is aggregated into three subsets following the method of aggregation outlined by Shively—namely, in the first subset 20% of the group are

The methods developed by Goodman admit of important applications, particularly when the variables of interest have nominal measures at the individual level. When these variables have at least interval measures at the individual level, ecological inference is subject to restrictions which, so far as empirical applications are concerned, are extremely severe. It is a rare case in which we can assume that the composition of real ecological units of the sort which are of interest to historians and social scientists is determined by random choice, or, for that matter, in which we have ecological units of equal size. Such cases do occur when the units are the results of standardized processes; for example, army units are of uniform size, and in some cases it may be justifiable to assume that men are assigned to such units at random, but certainly in the case of areal units such as counties or precincts the random choice hypothesis is too dubious to be seriously considered. It is often more plausible to assume that aggregation is based on scores of the independent variable, especially when this variable is a socially powerful factor, such as income. But even in such cases one is rarely in a position to hold that aggregation was not influenced by other variables such as race, ethnic stock, religion, age, etc. To the degree that such other variables exert an influence on aggregation, ecological inference becomes biased. The inferential difficulties which arise in empirical applications where there is at least interval measure-

---

x_1's, in the second 40% are x_1's, and in the third 60% are x_1's. Thus we have

I

	x_1	x_2	
y_1	1000	30000	31000
y_2	11000	18000	29000
	12000	48000	60000

II

	x_1	x_2	
y_1	6000	20000	26000
y_2	18000	16000	34000
	24000	36000	60000

III

	x_1	x_2	
y_1	24000	25000	49000
y_2	24000	7000	31000
	48000	32000	80000

But note that the proportion of x_1's who are y_1's is not constant here; for the first table it is .08, for the second .25, and for the third .50. Similarly, the proportion of x_2's who are y_1's is not constant: for the first table it is .63, for the second .56, and for the third .78. Hence nothing in the mode of aggregation itself guarantees that the linearity condition is met. In the second place, the fact that the method used in Case I sometimes yields proportions above one or below zero does not prove bias. The method is an estimating procedure; the estimators have a distribution with a non-zero variance, and where the parameters are near 1 or 0, it is only to be expected that some estimates will fall outside those limits. This fact is not inconsistent with the unbiased character of the estimators.

ment at both levels are therefore severely limiting. Where the variables are nominal at the individual level, the constraints arc less severe, but even here the necessary condition of linearity is not always met. It may well be, for example, that the voting behavior of a particular category of people varies depending upon whether they are a minority or a majority of the population of the political unit in question. It is therefore essential in applying this estimating procedure that the scatter diagram for the variables be examined to make sure that the linearity condition is met. Ecological inference is, then, a method which has to be used with considerable caution; nevertheless, it is one of the most important methods by which we can attack the problem of the confirmation of law-like hypotheses respecting past societies. Where it can be applied, it offers us a means of determining what patterns characterized the members of past societies, and so of putting general hypotheses to the test.*

The methods which we have been discussing depend upon the existence of aggregated data for either the whole population or a very large sample from it, and this is by no means a common situation. In the general case, we have to collect our own statistical data rather than relying upon what someone else has already collected. But how is this to be done? Consider

---

* Since this chapter is concerned with the confirmation or disconfirmation of general hypotheses regarding the individuals of a past population, I have limited the foregoing discussion to those aspects of the use of ecological data which involve inferences about individual behavior. This should not be taken to imply, however, that ecological data are of use solely in that respect. In the first place, the unit of interest may be the ecological unit, as e.g., in studies of New England towns, where it is not the individual inhabitants but the town itself with which we are concerned. Since historical data often give relatively more complete information about a population of ecological units in a given society than they do about the individual members of those units, there are many cases in which the study of the ecological units may be the more rewarding of the two. In the second place, we are often interested in the relation of individuals to the ecological units of which they are members. As the discussion of customary behavior above suggests, human behavior varies depending upon the social environment; membership in a given type of ecological unit may be a critical determinant of individual behavior. And in the third place, ecological units may themselves be composed of other ecological units, as states are of counties, and the objective may be to determine the relations among ecological units representing different levels of aggregation. Thus the problems of drawing inferences from ecological data are far more complex than those discussed above, and considerably more extensive than can be covered here. For an overview of the current state of research in these areas, the reader is referred to Mattei Dogan and Stein Rokkan, *Quantitative Ecological Analysis in the Social Sciences* (Cambridge: M.I.T. Press, 1969).

the problem of testing the applicability of a general hypothesis h to a society S of n members at time t. If this were a contemporary situation, the method to be used would be fairly obvious—we would draw some type of random sample of members of S and determine for each member of that sample whether or not the hypothesis h holds good. But if one attempts to apply such a procedure to a past society, one is met at once by a major difficulty. Consider the subset K of S, consisting of all members of S for whom data relevant to h has survived. Now we know enough about the processes of historical record creation and preservation to be certain at least of this—that K is not a random sample from S. Accordingly, no matter what sampling techniques we apply to K, we cannot obtain a random sample of S upon which to carry out our tests.

It therefore appears that we shall have to work with biased samples. But this is not an insuperable problem, provided we know something about the bias. The historian's problem is not unlike that faced by Inkeles and Bauer when they wrote *The Soviet Citizen*.[8] They wished to obtain information about the general population of the Soviet Union, but they were limited to subjects who were refugees from Russia and who were, for the most part, in camps in Europe. Some of them had been conscripted against their will by the Germans and brought to Germany as forced labor, but many others had voluntarily left Russia for Germany; accordingly, the sample was biased against the prevailing Russian regime. Nevertheless, knowing the direction of the sample bias, Inkeles and Bauer believed that they could use the sample to gain information about the Russian population. Essentially, they made two kinds of inferences. First, when they found the sample opposed to some aspect of the Soviet Regime, they could conclude nothing about the attitudes of the Russian people, since the finding might well be due to sample bias, but when they found the sample in favor of some aspect of the regime, they concluded that the Russian people as a whole favored this characteristic, since the anti-Soviet bias of the sample could hardly account for such a result. Secondly, they assumed that whatever factors had biased the sample had acted equally upon all subgroups within the sample. Thus, when they found that within the sample hostility to the Soviet regime was greatest in the lowest class and decreased as one ascended the class ladder, they concluded that this was also true for the Soviet population generally. As Inkeles and Bauer remark:

It is reasonable to assume that whatever selective factors account for the anti-Soviet bias of our sample operate relatively uniformly on all the subgroups in our sample, and that comparable groups in the Soviet population will stand in the same *relationship* to each other as do the members of our sample. It would, therefore, take a very tortured set of assumptions concerning the differential impact of sample bias on each of our subgroups to cause us to exhibit major hesitation about the main conclusion to be derived from these data, namely, that the lower classes are *relatively* more categorical in their opposition to the regime than are the upper classes.[9]

A few moments of reflection, however, will show that a not "very tortured set of assumptions" would explain these findings purely in terms of sample bias. Suppose it to be the case that, when the Nazis conscripted labor, they wanted better trained rather than poorer trained men, and so they conscripted most heavily from the upper classes and least heavily from the lower classes. This would mean that the proportion of a class which left Russia voluntarily would be inversely related to status—hence the proportion hostile to the regime would be inversely related to status, which is precisely what they found. Now I do not raise this point to challenge their study—such a possibility as I have suggested could be easily checked and undoubtedly was—but to point out that the same result can mean very different things depending upon how one assumes that the bias operates, and that hypotheses about the sample bias cannot be tested against that sample only. Inkeles and Bauer were able to make excellent use of their sample largely because they faced a relatively simple problem of bias; they knew on grounds independent of the sample itself the nature and direction of the major bias with which they had to deal. Hence they could use their added information to interpret the results obtained from that sample.

In the general case, the historian's problem of bias is not so simple as that which faced Inkeles and Bauer, since the number, magnitude, and direction of the biases affecting historical samples are largely unknown. Nevertheless, some interesting attacks have recently been made on this problem. In a study of bank deposits in the nineteenth century, Kindahl[10] found that the data-base consisted of two incomplete censuses of banks. To estimate characteristics of the total population of banks from these data—e.g., the total number of banks—he made an interesting application of the methods used in estimating the characteristics of populations of wildlife from different catches. In this technique, two catches of pre-determined size are made at times sufficiently far apart so that the natural geographical movements of the animals during the interim may plausibly be regarded as equivalent to reshuffling. Under these conditions, the two catches can be interpreted as independent random samples of prede-termined sizes, n_1 and n_2 respectively, drawn from a population of N unit. Where n_1 and n_2 are large relative to N, there will be items common to both catches—let there be c such items. It can be shown that c has a hyper-geometric distribution and an expected value of $\frac{n_1 n_2}{N}$. From these facts it is not difficult to show that the maximum likelihood estimator of N is $\frac{n_1 n_2}{c}$.

In applying this method to the historical case, neither of the two as-sumptions noted above holds true—i.e., the samples are not random and the sample sizes are not predetermined. If we examine the consequences of dropping the second assumption first, it is clear that n_1 and n_2 become random variables. Defining P_j $(j = 1,2)$ as the probability that any member of the population is drawn in the jth sample, we may regard n_j as the number of "successes" in N trials, with P_j as the probability of success and $1 - P_j$ as the probability of failure. Then n_j has a binomial distribution with $E(n_j) = NP_j$ and $E(c) = NP_1P_2$. Hence:

$$\frac{E(n_1)E(n_2)}{E(c)} = \frac{NP_1NP_2}{NP_1P_2} = N$$

$E\left(\frac{n_1 n_2}{c}\right) \neq \frac{E(n_1)E(n_2)}{E(c)}$; however, for N and P relatively large, Kin-dahl shows that

$$E\left(\frac{n_1 n_2}{c}\right) \doteq N + \frac{(1 - P_1)(1 - P_2)}{P_1 P_2}$$

so the bias is small relative to N if N and P_j are large.

So far we have assumed random sampling, and that, of course, cannot be assumed in the historical case. In surrendering this assumption, we must replace it by some hypothesis regarding the nature of the bias. Kindahl proposes a model in which the probability that a given element is chosen for the sample is a function of the variable of interest, x_i—in the case of his sample, size of bank deposits. He then suggests that the actual sampling pattern can be approximated by a step function such that sampling within each of R strata is random. Hence if $i = 1 \ldots R$, P_{ij} is constant for all members of the ith stratum but varies between strata. If we let $P_1^* = \max (P_{11} \ldots P_{R1})$ and $P_2^* = \max (P_{12} \ldots P_{R2})$, we can express the stratum probabilities as fractions of the maximum for the respective samples, e.g., $P_{i1} = k_{i1} P_1^*$ and $P_{i2} = k_{i2} P_2^*$ for appropriate choices of k. Then letting $k_{i2} = \alpha_i k_{i1}$ and $P_2^* = \beta P_1^*$ we have $P_{i2} = \alpha_i k_{i1} \beta P_1^*$, or letting $\gamma_i = \alpha_i \beta$, $P_{i2} = \gamma_i k_{i1} P_1^*$. If we then stratify each of the samples on the basis of x_i into R strata, and compute within each sample stratum the estimator

$$\hat{N}_i = \frac{n_{1i} n_{2i}}{c_i}$$

then $(\hat{N})^s \doteq \sum_{i=1}^{R} \hat{N}_i$ has the expected value

$$E(\hat{N})^s \doteq N + \sum_{i=1}^{R} \left\{ \left[\frac{1}{\gamma_i k_{i1} P_1^*} - 1 \right] \left[\frac{1}{k_{i1} P_1^*} - 1 \right] \right\}$$

and the variance

$$\text{Var} (\hat{N})^s \doteq \sum_{i=1}^{R} \left\{ N_i \left[\frac{1}{\gamma_i k_{i1} P_1^*} - 1 \right] \left[\frac{1}{k_{i1} P_1^*} - 1 \right] \right\}$$

Kindahl has derived similar results for estimators of the mean and total of x_i. Despite the crudity of these estimators and the fact that they are subject to unmeasurable error, they are the best available for this problem and the degree of bias may not be intolerable. Thus, if P_i is a monotonic increasing function of x_i, $\hat{N}$ is biased downward and $\hat{\bar{x}}$ is biased upward; hence, $\hat{N}\hat{\bar{x}}$, though still biased, may be reasonably close to the population value.

A second case which is of considerable interest is due to Hammarberg.[11] In a study of Indiana voters in the 1870s, he had as a data-base the manuscript returns of the United States Census for Indiana and a set of documents known as the *People's Guides*, which gave for nine Indiana counties a variety of data on individuals, including values for the variables political party identification, occupation, religion, place of birth, and so forth. Treating the census population as the total population (an assumption which appears admissible on the basis of what is known about that census for Indiana), he determined that the set of individuals listed in the *People's Guides* was a relatively small fraction of the total electorate. Since the concern of the study was with political party identification, and since this variable was determinable only from the *People's Guides*, Hammarberg faced a situation in which values for his dependent variable could be obtained for only a biased sample of the population, although a large number of other socially significant variables were determinable for both the census population and the subset of that population included in the *People's Guides*.

To deal with this problem, Hammarberg invoked a model of a sampling pattern not unlike Kindahl's: he assumed that the population consisted of R strata, such that sampling within each stratum could be treated as random although the probability of being chosen for inclusion in the *People's Guides* varied from stratum to stratum. But it could not be assumed in this model that stratification was a function of the variable of interest (e.g., party identification); accordingly, the problem was to identify the variables which defined the stratification, and to estimate the selection probabilities for at least the major strata. Since information on a large set of socially significant variables was available for both the sample and the total population (as defined by the Census), this problem could be attacked. Defining inclusion in the *People's Guides* as a dichotomous dependent variable, and taking the variables determinable from both the Census and the *People's Guides* as independent ones, Hammarberg used an analytic procedure that identified those factors which explained the largest percentage of the variance of the dependent variable. Having thus determined from the data which subgroups were most unequally represented in the sample, he was able to use those subgroups as strata for poststratification, and so to develop estimators for the population characteristics which had substantially reduced bias. Obviously, the applicability of this technique depends upon the availability of significant information for both the sample and the whole population. This is a severe limitation, since data about any whole population are rare. In those cases where the manuscript census is used to define the population, the information available is extremely limited, since the number of characteristics concerning which the census gives information rapidly dwindles into insignificance as one retreats from the present. Nevertheless, where the technique can be applied, it promises to yield significantly better estimates than could be obtained from biased samples alone.

In the cases just discussed, we have employed statistical methods to infer characteristics of past populations from the set K of members of that population for whom data relevant to our inquiry now exist. But there are two other applications of sampling theory which are of major importance for the study of the past. First, K may contain all the members of a particular social category of that past population. For example, K may well contain every person who has served in the United States Congress. Since these individuals are in K, data on them exist, but those data may be difficult to find, and the more obscure the individual the more difficult the search is likely to be. Thus if we set out to collect income data on the first five hundred men to serve in the Congress, we may well find that the cost of this inquiry, measured in time and money, is simply too great for a given investigator to undertake. But the cost of running down the requisite data for a simple random sample of fifty drawn from that population of five hundred might be well within the means of the investigator, and from such a ten-percent random sample quite precise estimates can be made concerning the characteristics of the population. In cases of this sort, standard sampling theory can be applied to very good effect.

Second, it often happens that the set K contains a large number of members. Whatever the difficulties may be in drawing inferences from K to the population N, one would rather try to make such inferences from K, particularly if K is large, than from a few arbitrarily chosen cases. But to determine what is true of all the members of K, where K is large, can present a very formidable research problem indeed. Here again one may attack the problem through standard sampling methods. In the first place, one must locate the data which define K. To do this, one must utilize to the fullest those considerations of document creation and preservation which were discussed in the preceding chapter. If one is sampling documents for which there exist institutionalized creation and preservation procedures, it may well be sufficient to sample these institutions directly. Thus, e.g., if one wishes to determine certain characteristics of state legislators, and the official records of the state legislatures are a sufficient data-base for the inquiry, it is quite sufficient to draw a first cluster sample of state legislatures, one being relatively certain of the existence and location of the documents. At the other extreme, if one wishes to determine certain attitudes of Union soldiers during the Civil War, and the data-base is letters written to their families, one has no institutionalized creation procedures with which to deal, and the only institutionalized preservation procedures which could form a feasible basis for this study would be the acquisitions procedures of institutional repositories, such as libraries and historical societies. Such institutions would therefore have to be chosen as clusters, but clearly the variability among such institutions is so great that one would want an initial stratification based upon such factors as size, location, and policy with respect to the acquisition of manuscript material. To carry through such a stratification would itself be a considerable research task. Furthermore, once a cluster sample has been obtained, we face the problem of sampling within the cluster. If our interest is in determining characteristics of individuals, the documents must be listed by the individuals for whom they provide data, whether these individuals are the authors, as in the case of letters, or the actors whose behavior is described in them, as in the case of the journals of state legislatures. From these lists, samples of individuals—i.e., samples of data-sets associated with individuals—can then be drawn by ordinary random sampling methods. We then face the problem of sampling within these data-sets. No matter how large these sets may be, it cannot be assumed that sampling is an adequate method of dealing with the data. Obviously, if the data were produced in a standard format, so that certain bits of information occur at particular places in the data, sampling would be irrelevant—one does not sample the pages of an autobiography to find out when the author was born. But regardless of format, sampling should not be applied at all unless we can assume that inscriptions encoding the needed bits of information occur frequently and more or less at random in the data, and that each inscription is equivalent to every other one. If these assumptions are met, and if the quantity of data on the individual is large, sampling techniques can be applied to lighten the load, and since documentary material is frequently serially ordered, systematic sampling is often used in such situations. Thus given certain conditions, it is possible to obtain probability samples from K which will permit a quite exact estimate of the characteristics of the members of K, and to do this through a multistage sampling process which will keep costs in time, money, and effort within reasonable bounds. Although such applications of sampling technique do not touch the fundamental inferential questions discussed above, they would nevertheless significantly increase the power and precision of historical study.

There would appear, however, to be another approach to the problem of confirming law-like statements about past populations which is acceptable in at least some social sciences and which does not involve the statistical difficulties we have just discussed. Of all the social sciences, anthropology has been the least statistical, yet anthropologists have succeeded in establishing a number of law-like generalizations about the societies which they have studied. In so doing, they have relied heavily upon "informants"—i.e., members of a native society who can tell them what the prevailing customs of that society are. But historical data are rich in descriptions of past societies written either by members of those societies or by visitors from other societies. These accounts typically contain descriptions of the behavior, beliefs, and attitudes of the members of those past societies, and are often very extensive and detailed. The commentaries of De Tocqueville,[12] and Bryce,[13] for example, are among the most famous and widely used sources of information about nineteenth-century American society. Why, then, cannot the historian treat such accounts as the anthropologist does the reports of his "informants" and hope to rival his success in deriving a description of the culture from them? This prospect is enormously attractive; but unfortunately there are difficulties involved. Both the historian and the anthropologist can and should use informants to generate hypotheses about a society, and the testimony of informants does certainly have evidential value. But informants are notably unreliable, whether they are contemporary natives or voices from the past—they are often in error and sometimes deliberately so. The testimony of informants therefore cannot be accepted without corroboration, and it is here that the anthropologist has available to him methods and opportunities which the historian lacks. First, the anthropologist can elicit information from his informants in a way that no historian can match. The anthropologist can cross-examine his informants and requestion them at different times and under different conditions; the historian must make do with whatever his informants chose to put down. Second, the anthropologist, what-

ever his reliance upon his informants, still observes the entire community which he is studying and, while there are always aspects of the
natives' behavior which he cannot observe, he is very often able to check
his informants' statements against his own empirical observation—something which the historian cannot do. And third, the anthropologist can
to a limited degree experiment with his community, observing how
people react when he deviates from their patterns or when he conforms
to them, in a way which no historian can ever hope to rival. It is, then,
incorrect to think of the anthropologist as limited in his access to his
society in the same way in which the historian is limited in his access to a
past society. If the anthropologist in the field usually foregoes the use
of statistics, this is because he deals with groups of people which are
small enough to permit him to observe all members of his society in
action and to satisfy himself directly regarding the generality of the pattern which he describes. The historian has no such privilege—the methods
of the field anthropologist are not applicable to his data.

It is customary to distinguish between those sciences which are experimental and those which are observational. Of the social sciences,
certainly psychology is the most experimental, but all of the others,
even—as the above remarks indicate—anthropology, involve at least
some degree of experimentation. History, on the other hand, is completely observational, for there is quite literally no way in which the
historian can manipulate the situation in which his data were created.
Those experimental controls, by which, in other fields, the influence of
disturbing variables can be eliminated or controlled so that the interaction of the variables of interest can be observed, are not among the
weapons upon which the historian can call. Accordingly, it is particularly
important for the historian to be able to apply to his data analytical procedures which will control the influence of these disturbing variables.
Like other observational scientists, he must substitute statistical controls
for experimental ones if he is to pick apart the complex situation confronting him and to discover how the various factors involved affect each
other. The applicability of such procedures to historical data depends
upon some of the considerations we have discussed above—notably, upon
sampling; but it also depends upon the level of measurement which the
data will bear. It is, therefore, particularly important to raise the question of what forms of measurement are possible with historical data.

The problem of measurement in history is, of course, part of the general problem of measurement; but it is complicated by certain peculiar features resulting from the nature of historical data. All measurement is based upon the establishment of a correspondence between an empirical relational system and a numerical relational system.* In the ordinary case, as, e.g., weight or height, the empirical objects whose relations are in question are directly accessible to examination, and the problem is one of establishing the appropriate numerical representation. Where the historian's problem is to establish a measure pertaining to observable characteristics of his data, as e.g., a measure of the frequency with which certain categories of symbols occur, his problem differs in no respect from that of any other empirical scientist. But the historian often wishes to establish a measure pertaining to past objects or events, which, by their very nature, are not available to present observation. Such entities are, as we have seen, postulated constructs of his theory, and measurements applied to them must be constructed by inference. Most of the measures which have thus far been applied in history involve relatively simple counting procedures—e.g., the number of individuals meeting a given criterion, the number of bales of cotton received at New Orleans in 1846, etc. In such cases, the problems have concerned the accuracy of the count, not the use of the cardinal numbers. But there are other cases in which the applicability of measurement is much less clear: for example, questions have been raised concerning the use of scalogram methods in the analysis of legislative roll calls. In these cases, it is not accuracy which is in question, but rather the applicability of the measurement model. These doubts appear to arise from two distinct sources: the interpretation of the model and the fragmentary character of the data. Let us examine these problems in order.

It would seem that there are two quite different sorts of measures with which we must be concerned. First, since our inscriptional data are always couched in terms of the perceptual-conceptual system of the culture which produced them, we are confronted with the problem of

---

* For general discussion of the theory of measurement, see Patrick Suppes and Joseph Zinnes, "Basic Measurement Theory," in R. Duncan Luce, Robert Bush, and Eugene Galanter (eds.), *Handbook of Mathematical Psychology* (New York: John Wiley & Sons, 1963) I: 1–76. For a less formal discussion, see Clyde H. Coombs et al., *Mathematical Psychology* (Englewood Cliffs, N.J.: Prentice-Hall, 1970), ch. 1.

inferring the measure relations obtaining in the world as viewed by that culture. But second, if we wish to move beyond this single culture to achieve a level of cross-cultural analysis, we shall also be faced with the problem of deriving measures of variables which were not part of the perceptual-conceptual system of the culture. Thus we may seek to determine a measure of perceived likeness or difference among subgroups within a given society and we may seek to relate this measure to measures of social interaction among the members of the subgroups, in order to test a general theory about the relation of perceived likeness or difference to social interaction in any society. In this case, we are relating a measure which involves the perceptual-conceptual system of the culture to one which does not. Accordingly, we must face the question of whether or not such measures can be established for historical data.

The fact that our inscriptional data come to us phrased in terms of the perceptual-conceptual system of a past culture means that our first problem is to gain access to the cognitive space shared by members of that culture. And to do this, we may turn to those methods used today to gain access to the cognitive space shared by individuals. A number of such methods have been devised in recent years by students of psychological measurement, and these developments have been codified into a general theory of data by Clyde Coombs, whose work is the basis for the discussion here.[14] In what follows, I shall be concerned with three measurement models only: parallelogram analysis, unfolding analysis, and scalogram analysis.

Parallelogram analysis is concerned with the relations obtaining between two different sets of items, for example a set of voters and a set of candidates. If we understand by a "dimension" a single attribute which can be possessed in different degrees by the candidate, e.g., conservatism, we may entertain the hypothesis that in the conceptual world of the voters the candidates are ordered along this dimension—i.e., that each candidate is regarded as having a different degree of conservatism. Thus we may think of the candidates as distributed along a line in space, where the line is taken to represent the dimension of conservatism and its two end points the extreme poles of radicalism and reaction. We assume that each voter prefers some particular degree of this attribute, so that a candidate located at just that point on the line would be his "ideal" choice. Thus to each voter there will correspond a point on the line which is his "ideal" point: his preferred degree of the attribute. If this situation, in fact, obtains, it is reasonable to say that the preference of each voter among the candidates will be determined by the distance between the voter's ideal point and the point representing each candidate's position: the nearer the candidate comes to the voter's ideal point the more the voter will prefer him, and the further he lies from the voter's ideal point the less the voter will prefer him. Suppose, then, that we have six candidates, represented by A, B, C, D, E, and F, and that each voter is asked to pick the three candidates whom he most prefers. If the hypotheses underlying the model are satisfied, there are four possible types of responses which form a perfect parallelogram pattern:

Figure 1

	A	B	C	D	E	F
1	x	x	x			
2		x	x	x		
3			x	x	x	
4				x	x	x

That this is so, may be seen intuitively by imagining the voter's ideal point translated along the length of the line from extreme left to extreme right. When the ideal point is at the extreme left, the choice must be ABC, since these three candidates lie closest to the ideal point. As the ideal point moves right, it will cross the midpoint between A and D; as soon as it does so, D becomes closer to the ideal point than A and so the response set becomes BCD. Obviously, only four such response types are possible if the model is true. Hence, if we have a significant number of subjects and if all show one of these four response types, we have a strong confirmation of the hypothesis that the parallelogram measurement model applies.

In practice, of course, the perfect parallelogram pattern is never found. Accordingly, we are faced with the question of how much deviation from the perfect pattern we can tolerate while still accepting the model. The usual measure of error applied in this case is Guttman's coefficient of reproducibility. The concept of reproducibility is intuitively obvious from the above figure. If I am told that a respondent falls into Category III response, for example, I can at once reproduce his response pattern; hence for the figure above the coefficient of reproducibility is one, since knowing the category into which any respondent falls would enable me to reproduce flawlessly his actual response pattern. Suppose, however, that one of the responses found in ABD. Whether we categorize this as a Category I or a Category II response, it is clear that the attempt to reproduce it from the knowledge of the category would lead to an error: we would either predict a C where a D occurs or a C where an A occurs. The coefficient of reproducibility is defined to be one minus the percentage of error that occurs among the responses—e.g., the percentage of responses which do not conform to the perfect parallelogram pattern. If this coefficient is .9 or higher, the hypothesis of the measurement model is usually accepted.

Parallelogram analysis as actually conducted may begin with hypotheses concerning the ordering of the items or with only the raw data: the choices of the respondents. In either case, we seek to arrange these responses in such a manner that the parallelogram pattern will be produced, or at least approximated. Where we succeed in achieving the pattern, we discover the ordering among the stimuli—here the candidates. But we also discover the ordering of the respondents: if A represents the liberal extreme and F the conservative extreme, then, clearly, respondents of Category I are more liberal than those of Category II. Thus by the analysis of the responses, which at first glance appear to contain no ordinal information and to be purely idiosyncratic choices, we are able to reconstruct the one-dimensional cognitive space shared by the respondents and so to determine the ordering of candidates and voters within that space.

A typical historical situation in which such a method of analysis might be applied concerns the analysis of children's literature to determine which acts of the child are regarded as praiseworthy. Here the acts praised are the stimuli, and the authors are the subjects. Assume for the moment that each author chooses three acts as praiseworthy. We can then examine the data to determine whether the parallelogram pattern is present or not; if it is, we so obtain an ordering of acts, and an ordering of the authors. What attribute underlies those acts the model does not tell us; that we shall have to determine from the analysis of the qualitative content of the data. All that the model tells us is that the acts are ranged along a single dimension. Similarly, the model has nothing to say about the variable which determines the ordering of the authors; all that the model shows us is that they are ordered in a particular way. Now it is, of course, likely that we would not have undertaken this analysis in the first place if we did not have in mind some hypothesis about the ordering of either acts or authors which we wished to test through the use of the model. But the point that must be made clear is that the model itself does not specify the empirical nature of the variables which produce these orderings—that is added by the substantive theory that we bring to bear upon the subject.

Of course, in practice the number of praiseworthy acts varies from author to author. It may be that for each author we can distinguish the k most praiseworthy acts and proceed as above. If this cannot be done, the analysis can be applied using different numbers of responses for each author. The resulting pattern is not, even in the ideal case, a perfect parallelogram, and no coefficient of error is available for such a case. Moreover, the order of the items and authors established is usually only a partial order. Nevertheless, partial orders can be used to yield very useful results, and any order is better than none. Parallelogram analysis is thus a technique which is fairly simple to use, which combines disparate choices into a single continuum, and which yields an ordinal level of measurement.

A surprisingly powerful measurement model due to Coombs is the unfolding technique. Unlike parallelogram analysis, this technique can be applied to n dimensional cases, but for simplicity we will restrict ourselves here to the one-dimensional case. We assume as before that the stimulus items are ordered along a continuum which is conceived to be defined by some attribute. Each respondent is conceived to prefer some specific degree of that attribute, and the point on the line corresponding to that specific degree of the attribute is called the respondent's "ideal point." As before, we assume that the respondent's preference for a given stimulus item is a function of its distance from his ideal point. Thus if we have five stimuli, represented by the first five letters of the alphabet, and if the respondent's ideal point is represented by x, we may conceive the underlying continuum (or J[oint] scale) as follows:

Figure 2

A	B		x C		D	E

For this case, the individual preference ordering (or I scale) of the respondent should be CBADE. All possible I scales consistent with this model can be generated by translating the ideal point from one end of the

J scale to the other, and the generation will follow the rule that each time the ideal point is conceived to cross the midpoint of the segment joining two stimuli, the preference ordering of those two stimuli will reverse, since crossing the midpoint means that the member of the pair which had been the closer (and hence the more preferred) is now the more distant (and hence the less preferred). Note too that each ordering will terminate in A or E, and that only two I scales are precise inverses of each other— namely, those obtained when the ideal point is at one extreme of the scale or the other. Suppose, then, that we find empirically that only the following I scales occur among our respondents:

> BACDE
> CDEBA
> DECBA
> ABCDE
> CBADE
> BCADE
> EDCBA
> CDBAE
> DCEBA
> CBDAE
> CDBEA

Even a casual inspection shows that these I scales are consistent with the one-dimensional model. The fourth and seventh scales are inverses, and starting from either of these it is easy to order the entire set, remembering that the follower of any member of the scale differs from its predecessor only by the inversion of a single pair of adjacent elements. Thus we have:

> ABCDE
> BACDE
> BCADE
> CBADE
> CBDAE
> CDBAE
> CDBEA
> CDEBA
> DCEBA
> DECBA
> EDCBA

The fact that the I scales can be ordered in this way shows that all respondents share a single cognitive space in which these five stimuli are regarded as ranged along a single dimension. Moreover, the order of the stimuli on that dimension is recoverable from the two inverse patterns. But from the ordering of the scales, one can also recover the ordering of the midpoints, since each inversion of a pair corresponds to the crossing of a midpoint. Thus if we represent the midpoint of the segment joining A and B by AB, we have in the above case the following order of the midpoints: AB, AC, BC, AD, BD, AE, BE, CD, CE, DE. That AB precedes AC is obvious from the order of the stimuli; that BC precedes AD, however, is not implied by the order of the stimuli, and one can easily show that the reverse order of the two midpoints is equally consistent with the order of the stimuli—thus

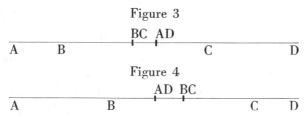

Figure 3

Figure 4

The midpoint ordering involves the ordering of *distances* between stimuli: thus if we represent the length of the segment joining A and B by $\overline{AB}$ and of that joining C and D by $\overline{CD}$, from the fact that BC precedes AD we can infer that $\overline{AB} < \overline{CD}$, while from the fact that AD precedes BC we can infer that $\overline{CD} < \overline{AB}$. The midpoint order permits the construction of a partial ordering of the distances between stimuli. Hence our I scales, which at first sight appeared to involve only ordinal information, turn out to involve metric information as well. For Figure 2 above, the partial order is

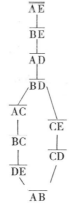

The fact that this partial order yields metric information suggests that it may be possible to introduce a form of measurement stronger than ordinal measurement—perhaps interval measurement. In recent years, a considerable amount of work has been done on this question, particularly with reference to the one-dimensional case. It now appears that the constraints imposed upon the possible assignments of interval scales to such data by the partial ordering of distances are actually very strong, and that for at least some types of cases they may be so strong that any two possible assignments will be highly correlated. Less work has been done on the n-dimensional case, but techniques now exist which make it possible to recover the ordering of stimuli on each dimension, and it seems likely that the same situation with respect to the introduction of interval scales obtains in the multidimensional case as in the unidimensional one. At the present time, however, results in this field are largely empirical and no definitive statement can be made.[15] In general, then, unfolding analysis permits the reconstruction of the arrangement of the stimuli in the cognitive space shared by the respondents, given nothing more than a complete set of I scales which meet the conditions of the model. Such a method is as applicable to patterns derived from historical sources as to those elicited from the trusty students of Psychology I. Unfortunately, there is no measure of error currently available for this model.

The model may be illustrated by an example which has considerable importance in the analysis of both historical and contemporary social data. Rokeach[16] collected similarities data from samples drawn from a variety of religious groups—Baptists, Methodists, Presbyterians, Catholics, Lutherans, and Episcopalians. Each respondent was asked to rate each of the other groups according to its degree of similarity to his own. Thus, for each respondent, the ideal point was his own religious group, and the stimuli were the six groups, one of which here coincided with his ideal point. By applying the unfolding technique, Rokeach was able, not only to show that all respondents shared a one-dimensional cognitive space and to reconstruct the order of the stimuli on that dimension, but also to introduce an interval scale which made distances between the groups comparable. The resulting scale is:

Figure 5

0	2.3		9.1		13.6	14.7	17
•	•		•		•	•	•
Cath.	Episc.		Luth.		Pres.	Meth.	Bapt.

The analysis does not demonstrate what the attribute is which defines this continuum, but it is reasonable to assume that it is a liturgical-evangelical dimension.

Perhaps the measurement model which is best known to historians is the scalogram due to Guttman. This model has been widely used by social scientists in the study of attitudes and by political scientists and historians in the study of roll-call votes.[17] In the scalogram model, there is a set of stimuli which may be illustrated by questions of different levels of difficulty. There is also a set of subjects, each of whom responds to each item or question. If, in the cognitive space shared by these subjects, the questions lie on one dimension, and the subjects are ordered with respect to their ability to answer the questions, a triangle pattern will result. Thus let P stand for pass and F for failure; let these be the only two responses possible and let there be four items. If the universe scales—that is, if for these subjects all questions lie on one dimension—then it should be possible to arrange the items and subjects so as to produce the pattern:

Figure 6

	A	B	C	D
I	P	P	P	P
II	F	P	P	P
III	F	F	P	P
IV	F	F	F	P
V	F	F	F	F

For those subjects in response pattern I, all the items were easy enough to pass; for those subjects in pattern III, the first two were too difficult to pass while the last two were passable; for those subjects in pattern V, all questions were too difficult. Clearly, the triangle pattern defines an order of the subjects in terms of ability and an order of the questions in terms of difficulty.

In practice, of course, the perfect triangle pattern, like the perfect parallelogram pattern or the perfect unfolding pattern, is not to be found. Guttman's coefficient of reproducibility defined above is usually taken to be the appropriate measure of scalability for this procedure, and the hypothesis that the universe scales is accepted if the coefficient equals or exceeds .9.

The major application of scalogram analysis to history has been in the analysis of roll calls. The objective has been to identify issues which have a common underlying dimension, and to order the legislators by response types. Thus if A, B, C, and D above represent civil rights bills of varying degrees of firmness, legislators may be expected to vote according to how difficult they find it to accept the proposals of the bills: some conservatives would accept none, some liberals would accept all, and many would accept some and reject others. The bills voted on are thus scaled according to the difficulty legislators found in voting for them, and the legislators themselves are scaled by their attitudes.

In presenting these measurement models, I have used an interpretation of them which is conventional in current psychology— namely, I have treated them as if what they yield is the structure of the cognitive space shared by the respondents. But this interpretation is gratuitous; the formal model is independent of any given interpretation. Thus consider the case where the data yield frequency of interaction among members of different religious groups. Here we have data which can be analyzed in terms of an ordering relation upon dyads of points from a single set—i.e., does w (member of group A) interact more frequently with z (member of group B) than with y (member of group C)? If, to fix ideas, we take the religious groups to be Catholic, Episcopal, Lutheran, Presbyterian, Methodist, and Baptist, and each respondent to be a member of one of these groups, we obtain for each respondent x an I scale, where the order of the groups in his I scale is determined by the frequency with which he interacts with members of those groups. With an adequate number of respondents representing each of the religious groups, we may then test the applicability of a one-dimesional model through the unfolding technique. If, in fact, the applicability of the model is confirmed, what we shall have established is that the frequency of social interaction among the members of these groups is a function of their distance from one another, measured along an unnamed but determinate dimension. This claim involves no reference to the perceptual-conceptual system of a culture, except insofar as an understanding of that system is prerequisite to the interpretation of any data from that culture. We can, of course, hypothesize that frequency of interaction is a function of perceived similarity, and proceed to correlate distances on the dimension of perceived similarity with those on the interaction J scale, but we are then testing a relation between a variable which does explicitly involve the perceptual-conceptual system of the culture and one which does not.

Moreover, such a hypothesis leads easily to quite general hypotheses of a cross-cultural nature—i.e., that, for any society, frequency of social inter-action among the members of social positions is a function of perceived similarity. Such a hypothesis, of course, assumes that concepts such as "social interaction" can be formulated in a manner which is either culture-free or capable of being operationalized in different but equivalent ways in different cultures. Nevertheless, it is a hypothesis which begins to carry us from the study of a particular society at a given time to societies in general.

A similar point needs to be made concerning scalogram analysis. One objection which has been made repeatedly to the application of scalogram analysis to roll calls is that such an application makes the assumption that legislative voting is a direct function of attitude. This objection is certainly well taken, since, in fact, the dimensions which have been identified as determining voting in such analyses have usually been attitudinal. But there is nothing in the scalogram model itself which compels this interpretation. What the model does is to test the scalability of the universe of items and respondents—to test whether or not one-dimensional orderings of the items and the respondents can be assumed, given the response patterns. The model itself has nothing to say about the nature of the variables which determine those orderings. They may, of course, be due to attitudes; but they may be due to length of time in office, or to the income of the legislator, or to his wife's age, or to any one of an infinite set of variables, some of which do and some of which do not involve explicit reference to the perceptual-conceptual system of the culture. Thus here, as in the case of other measurement models, the models themselves are formal and require no particular empirical interpretation of their results.

The measurement models discussed above are applicable wherever their underlying assumptions can be met. That they are widely applicable in the social sciences is due in part to the methods of data collection which are used in those fields. Whether these methods are experimental, as is frequently the case in psychology, or observational, as is usually the case in the other social sciences, they have certain common features. Thus, whether we use an observation schedule, an interview, a questionnaire, or an experimental treatment, what we obtain, if the method is properly used, is a standard set of responses for each subject. Moreover, except in cases where unstructured behavior is being observed and recorded, these responses are made to a standard set of stimuli (the questions asked or treatments given) which are put to each subject in turn. It is thus possible in principle to obtain for each subject a response to every stimulus presented. This is, of course, not possible in practice: subjects may be unwilling or unable to answer, or they may prove to be unobtainable. But it is generally agreed that some amount of nonresponse can be tolerated without calling the results into serious question. The general rule of thumb for sample survey work is that the nonresponse rate must not exceed twenty percent; if it does, some further procedure, such as obtaining data from a special sample of nonrespondents, must be introduced. But in general it is possible in the social sciences to obtain data in sufficiently complete form to permit the applications of statistical techniques.

The situation facing the historian is very different. One cannot give questionnaires or interviews or experimental treatments to the dead. In order to collect data from historical respondents, one must convert the questionnaire or interview schedule into a form which can be applied by content analysis to some type of inscriptional trace. Thus to a given question on the questionnaire there corresponds a question to be put to a document, together with the specification as to which features of the document are to be interpreted as an affirmative reply and which as a negative one. Now any historian who has attempted to apply such a set of standard questions to documentary materials knows that he is doing very well indeed if he can muster a fifty-percent response rate on any given question. Unless the questions are made extremely general, and hence largely useless, or the data were originally created in a standard format which guarantees that virtually every document will carry certain information (e.g., as every letter has a salutation), the historian must settle for a nonresponse rate so high that it would automatically vitiate his results if they were to be evaluated in terms of the current standards of the social sciences.

There are several ways of approaching this problem, but perhaps the first step is to raise the question as to whether or not the problem is properly viewed as one of nonresponse. Because of the nature of the data-collection methods employed in the social sciences, it is always clear that nonrespondents must be considered as differing in important ways from respondents. Those who are not at home when the survey taker calls are likely to differ from those who are in essential respects, such as being employed in activities different from those of the respondents, and those who cannot or will not answer are obviously giving a different response to a given stimulus than are those who can and will. But the meaning of nonresponse is much less clear for historical data because the stimuli which evoke the response are uncontrolled. When one is content-analyzing a letter for particular indicators, one has no control over the creation of the letter—one cannot present the writer with a stimulus which should evoke the response—one simply has to look for certain responses, hoping that stimuli occurred to the writer which did evoke them. The failure of Jones to mention the same subject as Smith proves nothing about how Jones would have responded had he been presented with the same stimulus which led Smith to respond. Instead of facing a standard set of stimuli, the subject in the historical case draws stimuli more or less at random, and the failure to draw one which evokes the desired response may be a matter of chance. It is, therefore, not at all clear that those who fail to produce the desired indicators in their inscriptions should be considered as nonrespondents in the same sense in which that term is currently used in the social sciences. Indeed, there appears to be at least a presumption on the basis of the above analysis that the responses actually made might be considered to be a random sample drawn from a population of possible responses.

To put the matter more precisely, we must restrict our attention to a given content domain, e.g., kinship, visiting, etc., and to a set of historical subjects. The restriction to a content domain is essential, since otherwise, by arbitrarily changing domains, we could artificially induce an apparently random pattern. Let us suppose, then, that within the domain the historical subject is faced with a set of stimuli from which he selects randomly. Let us further suppose that in a population of N stimuli confronting our respondent, there are n independent stimuli related to our question i, and that the probability of his drawing a particular one of these n stimuli is Pj ($j = 1 \ldots n$). Let us also suppose that our subject is a perfect respondent: he never refuses to answer. Then the probability that we get a response from him which is scorable for question i is $\Sigma_j P_j$, that is, the sum of the probabilities of the selection of the separate stimuli related to our question i. We will then have more answers to some questions than to others, since there may be more related stimuli for some questions than for others. What we should not get, however, is a set of people who answer all questions and a set of people who answer no questions, or a set of questions which everyone answers and a set of questions which no one answers. We may, to fix ideas, think of the data matrix with questions horizontally in random order and subjects vertically, also in random order, thus:

Figure 7

	a	b	c	d	e	f
1	x	o	x	o	x	x
2	x	x	o	x	x	o
3	x	o	x	o	x	x
4	x	x	o	x	x	o
5	o	x	o	o	o	x
6	o	o	x	o	x	o

The x's here simply stand for responses, regardless of their quality, and the o's for nonresponses. Thus the problem may now be formulated as follows: are the x's which appear a random sample of the x's which would have appeared if each respondent had drawn a stimulus related to each question? We can, in fact, answer this question by applying a one-sample runs test to the columns and rows of the data matrix. For the purposes of this test, we define a run as an uninterrupted sequence of x's or an uninterrupted sequence of o's, where the columns (or rows) are conceived as running continuously into one another—e.g., the last response of column e and the first response of column f form a single run. There are then 24 runs in the columns of the data matrix, and also 24 runs in the rows. If the five-percent criterion is adopted, the critical values for this case are 12 and 25—hence the hypothesis of randomness can be adopted. We can, therefore, treat the responses which we have as a random sample from a universe of potential responses, and so infer the characteristics of that universe from our sample. Where the measurement model is one involving simple counting, such a method can often yield adequate results.

But where we turn to more complicated measurement models such as parallelogram analysis, unfolding analysis, or scalogram analysis, such a sampling approach is not adequate. This is true not because the sampling distributions of these measures are unknown, although that is generally true, but rather because these models assume complete response sets from every member of a sample of individuals. When the data are incomplete, serious problems arise. There are two sorts of incompleteness with which we must deal: we may not have data for some individuals; and the response sets which we have for any one individual may not be complete. The first sort of incompleteness can be dealt with practically by making the set of respondents sufficiently large that every response category is virtually certain to occur. Nevertheless, the possibility remains that even for large sets some category will not appear. Thus in the unfolding analysis, if the isotonic region, or segment of the J scale, to which a given I scale corresponds is extremely short, it may be that no respondent even in a large set will realize that scale. Should this be the case, the only adequate recourse is to increase the set of respondents still further until the scale is realized. But if only one scale is missing and if scalability is assumed, the missing scale is easily inferred from the others. It is the second sort of incompleteness which particularly characterizes the historical case and which must occupy us here. And the effect of this sort of incompleteness is to render the use of these measurement models at least questionable. To see that this is so, consider the following simple problem in scalogram analysis. Suppose we have four items and five respondents, each of whom is a perfect example of a distinct response type:

Figure 8

	A	B	C	D
I	P	P	P	P
II	F	P	P	P
III	F	F	P	P
IV	F	F	F	P
V	F	F	F	F

Suppose that we knew the order of the items on a priori grounds and that our only problem was ordering the respondents, and suppose that we could obtain a fifty-percent random sample of the response universe given above. Could we, in fact, order the respondents? Note first that this ordering depends upon certain pairs; thus, even assuming scalability, we need at least the following:

Figure 9

	A	B	C	D
I	P			
II	F	P		
III		F	P	
IV			F	P
V				F

To get a simple ordering of respondents, these eight responses would have to occur among the ten chosen at random—a result which would be, to put it mildly, unlikely. Moreover, if we construct a case in which the actual responses really are a random sample of that universe, the difficulty becomes quite obvious. Consider, for example, the following case in which ten responses have been chosen at random from the universe of twenty:

Figure 10

	A	B	C	D
I	P	P		
II	F		P	P
III	F	F		
IV		F	F	
V	F			

Even *assuming* scalability, it is impossible from such data to construct an ordering of any utility, and it is senseless even to talk of testing scalability on the basis of them.[18] Nor is the situation with respect to the unfolding technique any better. Even a fifty-percent random sample will not permit the J scale to be recovered. On the other hand, if parallelogram analysis is applied to a fifty-percent random sample of the response universe, at least a partial order is usually forthcoming, provided that the order of the items is given a priori and that scalability is assumed. Thus parallelogram analysis stands up slightly better under missing data than do the other two models.

We shall not, therefore, be able to utilize such models without further assumptions. So far as unfolding analysis and parallelogram analysis are concerned, the simplest such assumption would appear to be that the responses which do occur are those closest to the ideal point. This assumption has some intuitive justification, at least for preferential choice data and similarities data, for it seems reasonable to hold that stimuli close to the ideal point are more salient than those distant from it, and so more likely to be mentioned. However, this justification of the assumption is empirical rather than formal, and its reasonableness will depend upon the particular interpretation given to the model. When the assumption can be justified, it proves to be extremely powerful. Let us first assume scalability and unidimensionality, and explore what unfolding analysis would yield with fifty percent of the responses. Suppose, first, that we have the following I scales, which for simplicity we shall consider to be an ordered pair of stimuli for each respondent:

$$xy$$
$$yz$$
$$xw$$
$$yx$$
$$yz$$
$$zy$$
$$xy$$
$$wx$$

Can we reconstruct the missing data? Almost. Our ability to do this rests upon certain principles which will be evident from an inspection of the I scales and the figures on pages 183-84. Note first that in the example on page 184 there are only two I scales whose initial stimuli occur in the first position in no other I scales: ABCDE and EDCBA. In every other case, there are at least two I scales with the same stimulus in column one but different stimuli in column two. That this must be so is evident from the consideration of Figure 2. As the ideal point is translated to the right, the first midpoint it crosses is AB, and the last is DE—hence, A and E can occur in column one only once. But for any other three stimuli —let them be called r, s, and t—so ordered on the continuum that s succeeds r and t succeeds s, there will be an I scale beginning with the pair sr which is generated when the ideal point crosses the rs midpoint, and an I scale beginning with st generated when the ideal point crosses the rt midpoint. But every stimulus except the terminal ones has a preceding and succeeding stimulus; hence, every stimulus except the terminal ones is the initial stimulus of at least two I scales which differ in their second elements. Thus in the above data, zy and wx must be the terminal scales and z and w the terminal stimuli. Second, in the I-scale ordering on page 184, the scales which are next to the terminal scales differ from them only in the inversion of the first two stimuli. Again an

inspection of Figure 2 shows that this is a necessary property of the
unidimensional ordering. Hence we have:

zy
yz
•
•
•
xw
wx

Third, once a stimulus leaves column one, it cannot return. Again this
follows from the linear order of the stimuli: once a stimulus has ceased
to be the one nearest the ideal point, it cannot again become so. Hence
we have:

zy
yz
yx
•
xy
xw
wx

Since yx follows yz, we know that x must have occupied the third position
in the second I scale, and that z must move to the second position in the
third I scale. Hence we have:

zy
yzx
yxz
•
xyw
xwy
wx

Since each I scale is followed by an I scale which differs from it only by
the inversion of one pair of adjacent elements, we have:

zyx
yzx
yxz
•
xyw
xwy
wxy

Knowing that the first and last I scales are inverses, and applying the above rules we have:

zyxw

yzxw

yxzw

•

xywz

xwyz

wxyz

The missing scale is obviously either xyzw or yxwz. But we have no way to decide between these. The fact that we have another xy among the responses in the data proves nothing, for this may be a repetition of xywz. Hence we cannot recover from such incomplete data the full partial ordering of distances, but we can recover the order of stimuli on the continuum, and this is a major gain.

To reach this result, we assumed both scalability—i.e., the applicability of unfolding analysis—and unidimensionality. Need we make such severe assumptions? The answer is no. Suppose our fragmentary I scales were:

xy

yz

xw

yx

zv

wx

wy

zx

These data could not be given a linear order on one dimension, for there is no I scale the first stimulus of which appears as the first stimulus of no other I scale. In general, if two or more dimensions are required for the unfolding, every stimulus will appear as the initial stimulus of at least two I scales which differ in their second elements. Hence, even with such fragmentary data, we can test for the difference between unidimensional and multidimensional models, *if the general model applies at all.* And this is the rub. For even in the apparently unidimensional case examined above, the true I scales may well be:

zyxw
yzwx
yxwz
yxzw
xyzw
xwzy
wxzy

Unfolding analysis is simply inapplicable to these data; the assumptions underlying the model are violated by the data. But we could not tell that this was the case, given only the first pair of elements in each scale. Hence, we could not test the applicability of the method as a whole.

It thus appears that the application of measurement models to historical data faces some very severe difficulties because of the fragmentary character of the data. With respect to certain sorts of measurement models, the application of sampling techniques offers a possible solution, provided that the responses obtained form a random pattern. But other models can only be applied when they are supplemented by rather strong assumptions about what data are missing, and even then we generally cannot test the applicability of these models. These restrictions are sufficiently severe to raise real questions concerning our ability to apply statistical or quantitative methods to certain types of historical data, even when these data relate to subjects to which the measures are applied in contemporary social science.

The approaches to the confirmation of law-like hypotheses which I have discussed so far have been chiefly statistical and have been based upon the assumption that, to determine whether or not a given generalization holds true of a population, we must examine at least a sample of that population. This assumption, however, is not always true: there are situations in which we can draw inferences regarding the prevalence of a behavioral pattern by other methods. This is particularly true of certain categories of custom. By definition, customs are behavioral patterns which are expected of members of a social position and which are enforced by positive and/or negative sanctions applied to the members of that social position by at least one (and often more than one) sanctioning group. It is often relatively easy to determine from historical data what the norms and expectations involved in a given custom are—easier, certainly, than to determine how closely behavior conforms to these norms and expectations. But with respect to some customs, the sanctioning groups have sanctioning methods which involve the creation of a record of each case in which sanctions are applied. This, of course, is not true for every custom or every sanctioning group, but it is true for some —particularly for those whose sanctioners are themselves members of a social position whose role involves the levying of these sanctions. Thus if deviation from a custom is proscribed by civil law, sanctions against deviants will be levied by a public agency such as the police; similarly, deviations from the accepted operating procedures of a corporation will likely bring negative sanctions from a supervisory group within the institution. In such cases, records of negative sanctioning activity are generally made and kept, at least for some time. Hence, while we may not be able to obtain data on individuals who conform to a custom, we may through such records be able to determine the amount of deviance from it, and so infer the amount of conformity.

Several rather obvious difficulties restrict the applicability of this approach. First, even when such records are created, they are often not preserved for long periods and are, in fact, sometimes deliberately destroyed after a set period. Hence the data are not easy to find and are often incomplete. Second, deviation which is noted in records is usually that of the more extreme kind. Negative sanctions which involve the creation of a record are usually reserved only for the most severe deviations from the custom—lesser deviations are dealt with by more informal means. Third, the recording of deviance is a function of the observability of the deviation and the willingness and ability of the sanctioning group to act. Deviations differ markedly in their observability: murder, as every reader of detective stories knows, leaves a corpse which is notably difficult to hide, while rape generally produces no result which is immediately detectable by society at large. Similarly, the victim of theft has every reason to report the crime and to insist upon something being done about it, while the victim of rape very often conceals what has occurred out of feelings of shame. Thus, the number of reported cases of rape will not only be smaller than the actual incidence of the crime, but the difference between the number of reported cases and the number of actual cases will be greater for rape than for theft or murder. But observability is not the only variable which affects the recording of deviance. Enforcement agencies differ from place to place and from time to time in their size, adequacy, and vigor. Even within a given city, enforcement

varies by neighborhood according to patterns well documented by crim-
inologists. Hence any use of court records, arrest statistics, disciplinary
records, etc., to establish the incidence of types of deviations from custom
is almost certain to yield biased estimates which are too low and in which
the amount of bias can only be guessed at. Nevertheless, when all this is
said, the records of sanctioning groups provide one of the relatively few
ways in which we can hope to determine the degree of conformity to
customary patterns. This method is very limited in its applicability, and
is crude at best, but where it can be systematically applied it offers at
least some basis for assessing the degree of conformity of behavior to
custom.

In the foregoing discussion, I have reviewed a variety of problems
which confront the student of the past as he attempts to confirm law-like
generalizations regarding past populations. The seriousness of these
problems becomes evident when one considers the types of data which
can possibly be used for this purpose. There are essentially eight such
types of data:

    (1) testimonial data collected by contemporary observers
    (2) data relating to deviance
    (3) complete data respecting every member of the population
    (4) incomplete data respecting every member of the population
    (5) complete data respecting some members of the population
    (6) incomplete data respecting some members of the population
    (7) aggregated data respecting all members of the population
    (8) aggregated data respecting some members of the population

I have already discussed the limitations of (1), observing that such testimony, while it has evidential value, must be confirmed by other means.
(2) can be used effectively for dealing with a small number of cases. As
regards (4) and (6), we can in some cases use sampling methods to deal
with incompleteness, and in other cases we can add assumptions to the
models to guarantee applicability, but our present methods for dealing
with data of this sort are limited and unsatisfactory. In the case of (5)
and of (6), we have no general solutions to the sampling problems involved, and very few specific solutions applicable to particular types of
cases. For (7) and (8) we have some viable methods, depending upon
the type of measurement involved at the individual level and the satisfaction of general linearity requirements. Only in the case of (3) are we

really in a position comparable to that of a contemporary social investigator, and the tragedy is simply that, aside from the manuscript returns of the United States Census, it is a type of data which arises so seldom that it offers little hope. It thus appears that our present methods for confirming general hypotheses regarding past populations cannot meet the standards which now prevail in the social sciences.

NOTES

1. V. O. Key, *Southern Politics* (New York: Alfred A. Knopf, 1949).

2. W. S. Robinson, "Ecological Correlations and the Behavior of Individuals," *American Sociological Review* 15 (1950): 351–57.

3. Otis Dudley Duncan, Ray P. Cuzzort, and Beverly Duncan, *Statistical Geography* (Glencoe, Ill.: Free Press, 1961), pp. 65–66.

4. Leo Goodman, "Some Alternatives to Ecological Correlation," *American Journal of Sociology* 64 (1959): 610–25.

5. Gudmund R. Iversen, "Estimation of Cell Entries in Contingency Tables When Only Marginals are Observed" (Ph.D. diss., Harvard University, 1969).

6. Hubert M. Blalock, Jr., *Causal Inference in Nonexperimental Research* (Chapel Hill: University of North Carolina Press, 1961).

7. W. Phillips Shively, "Ecological Inference: The Use of Aggregate Data to Study Individuals," *American Political Science Review* 63 (1969): 1183–96.

8. Alex Inkeles and Raymond A. Bauer, *The Soviet Citizen* (Cambridge: Harvard University Press, 1959).

9. Inkeles and Bauer, *The Soviet Citizen*, p. 27.

10. James K. Kindahl, "Estimation of Means and Totals from Finite Populations of Unknown Size," *American Statistical Association Journal* 57 (1962): 61–91.

11. Melvyn Hammarberg, "The Indiana Voter" (Ph.D. diss., University of Pennsylvania, 1970); "Designing a Sample from Incomplete Historical Lists," *American Quarterly* 28 (1971): 542–61.

12. Alexis De Tocqueville, *Democracy in America*, trans. Reeve (London: 1835).

13. James B. Bryce, *The American Commonwealth* (New York: Macmillan Co., 1888), 3 vols.

14. Clyde H. Coombs, *A Theory of Data* (New York: John Wiley & Sons, 1964).

15. Robert Abelson and John Tukey, "Efficient Conversion of Non-metric Information into Metric Information," *American Statistical Association: Proceedings of the Social Statistics Section* 1959: 226–30; Robert Abelson and John Tukey, "Efficient Utilization of Non-numerical Information in Quantitative Analysis: General Theory and the Case of Simple Order," *Annals of Mathematical Statistics* 34 (1963): 1347–69; J. P. Benzecri, "Sur l'Analyse Factorielle des Proximités," *Publications*, Institut de Statistique, Université de Paris, 13 (1964): 235–82; J. P. Benzecri, "Sur l'Analyse Factorielle des Proximités (suite)," *Publications*, Institut de Statistique, Université de Paris, 14 (1965): 65–80; J. B. Kruskal, "Multidimensional Scaling by Optimizing Goodness of Fit to a Non-metric Hypothesis," *Psychometrica* 29 (1964): 1–27.

16. Coombs, *Data*, pp. 456–57.

17. Thomas B. Alexander, *Sectional Stress and Party Strength* (Nashville: Vanderbilt University Press, 1967); Joel Silbey, *The Shrine of Party* (Pittsburgh: University of Pittsburgh Press, 1967).

18. See, however, the treatment of absences in Duncan MacRae, Jr., *Issues and Parties in Legislative Voting* (New York: Harper and Row, 1970), pt. I.

Conclusion

During the past thirty years, there has been a great deal of controversy about the nature of historical knowledge. The argument has centered about the question of whether or not history is a science. I am not certain what this question means, for I find it very difficult to define the term "science." But since history, if a "science," is clearly a social science, it is perhaps desirable to rephrase the question as follows: are the methods and standards of the contemporary social sciences used (or usable) in history? In most of the recent literature, it has been assumed that the answer to this question will be determined once we know what sort of explanation is used in history. Hence the crux of the modern debate has been the nature of historical explanation. But, as I hope that the foregoing discussion has demonstrated, the problem of the nature of historical knowledge is considerably more complex than this formulation suggests. If historical explanations involve laws of limited scope which must be discovered by historians themselves, or if the applicability to a past society of laws and theories borrowed from other disciplines must be tested against data from that past society, then questions respecting the possibility of confirming law-like hypotheses about the past must be faced. These questions have not been discussed in recent literature concerning the nature of historical knowledge, but they are clearly of crucial importance for our knowledge of the past.

If the argument of the last two chapters is accepted, it seems clear that the methods and standards of the contemporary social sciences can be applied only imperfectly to the study of the past. So far as the confirmation of law-like hypotheses respecting historical societies is concerned, we are faced with a series of problems for which no solutions are available at present. Whether or not these problems are solvable it is, of course, impossible to say, but it does seem clear that their solutions will not come from the application to historical data of techniques already in existence: new techniques will have to be forthcoming. As to the likelihood that such new developments will occur, one can only offer speculation, but it may not be amiss to do so. The reader, I am sure, will have been struck by the contrast between the present state of the ecological problem and that of the sampling and measurement problems. Significant advances have been made on the ecological problem since Robinson published. Moreover, those who are working on it are either mathematically sophisticated social scientists or mathematical statisticians. This is by no means accidental. The ecological problem has broad applicability in many domains of social analysis and has therefore attracted wide attention. Furthermore, it admits of formulation in such a way that it can be attacked as a purely mathematical problem rather than as a substantive one. And finally the problem is one which has considerable importance in probability theory. This will not be obvious from the discussions offered above; but what we have called Case I—i.e., the problem of inferring T-probabilities from the marginals where there is nominal measurement at the individual level and at least interval measurement at the aggregate level—is formally identical with the problem of estimating the stationary transition probabilities of a Markov chain from empirical data.[1] Hence the ecological problem is one which has drawn the attention of mathematicians and which is amenable to purely mathematical attack.

The situation with respect to the sampling problem is markedly different. The results cited above have been achieved by historians and social scientists, not by mathematicians. Moreover, it is doubtful whether the problem can be stated at present in a form which admits of purely mathematical attack. To say that samples obtainable from past populations are biased is no doubt true, but it tells us nothing about the bias and so offers no opening through which the problem can be approached. It will be remarked that the problems dealt with by Kindahl and Hammarberg are defined by particular combinations of records: for Kindahl, by two incomplete censuses; for Hammarberg, by a complete list giving values for many of the independent variables but not for the dependent variable, and a partial list giving values for both sets of variables. It was these particular characteristics of the data-bases which determined how the problems of bias could be approached in these problems. I suspect that the pattern evident here will hold for the immediate future: that what we will see during the next ten years will be a series of very specific studies in which the problem of controlling the bias will be attacked in terms of the particular characteristics of the data-bases. Perhaps, when enough studies of this sort have been done, some common features of these special cases will emerge which will make possible a more general characterization of the problem or problems involved—one which hopefully will admit of mathematical attack.

With respect to the problem of measurement as applied to historical data, so little has been done that even speculation seems ill-advised. Yet one may hope for progress here, both from studies in psychological* measurement, where problems of missing data are of recognized importance, and from content analysis, since many of the problems of analyzing historical documentary material are the same as those of analyzing any documentary material. But one would need a crystal ball indeed to foresee what the next ten years are likely to bring in this area.

If, then, one seeks to assess the "scientific" status of history as a discipline at the present time, no very conclusive answers can be offered. On the one hand, we are clearly seeing a rapid increase in the use of social science concepts and social science theories, and a growing acceptance of the covering law model of explanation, at least in principle. On the other hand, it seems clear that historians are unable to use the methods or meet the standards for the confirmation of hypotheses and theories which are prevalent in the contemporary social sciences, and that this inability is a function of the character of historical data and of the problems respecting confirmation which they generate. I do not know of any reason to believe that these problems are not solvable, but in point of fact they have not been solved, and, if one assumes that they will be solved, one does so in the optimistic faith that our knowledge can be indefinitely extended, even into the abyss of time.

But the question of whether or not history is a science is, after all, a relatively trivial one, if indeed it is meaningful at all. What is not trivial is the question of the nature of historical knowledge, and particularly of the warrants for those statements which deal with objects and events of the past. It is for this reason that we must be so concerned with the confirmation of such statements and with the problems which are involved in their confirmation. As I trust the discussions of the last two chapters have shown, we can hardly rest content with the current state of our methods of confirmation in history. It is in this area that further work is most urgently needed. Whether such work takes a form which increases the similarity of history to the social sciences or whether it takes some other direction, the important thing is that we develop better ways of testing our statements about the past against the data which the past has left us. If truth is to be the daughter of time, it is the historian who must make the delivery, and the quality of his midwifery could stand improvement.

NOTES

1. Lester G. Telser, "Least Squares Estimates of Transition Probabilities" in *Measurement in Economics*, ed. Carl Christ (Stanford: Stanford University Press, 1963), pp. 270–92.

Index